The Production of
the Muslim Woman

After the Empire:
The Francophone World and
Postcolonial France

Series Editor

Valérie Orlando, Illinois Wesleyan University

Advisory Board

Robert Bernasconi, Memphis University
Alec Hargreaves, Florida State University
Chima Korieh, Central Michigan University
Françoise Lionnet, UCLA
Obioma Nnaemeka, Indiana University
Kamal Salhi, University of Leeds
Tracy D. Sharpley-Whiting, Hamilton College
Frank Ukadike, Tulane University

Dedicated to the promotion of intellectual thought on and about the Francophone world, *After the Empire* publishes original works that explore the arts, politics, history, and culture that have developed in complex negotiations with the French colonial influence. The series also looks at the Hexagon and its borders, and at the transgressions of those borders that problematize notions of French identity and expression.

Of Suffocated Hearts and Tortured Souls: Seeking Subjecthood through Madness in Francophone Women's Writing of Africa and the Caribbean, by Valérie Orlando

Francophone Post-Colonial Cultures: Critical Essays, edited by Kamal Salhi

In Search of Shelter: Subjectivity and Spaces of Loss in the Fiction of Paule Constant, by Margot Miller

French Civilization and Its Discontents: Nationalism, Colonialism, Race, edited by Tyler Stovall and Georges Van Den Abbeele

After the Deluge: New Perspectives on Postwar French Intellectual and Cultural History, edited by Julian Bourg with an Afterword by François Dosse

Remnants of Empire in Algeria and Vietnam: Women, Words, and War, by Pamela A. Pears

Packaging Post/Coloniality: The Manufacture of Literary Identity in the Francophone World, by Richard Watts

The Production of the Muslim Woman: Negotiating Text, History, and Ideology, by Lamia Ben Youssef Zayzafoon

The Production of the Muslim Woman

Negotiating Text, History, and Ideology

Lamia Ben Youssef Zayzafoon

LEXINGTON BOOKS
Lanham • Boulder • New York • Toronto • Oxford

LEXINGTON BOOKS

Published in the United States of America
by Lexington Books
An imprint of The Rowman & Littlefield Publishing Group, Inc.
4501 Forbes Boulevard, Suite 200, Lanham, Maryland 20706

PO Box 317
Oxford
OX2 9RU, UK

Copyright © 2005 by Lexington Books

All efforts have been made by the author of this work to obtain copyright and reproduction permissions. If any of these have been accidentally omitted, kindly inform the author and the errors will be corrected in subsequent editions.

Cover image: 'Amor al Ghrayri, "The Doctor to the Pharmacist: 'Prepare for Her This Medicine and She Will Be Cured, God Willing!'" Source: Ed. Mahmud Beyram al Tunsi. *Al Shabab*, no. 4, 19 November 1936, 1(N). Tunis: Dar al Kutub al Wataniya, 2004. 20 vols. 29 October 1936–12 March 1937.

British Library Cataloguing in Publication Information Available

Library of Congress Cataloging-in-Publication Data

Zayzafoon, Lamia Ben Youssef, 1966–
   The production of the Muslim woman : negotiating text, history, and ideology / Lamia Ben Youssef Zayzafoon.
      p. cm. — (After the empire)
   Includes bibliographical references and index.
   ISBN 0-7391-0962-6 (cloth : alk. paper) — ISBN 0-7391-1078-0 (pbk. : alk. paper)
   1. Muslim women. 2. Women in Islam. 3. Women's studies. I. Title. II. Series.

HQ1170.Z37 2005
305.48'697—dc22   2004019998

Printed in the United States of America

⊗™ The paper used in this publication meets the minimum requirements of American National Standard for Information Sciences—Permanence of Paper for Printed Library Materials, ANSI/NISO Z39.48–1992.

To my parents, my children, and my husband

Contents

Illustrations

Acknowledgments

This project began with the doctoral dissertation I defended at Michigan State University in 2002. I would like to express here my heartfelt gratitude to my two directors, Dr. Kenneth W. Harrow and Dr. Salah Dean Assaf Hassan, for their assistance and guidance during my doctoral program at MSU. I also want to thank the other members of my Ph.D. committee, namely, Dr. Dianne Brunner and Dr. Surjit Dulai, for their advice and insight.

This publication would not have been possible without the generosity of Valérie Orlando, series editor of After the Empire: The Francophone World and Postcolonial France, at Lexington Books, who offered to read my work after an informal discussion on gender and power in Tunisian academia. I also would like to note a special debt of thanks to other senior editors at Lexington Books, namely, Serena Leigh Krombach, Brian Richards, Sarah Fell, and Erin Hill-Parks, for their patience and thoroughgoing editing of this manuscript. I also thank Sharon Harrow, Emily Lemoine, and Mary McCullough for their help and thoughtful editing.

In Tunisia, I wish to acknowledge my debt to Mrs. Kerkeni and Dr. Nassima Tarchouna for planting in me the love of English literature. I extend as well my heartfelt thanks to Dr. Hedi Sioud and the Tunisian Ministry of Education for sponsoring my M.A. program at Michigan State University, and to AMIDEAST for granting me a Fulbright Scholarship during the first two years of my doctoral program at MSU. At the University Tunis, I would like to extend my thanks to Dr. Hachmi Trabelsi, Dr. Fethi Dali, and Dr. Ali Mahjoubi for encouraging me to resume my doctoral studies at MSU.

A special mention is in order for my Tunisian friends and colleagues, especially Selma Ben Abdallah, Nejat Mchela, Samira Mechri, Omar Bouraoui, Kamel and Monia Jerfel, Khaled Abid, Boutheina Ben Hassine, Inaam Mrabet, Slah Kefi, Olfa Bayoudh, and Naima and Muhammad Idris for their invaluable source of support and information. Selma and Nejat must be singled out for their meticulous proofreading and generous feedback. I also offer my humble thanks to the personnel at the Tunisian National Library, the National Center of Documentation, the RCD, the CREDIF Center, and the Tunisian Ministry of Culture for their generous help during my research on gender and Tunisian nationalism. Thanks as well to *Le Renouveau* for giving me permission to reproduce political cartoons from the Tunisian nationalist press.

And last but not least, I wish to thank my parents, who passed on to me their love of French literature and ancient Arabic poetry. I am eternally grateful to my mother, Aïsha Ben Youssef, for staying up all night taking care of my newborn while I was working on my dissertation. I am equally grateful to my father, Hichem Ben Youssef, who helped me not only by babysitting and making mint tea but also by buying me almost every pamphlet/book available in Tunisia on women's issues. I am also very thankful to my husband, Majd Zayzafoon, for printing and formatting the figures of this manuscript. Many thanks also go out to my sister Najla, my brother Zoubeir, my babysitter Amna, and my extended family in Béja and Tunis for their unquestioned support and encouragement. Lastly, I wish to express my love and affection for my two sons, Alexander and Abraham, whose laughter and cooing were refueling breaks amidst the difficult process of writing this book.

Introduction

The Production of the Muslim Woman: Negotiating Text, History, and Ideology investigates the configurations of power implicated in the production of the discourses on the "Muslim woman" in the West and North Africa. In contrast with the Western narrative of the victimized "Muslim woman," and in opposition to the Arabocentric narrative in which "the Muslim woman" has no claims because Islam elevated her position fifteen hundred years ago, this book argues that as a single "category,"[1] the "Muslim woman" is an "invention," whether in the Western discourses of Orientalism and Western psychoanalytic feminism or in the discourses of Arab nationalism and Islamic feminism in colonial and postcolonial North Africa. Against the term "representation," which posits a binary opposition between true and false representation, the word "invention" presents the "Muslim woman" as an unfixed yet situated signifier.

As a fixed category, the "Muslim woman" functions metaphorically[2] to produce the alterity and inferiority of Islam as in the discourse of Orientalism or to symbolize Tunisian identity as in the nationalist master narratives of Tahar al Haddad and President Habib Bourguiba. Whereas the metaphoric usage of the "Muslim woman" in the discourses of Orientalism and Maghrebian nationalism is sutured, the metonymic deployment of the "Muslim woman" in the writings of Assia Djebar resists closure and produces the "Muslim woman" as an unfixed and plural signifier. Resisting all claims to presence and identity, this study constructs the "Muslim woman" in view of Jacques Derrida's notion of "excess" or "supplementarity."[3] As such, rather than being fixed, the "Muslim woman" occupies an "in-between"[4] space, one that cuts across the binary oppositions of self and other or "slave and master."

Besides taking into account the racial diversity of Muslim women in the Maghreb—Arabs, Berbers, and blacks—and their differences of class and

1

education, I view the word "Muslim" as heterogeneous. Even though Islam is not the focus of this book, this study is aware of the different Islamic groups and subgroups living in the Maghreb, namely, the Sunna with its Hanafi, Maliki, Hanbali, and Shafi'i schools and the Sufi brotherhoods like the Tijaniya and al Kadiriya. This heterogeneity, however, is to be viewed in terms of Derrida's concept of *différance*, rather than the "arrested" or "fixated"[5] differences that Bhabha describes in his discussion of colonial discourse.

The second claim I make in this book is that the "Muslim woman" is a semiotic subject who is produced according to the law of supply and demand to serve various political and ideological ends. I understand semiotic subject to mean a subject who is constituted through previous discourses, but who is historically situated. Building on Teresa de Lauretis's three claims—(1) that the human subject is always "gendered"[6] and "produced through language"; (2) that gender is "the representation of a relation"; and (3) that it is "the product and the process of both representation and self-representation"[7]—this study argues that "the Muslim woman" is essentially a semiotic subject that is produced and reproduced by Orientalist, Islamic, feminist, and nationalistic discourses. A major focus shall be placed on the situatedness of these discourses produced on the North African "Muslim woman": Where do writers like Isabelle Eberhardt, Jacques Lacan, Hélène Cixous, Tahar al Haddad, Habib Bourguiba, Fatima Mernissi, Assia Djebar, and Abul 'Alâ al Ma'arri come from when they receive/manufacture/transform images of the "Muslim woman"?[8]

The third argument of this book is that cultures are invented and maintained to express relations of power. Just as the "Muslim woman" is invented to negotiate European identity or national identity in the discourse of Orientalism or Arab nationalism, cultural differences are also invented to negotiate one's place and identity. Dismissing the conventional anthropological notion of culture as a set of social practices common to a special locale, nation, or tribe, and the assumptions of Muslim feminists like Mernissi about the territorialized oppressive Islamic culture of the Maghreb, this book argues not only that there is no homogeneous or unifying Islamic culture in the Maghreb, but more important, that the so-called Islamic culture that Mernissi denounces is in fact nothing but a current ideological or political invention that masquerades as an authentic Islamic tradition.[9] It is the objective of this study to demonstrate that cultural identity, as Kenneth W. Harrow puts it, emerges from "contestation," from setting oneself against another; hence, it cannot be "confined within established borders."[10] Rather than focusing on the cultural differences between the Maghreb and the West, I investigate in this work the hegemonic positions from which a discourse articulating cultural and gender difference is enunciated, and the processes through which cultures are imposed, invented, and transformed.

The fourth and final claim of this study is that Orientalist, feminist, or nationalist discourses on the "Muslim woman" are always ambivalent. In contrast with Edward W. Said's monolithic presentation of Orientalism as a homogeneous Western discourse that aims at dominating and subduing an immoral and effeminate Orient, the present study argues that the Orientalist discourses on the "Muslim woman" are always ambivalent. This ambivalence is caused by the enunciator's location within an apparatus of power,[11] as she/he negotiates a position from which to speak. This study takes upon itself the task of investigating the racial, social, educational, and gender privileges that allow Western female travelers in the Maghreb, Western and Muslim feminists, and North African nationalist revolutionaries to speak on behalf of the "Muslim woman." The following section explains more fully in what way this book departs from Said's study of gender and colonialism in *Orientalism*[12] and *Culture and Imperialism*.[13]

Many feminists criticized Said for his gender politics. For instance, in "Presences and Absences in Edward Said's *Culture and Imperialism*," Harriet D. Lyons points to the omission in Said's work of African women's struggle against colonialism: "The Igbo Women's War of 1929 is nowhere mentioned, though it was prominently reported and brought the dysphoria of colonized women to the attention of the British public."[14] To the aforesaid criticism, I shall add that nowhere in his work does Said cite Arab women writers and feminists, let alone mention Arab women's struggle against French and British imperialism. In an interview with Jacqueline Rose, Said provides an excuse for the conspicuous absence of women from his work, which he explains by the phallocentrism underlying his British education:

> And I always went to all-male schools, and the ethos—I think you have to blame this on the British a little bit—the ethos was terribly masculine. In my higher education, there were no women as students, none as professors, neither at Princeton when I was an undergraduate nor at Harvard. . . . Then I've tried to educate myself, but too late probably, in the history and writing by women about women of the last few years [i.e., after *Orientalism*].[15]

This explanation is unconvincing, for if Said had been able to denounce the racism in the British and American academy and attack an ethnocentric book like Allan D. Bloom's *The Closing of the American Mind*,[16] he should have been able to escape the sexism of his British education.

In *Orientalism*, Said's study of the image of the "Muslim woman" in the works of the nineteenth-century French writers (Gustave Flaubert, Gérard de Nerval, François René Chateaubriand, and Charles Baudelaire) reveals two sets of imagery. In the first set, the "Muslim woman" appears as a licentious sexual creature. She is often working as a prostitute or a courtesan like Flaubert's Kuchuk Hanem.[17] Because of her excessive sexuality, the "Oriental woman" becomes a femme fatale, similar to the legendary type of Isis, Cleopatra, and Salome.[18] In the second type, the "Muslim woman" epitomizes the exotic essence of the Orient, which the European male traveler covets and tries to possess. Commenting on the function of the "Oriental woman" in Nerval's *Vaisseau d'Orient*, Said writes:

> The Orient symbolizes Nerval's dream quest and the fugitive woman central to it, both as desire and as loss. Vaisseau d'Orient—vessel of the Orient—refers enigmatically either to the woman as the vessel carrying the Orient, or possibly, to Nerval's own vessel for the Orient, his prose voyage.[19]

Whether a prostitute or the symbol of a mysterious Orient, these two sets of imagery associated with the "Muslim woman" are constitutive of the discourse of Orientalism, which constructs/uses the degeneracy and effeminacy of the Oriental as an excuse to invade/penetrate the Middle East under the cloak of the French civilizing mission. Showing the deep complicity between literary knowledge and the institutions of power, Said demonstrates how the image of the "Oriental woman" as a prostitute or a barren woman[20] is complicit with the European imperialist project of conquering and civilizing a lifeless, feminine, and immoral East. As Said puts it: "My argument is that Flaubert's situation of strength in relation to Kuchuk Hanem was not an isolated instance. It fairly stands for the pattern of relative strength between East and West, and the discourse about the Orient that it enabled."[21]

Said's discussion of male Orientalism seems to derive from the Freudian distinction between the surface and latent meaning of a text. As a prostitute or a barren "femme fatale," the "Oriental woman" functions on the surface level as a metaphor for the Orient's need for Europe's civilizing mission. On a deeper level, she is a "sort of surrogate and even underground self"[22] for Europe. The excessive sexuality of Flaubert's Kuchuk Hanem as well as his obsession with harems and dancing women illustrate the "escapism of sexual fantasy." For Said, the sexual indulgence of the Orientals compensates for Flaubert's sexual frustration under Europe's bourgeois morality.[23]

The excessive sexuality of the Oriental (the surface meaning of Flaubert's text) could be, as Said says, a trope to compensate for Flaubert's sexual repression under bourgeois morality (latent meaning), but what appears here to be a latent meaning (the sexual repression following the embourgeoisement of European society), could also be a displacement for an earlier act of repression; the repression of Flaubert's homoerotic desire. In "Vacation Cruises: or, the Homoerotics of Orientalism," Joseph Boone rightly criticizes

Said for his silence over the homoerotic in his discussion of Orientalism. Boone writes that Flaubert was in fact fascinated with "Hassan el Belbeissi," an Egyptian male dancer, not "Kuchuk Hanem."[24] Even though Jean-Léon Gérome's painting "The Snake Charmer"—a voyeuristic spectacle where eleven Oriental men gaze at the penis of a young Arab boy—appears on the cover of *Orientalism*, nowhere in his book does Said discuss this painting's voyeuristic economy of desire. In this tableau, only the Arab men can see the young boy's penis, which seems to be deliberately hidden from the painting's viewers. This veiling or artistic prohibition is instrumental in kindling the spectator's desire. Because desire always involves the substitution of one word for another (Lacan), the snake, as a phallic symbol, should be seen as a substitute for the absent object of desire, that is, the young boy's penis. As he plays with the snake, the young boy acts out the masturbatory fantasies of the male imperial painter/viewer, who exclusively sees and exoticizes the young boy's buttocks.

Gérome's painting recalls a similar scene in *Flaubert in Egypt: A Sensibility on Tour*,[25] where a young snake charmer enters the French man's room and undresses in front of him to show him that there is no trickery. In this scene, the snake appears as a third body where the homoerotic encounter between Flaubert and the young boy takes place:

> He lifted the snake to my ear; *it bit me hard*; with a finger he took the blood from the bite and spread it on the ground; then *he breathed twice into my mouth, made me breathe twice on the large black snake*, which he had wrapped around my neck, *twice rubbed my bloody ear with his hand that he had moistened with his saliva*, once again asked me for "a big tip"—and the thing was done. [emphasis added][26]

Even though his narrative suggests the primitiveness of the Orient and its strange cultural practices, Flaubert's writings about his sexual adventures in Egypt are quite subversive of the French civilizing mission in the Orient. After noting how sodomy is accepted in the East, Flaubert confesses in a letter to his friend Louis Bouilhet (15 January 1850)—and not without irony—that "traveling as [he was] for educational purposes, and charged with a mission by the government, [he has] considered it [his] duty to indulge in this form of ejaculation."[27] In the Turkish bath, the Kellaa "was rubbing him gently," and "lifted up [his] *boules d'amour* to clean them," put his right hand on his "prick," and asked for baksheesh. Flaubert pushed him away. Yet, far from being "angry," Flaubert "laughed aloud like a dirty old man."[28] In another letter to Bouilhet (2 June 1850), Flaubert wrote that he finally "consumed that business at the baths." It was "on a pockmarked young rascal wearing a white turban. It made [Flaubert] laugh, that's all. But [he'll] be at it again. To be done well, an experiment must be repeated."[29] Flaubert might be complicit with the French civilizing mission as Said claims, but in presenting these homoerotic encounters as part of his official mission in Egypt, he is undermining the dichotomy between Eastern degeneracy and Occidental morality, which is at the heart of the French civilizing mission in the Middle East. Hence, Orientalism rather than being a monolithic discourse as Said presents it, is always ambivalent.

Similarly, Flaubert's self-presentation as a "frequenter" of Parisian brothels and prostitutes is subversive of the French civilizing mission, which locates degeneracy outside its national borders, that is, in those countries to be conquered. For Flaubert, prostitution, indeed, seems to have a "particular mystique":

> It may be a perverted taste . . . but I love prostitution, and for itself, too, quite apart from its carnal aspects. My heart begins to pound every time I see one of those women in low-cut dresses walking under the lamplight in the rain, just as monks in their corded robes have always excited some deep, ascetic corner of my soul.[30]

Subverting the moral superiority underlying the French civilizing mission, Flaubert compares the Muslim prostitutes to the Christian prostitutes he encountered in the brothels of France: "Kuchuk dances with my tarboosh on her head. Then she accompanies us to the end of her quarter, climbing up on our backs and making faces and jokes like any Christian tart."[31] In another letter, he writes that the "word *almeh* means 'learned woman,' 'bluestocking,' or 'whore'—which proves, Monsieur, that in all countries women of letters. . . !!!"[32] The footnote accompanying the letter states that Flaubert is referring here to his French mistress Louise Colet. Thus, Flaubert's depiction of the Oriental woman as a prostitute reveals not only the French colonial desire to dominate and subdue the East, but also Flaubert's own misogynistic attitude toward women in general whether they be Colets or Kuchuk Hanems.[33]

Flaubert's discourses on the "Oriental woman" depend on the context in which they have been articulated. When Louise Colet wrote Flaubert a letter in which she expressed her jealousy of Kuchuk Hanem, to appease her anger, Flaubert painted her an appalling picture of the "Egyptian woman":

> The Oriental woman is no more than a machine: she makes no distinction between one man and another man. Smoking, going to the baths, painting her eyelids and drinking coffee—such is the circle of occupations within which her existence confined. As for physical pleasure, it must be very slight, since the well known button, the seat of same, is sliced off at an early age.[34]

In a letter to Sainte-Beuve (23–24 December 1862), Flaubert compares Amilcar's daughter Salammbô to Saint Thérèse. And in contrast with his previous assertion to Colet that the "Oriental woman" is a "machine," he now claims that all knowledge of the "Oriental woman" is impossible:

> Mme Bovary est agitée par des passions multiples; Salammbô au contraire demeure clouée par l'idée fixe. C'est une maniaque, une espèce de Sainte Thérèse. N'importe! Je ne suis pas sûr de sa réalité; car ni moi, ni vous, ni personne, aucun ancien et aucun moderne, ne peut connaître la femme orientale, par la raison qu'il est impossible de la fréquenter.[35]

In Arabic, the word *Maghreb* ("North Africa") means "West." Said's discussion of French Orientalism betrays a Levantocentric point of view, which excludes and constructs the Maghreb as an African/Western Other. Despite the long history of French colonialism in Algeria (1830–1962), Tunisia (1881–1956), and Morocco (1912–1956), in Said's text, the Maghreb with its women and the entire history of its people is ignored and dismissed to a footnote. In opposition to Said, Flaubert does not see the Maghreb as totally Other. In *Salammbô* (1862), which is set during the Mercenaries' War (241–38 B.C.) between Carthage and the Numidians—just after Carthage lost the First Punic War against Rome—Flaubert points to the heterogeneity of the Orient and to the ethnic and political conflicts setting on the one hand the Carthagenians/Phoenicians against the "Barbarians"/Africans, and against the Romans on the other hand. In this historical novel, Flaubert identifies with the Romans, the Carthagenians, and the "Barbarians." For instance, Mâtho, the Numidian or "Barbarian" hero who fell in love with the Canaanite Salammbô, is presented as a Christlike figure. He dies a horrible death at the hands of an angry mob: his ears torn, his cheeks slit with needles, his face smeared in filth, his chest branded with "a red-hot bar" before being opened with a knife.[36] Even though he identifies with Rome because it is the emblem of the Western world, Flaubert still feels sympathy for the Barbarian Matho and expresses his admiration for the Canaanite King Amilcar.

Historicizing this process of identification, Lisa Lowe observes that the repeated defeats of Carthage echo the repeated defeats of Napoleon and "France's international losses" during the unstable period of the "bourgeois revolt" known as "the July Monarchy of 1830."[37] According to Michel Butor, Salammbô is a "double text"[38] where Carthage appears as "the hidden face of ancient Rome," or the Other "buried" and "denied" at first by Rome, then by France. Despite its colonial undertones, Flaubert's novel situates Carthage halfway between East and West; the same Greek, Mycenaean, Phoenician, and Egyptian influences that gave birth to Carthage have also generated Western culture.

Another problem Dennis Porter identifies in *Orientalism* is Said's reluctance to consider other alternatives to Orientalism.[39] Even though he wonders if there could ever be "nonrepressive and nonmanipulative"[40] Western studies of the Orient, Said does not return to this issue later. This book takes issue with Said's pessimistic view—in *Orientalism*[41] at least—that knowledge of the Other is impossible. Said's premise might have drastic implications on the political activism of North African feminists, such as stripping the latter from the incentive to reach out and understand the problems of other women across the boundaries of class, race, and nation. Finally, whereas Said deemphasizes class and gender to focus exclusively on the Orient's subjection to Western hegemony, *The Production of the Muslim Woman* goes beyond the stereotypical vision of the victimized "Muslim woman" in the discourses of Orientalism and Arab nationalism to examine patriarchy in terms of different configurations of power such as class, education, race, and gender.

From a methodological point of view, *The Production of the Muslim Woman* is a hybrid work combining Western and Islamic feminist theory as well as psychoanalytic and historicist approaches. Going beyond the ghetto of ethno-theory, this study tries to overcome the shortcomings and limits of any single approach; its primary objective is to interrogate the text, generate meanings, and disclose relations and concepts that would remain hidden were it to rely exclusively on one approach and not the other. It is the task of the postcolonial writer/critic/reader to interrogate her/his own premises and throw the theory against itself. As Judith Butler puts it, to deconstruct does not mean to dismiss, but to put into question:

> To deconstruct the concept of matter or that of bodies is not to negate or refuse either term. To deconstruct these terms means, rather, to continue to use them, to repeat them, to repeat them subversively, and to displace them from the contexts in which they have been deployed as instruments of oppressive power. . . . To call a presupposition into question is not the same as doing away with it; rather, it is to free it up from its metaphysical lodgings in order to occupy and to serve very different political aims.[42]

Endorsing Butler's warnings against "a transcultural notion of patriarchy,"[43] this study makes the claim that almost all societies are patriarchal, but that patriarchal oppression takes on different forms; hence the need for a localized strategic feminism, one in alliance with Western feminism, yet aware of the different forms of local patriarchies; and hence also the need to devise an appropriate in-situ feminist agenda. Even though this book engages with Western feminist theory, it also interrogates its viability when applied to the North African context. If we grant that the image of the "Muslim woman" is invented, does this mean that the different forms of oppression she is subjected to are also invented? How can we reject state authority (Butler) in the North African context where Muslim feminists, in their dedication to social and political commitment, want to involve the state in promulgating laws that protect women's rights? What are the limits of constructedness? What problems accompany the idealization of agency and women's voices?

This study also shows the limits of using Lacanian theory in the Maghrebian context. For instance, what are the consequences of applying Lacan's notion that the phallus works best when veiled to the Algerian context where the Islamic Salvation Front (FIS) holds that the glory of Islam consists in the control of the female body through seclusion and veiling? Should we dismiss psychoanalysis altogether? It is a common misconception indeed to dismiss psychoanalysis because of its Western universalism. In his essay "The Function and Field of Speech and Language in Psychoanalysis," Lacan stands against the American "ahistoricism" and states that the symbolic is always mediated through the local culture:[44]

> In the symbolic order first of all, one cannot neglect the importance of the c factor, which I noted at the Congress of Psychiatry in 1950 as being the constant characteristic of any given cultural milieu: the condition here of the ahistoricism, which, by common accord, is recognized as being the principle feature of "communication" in the United States, and which, in my opinion, is at the antipodes of the psychoanalytic experience."[45]

However, one has to be aware of the limits of psychoanalysis, notably of its overemphasis on "sexual matters" and "exclusion" of racial and social issues. As Claudia Tate[46] puts it, rather than dismissing psychoanalysis because of Freud's "Negro jokes"[47] or because it is a white practice intended for the white "well-to-do," psychoanalysis needs to be critiqued and revised in order "to address more pressing concerns—such as Western cultural crises in which the family, race, and cultural difference play critical roles," and be put "in a much larger cultural context than the white bourgeois family."[48] Just as psychoanalysis is useful in illuminating the not so obvious meanings of a text, a historicist approach is also instrumental in situating the ideological production and deployment of the "Muslim woman" within a certain historical and political conjuncture.

This book is divided into five chapters. The first, "A Semiotic Reading of Islamic Feminism: Hybridity, Authority, and the Strategic Reinvention of the 'Muslim Woman' in Fatima Mernissi," focuses on the production of the "Muslim woman" in the discourse of the Moroccan sociologist Fatima Mernissi. In opposition to the Western monolithic perception of the "Muslim woman," Mernissi reinvents the "Muslim woman" as a plural yet situated signifier. Just like the "Muslim woman" fabricated by the Islamist discourse, the "Muslim women" produced by Mernissi are strategic inventions that ought to be examined in view of the current cartography of power in Morocco. However, by marking *Jahiliya* as the original point of Islamic culture, Mernissi undercuts any notion of Islam being heir to the earlier Middle Eastern cultures, falling therefore in the originary thinking of Islamic Orthodoxy. This chapter also questions Mernissi's use of Freudian theory to analyze the psyche of Muslim societies as well as the sources of her authority to write on behalf of Moroccan women.

The second chapter fills out Said's silence over female Orientalism. "Isabelle Eberhardt, *ou 'La Roumia Convertie'*: A Case Study in Female Orientalism" focuses on the relationship of Western women with North African women and on their understanding of gender as white women residing in the Arab world. The production of the "Muslim woman" in Eberhardt's autobiographical and fictional writings will be investigated in view of the fin de siècle French colonial culture. This chapter demonstrates how Eberhardt's ambivalence vis-à-vis the "Muslim woman" and the French civilizing mission in the Maghreb depends on her position inside/outside the French imperial world. This corroborates the view that culture is a relation of power (Amselle), not something specific to an ethnicity or locale. This chapter also uses Eberhardt to critique Bhabha for his androcentric view of the hybrid.

Relying on de Lauretis's notion of gender as "representation," the third chapter, "The 'Muslim Woman' and the Iconography of the Veil in French Feminism and Psychoanalysis," discusses the viability of Western feminist and psychoanalytic theory in the North African context and argues that these discourses derive at times from the same Orientalist impulse we find in the male Orientalism discussed by Said. The first part of this chapter argues that even though he is situated on the left, Frantz Fanon's discourse on the veil in "Algeria Unveiled" is both patriarchal and Orientalist. The second section traces Lacan's notion of the "veiled phallus" to the primacy of the specular in Western metaphysics and to the discourses of the veil produced during the Algerian Revolution. The third part of this chapter examines how French feminists like Simone de Beauvoir and Luce Irigaray recycle the earlier Orientalist discourses on the "Muslim woman." In contrast with the other French feminists, Cixous's discourse on the "Muslim woman" stands inside/outside French imperial ideology. The final part of this chapter examines how Cixous's *Les Rêveries de la femme sauvage: Scènes primitives* (2000) presents a "doubled vision"[49] vis-à-vis the veil and Algerian Muslim women. Cixous's ambivalence will be examined against her self-proclaimed "literary nationality,"[50] her autobiography, and the Frenchification of the Algerian Jews.

The fourth chapter, "Body, Home, and Nation: The Production of the Tunisian 'Muslim Woman' in the Reformist Thought of Tahar al Haddad and

Habib Bourguiba," focuses on the invention of the "Tunisian Muslim woman" in the feminist and nationalist discourses of Habib Bourguiba (1903–2000) and Tahar al Haddad (1899–1935). This chapter examines how the double privilege of gender and education gives al Haddad and Bourguiba not only the authority to speak on behalf of the "Tunisian woman," but also the power to claim for her a traditional past and a future.

The last chapter, "The House of the Prophet as a Technology of Power: Reinventing Domesticity and the Sacred in the Texts of Al Ma'arri, Al Naluti, Djebar, and Rushdie," makes the claim that as a technology of power, the House of the Prophet is claimed not only by hegemonic Islamic groups but also by those who are situated on the margin of Islamic Orthodoxy. This chapter argues that in contrast with the cynicism of Abul 'Alâ al Ma'arri in *The Epistle of Forgiveness* (1032), which makes him reject the House of the Prophet as an instrument of political legitimation, Djebar's political commitment in *Loin de Médine* (1991) makes her engage in the dominant discourse of Islamic orthodoxy and reinvent the House of the Prophet through the lens of both *écriture feminine* and Islamic feminism. This chapter will also briefly examine the invention of the House of the Prophet in Salman Rushdie's *The Satanic Verses* (1988) and *Al Tawba*, a 1992 theatrical readaptation of al Ma'arri's divine comedy by the Tunisian novelist Arusiyya al Naluti.

NOTES

1. Chandra Talpade Mohanty, "Under Western Eyes: Feminist Scholarship and Colonial Discourses," in *Colonial Discourse and Postcolonial Theory*, ed. Patrick Williams and Laura Chrisman (New York: Columbia University Press, 1994), 196–220.
2. I am relying here on Homi K. Bhabha's distinction between metonymy and metaphor: Whereas the first is a "supplementary strategy" that is open and based on difference, the second is closed and sutured as it conflates "the many as one," and "totalize[s] the social in a homogenous empty time." See *The Location of Culture* (London: Routledge, 1994), 155.
3. Derrida Jacques, *Of Grammatology*, trans. Gayatri Chakravorti Spivak (Baltimore: Johns Hopkins University Press, 1976), 145.
4. Bhabha, *The Location of Culture*, 55.
5. Bhabha, *The Location of Culture*, 75.
6. Teresa de Lauretis, *Technologies of Gender: Essays on Theory, Film, and Fiction* (Bloomington: Indiana University Press, 1987), 19.
7. De Lauretis, *Technologies of Gender*, 9.
8. My own claim that the "Muslim woman" is a political invention derives from my privileges of class and Western education, and the colonial status of my ancestry,

the Turks, who confiscated almost the whole region of Beja, the most fertile land in Tunisia, and formerly known as "The Basket of Rome." During my visit to Tunisia in May 2001, I realized how deep the gap was between the preoccupations of upper- and middle-class Muslim women studying in American universities, and the Muslim female students from the lower classes who work as maids and in slavelike conditions to support their families and buy schoolbooks. One of these young women was Amna, whom I hired as a babysitter so that I could go to the Tunisian National Archives and The National Library and write about Bourguiba and al Haddad. I realized (and not without guilt) that intellectual pursuits like the present study are the domain of the privileged; Muslim women like Amna worry about food and still go to school on an empty stomach. Not once did Amna complain about Tunisian men or Islamic patriarchy. Her main concern was feeding her sick old mother—that is to say, survival. My contact with Tunisian women from the lower classes made me realize that patriarchy is a matter of power and social class, not simply gender.

9. Jean-Loup Amselle, *Mestizo Logics: Anthropology of Identity in Africa and Elsewhere*, trans. Claudia Royal (Stanford: Stanford University Press, 1988), 3.

10. Kenneth W. Harrow, "Shibboleths in the Production of Culture" (Paper presented at the 27th annual meeting of the African Literature Association in Richmond, Virginia, 4–8 April 2001). n.p.

11. Bhabha, *The Location of Culture*, 1.

12. Edward W. Said, *Orientalism* (New York: Vintage Books, 1979).

13. Said, *Culture and Imperialism* (New York: Vintage Books, 1993).

14. Harriet D. Lyons, "Presences and Absences in Edward Said's Culture and Imperialism," *Canadian Journal of African Studies* 28, no. 1 (1994): 102.

15. Jacqueline Rose, "Edward Said Talks to Jacqueline Rose," *Critical Quarterly* 40, no. 1 (Spring 1998): 87.

16. Said, "Identity, Authority, and Freedom: The Potentate and the Traveler," *Boundary 2* (Fall 1992): 5.

17. Said, *Orientalism*, 6.

18. Said, *Orientalism*, 180.

19. Said, *Orientalism*, 184.

20. Said, *Orientalism*, 187.

21. Said, *Orientalism*, 6.

22. Said, *Orientalism*, 3.

23. Said, *Orientalism*, 90.

24. Joseph A. Boone, "Vacation Cruises; or, the Homoerotics of Orientalism," *Modern Language Association of America* 110, no. 1 (Jan. 1995): 92.

25. Gustave Flaubert, *Flaubert in Egypt: A Sensibility Tour*, trans. Francis Steegmuller (Boston: Little, Brown, and Company, 1972).

26. Flaubert, *Flaubert in Egypt*, 89.

27. Flaubert, *Flaubert in Egypt*, 84.

28. Flaubert, *Flaubert in Egypt*, 83.

29. Flaubert, *Flaubert in Egypt*, 203–4.

30. Flaubert, *Flaubert in Egypt*, 9–10.

31. Flaubert, *Flaubert in Egypt*, 116.

32. Flaubert, *Flaubert in Egypt*, 129.

33. Flaubert's mystical interest in prostitutes could also be explained by the teachings of the Saint Simonians who preached free love and destigmatized prostitution in early-nineteenth-century France.

34. Flaubert, *Flaubert in Egypt*, 220.

35. Quoted by Lawrence R. Schehr, "*Salammbô* as the Novel of Alterity," *Nineteenth Century Studies* 17, nos. 3–4 (Spring–Summer 1989): 328.

36. Flaubert, *Salammbô* (New York: Modern Library, 1929), 350–53.

37. Lisa Lowe, "The Orient as Woman in Flaubert's *Salammbô* and *Voyage en Orient*," *Comparative Literature Studies* 23, no. 1 (Spring 1986): 46.

38. Quoted by Lowe, "The Orient as Woman," 47.

39. Dennis Porter, "Orientalism and Its Problems," in *Colonial Discourse and Postcolonial Theory*, ed. Patrick Williams and Laura Chrisman (New York: Columbia University Press, 1994), 151.

40. Said, *Orientalism*, 24.

41. Said's political commitment for the Palestinian people made him later change this position. See Bruce Robbins, "Race, Gender, Class, Postcolonialism: Toward a New Humanistic Paradigm?" *A Companion to Postcolonial Studies*, ed. Henry Schwarz and Sangeeta Ray (Malden: Blackwell, 2000), 556–73.

42. Judith Butler, *Feminists Theorize the Political* (New York: Routledge, 1992), 17.

43. Butler, *Gender Trouble: Feminism and the Subversion of Identity* (New York: Routledge, 1990), 35.

44. This book views "local culture" as a set of power relations temporarily characterizing a specific locale, rather than a set of misogynistic cultural practices that are fixed in time and space. In this study, the concept of "cultural difference" refers to the different power relations, which govern all human societies, whether Eastern or Western.

45. Jacques Lacan, *Écrits*, trans. Alan Sheridan (New York: W. W. Norton & Company, 1977), 37–38.

46. Claudia Tate, "Freud and His 'Negro': Psychoanalysis as Ally and Enemy of African Americans," *Journal for the Psychoanalysis of Culture & Society* 1, no. 1 (Spring 1999): 53–62.

47. Tate, "Freud and His 'Negro,'" 56.

48. Tate, "Freud and His 'Negro,'" 61.

49. De Lauretis, *Technologies of Gender*, 10.

50. Hélène Cixous, *Hélène Cixous: Photos de Racines* (Paris: Des Femmes, 1994), 207.

Chapter One

A Semiotic Reading of Islamic Feminism: Hybridity, Authority, and the Strategic Reinvention of the "Muslim Woman" in Fatima Mernissi

This chapter examines how the "Muslim woman" has been constructed, even by Muslim women feminists, within the binary of the West and Islam. Using de Lauretis's claim that gender is representation, the first part of this chapter argues that Mernissi's reinvention of the "Muslim woman" stands outside/ inside Western and Islamic ideologies. Whereas Mernissi's presentation of the "Muslim woman" as a plural signifier and her revision of Islamic tradition constitute a break with the earlier Orientalist and Islamic discourses on the "Muslim woman," her reliance on the opposition between "tradition" and "modernity" and her reauthentication of the hadith as sources of authority are in continuity with those earlier discourses on the "Muslim woman." The second section of this chapter examines the contradictions in Mernissi's construction of the "Muslim woman" and refashioning of Islamic tradition in view of the current power politics in Morocco and the Muslim world. The third section investigates the sources of Mernissi's authority to claim a past Islamic tradition for the "Muslim woman" as well as the implications of her invention of a homogenous "Islamic culture." The final section of this chapter questions Mernissi's reliance on a Freudian paradigm to study the consciousness of all Muslim societies.

Born in 1940 in a religious and conservative well-to-do family in Fez, Mernissi spent the first few years of her life in a harem before receiving a dual French and Arabic education in French colonial Morocco.[1] She was formerly a professor at the University of Muhammad V at Rabat, and is currently a member of the United Nations' University Council. Because of her dual cultural background, Mernissi's construction of the "Muslim woman" rests on the double bind to reproduce and resist the discourses of both the Orientalist and Islamic tradition.

MERNISSI'S STRATEGIC DEPLOYMENT OF IJTIHAD

Far from the metaphoric usage of the "Muslim woman" as a symbol for Islam or Muhammad's *umma* ("nation") in the respective discourses of Orientalism and Islamism, Mernissi's "Muslim woman" is deployed metonymically[2] to express the plurality and diversity of Muslim women's experiences. Unlike the Orientalist male invention of the "Muslim woman" as a prostitute or "victim of male violence"[3] in Western feminist scholarship or the subsequent scenario of her rape and abduction by imperial powers in Arab nationalist discourses, Mernissi reinvents "the Muslim woman" as an unfixed and plural signifier. In her investigation of the desegregation of the sexes in Moroccan society, Mernissi focuses on the differences between the women she is interviewing: "The categories 'modern' and 'traditional'[4] cover a range of differences in age, education, employment, and so on."[5] In *Chahrazad n'est pas marocaine*, she makes the claim that illiteracy is the major challenge facing rural Moroccan women in the twenty-first century. Unlike the mythical Chahrazad, who saved her life through her erudition, the illiteracy of Moroccan women (estimated at 95 percent in the rural areas and 57 percent in the cities during the 1980s) foreclosed and doomed their future.[6]

In contrast with colonial feminism's uniform perception of the veil as a marker of Muslim women's oppression and the radical difference of Islam, the veil in Mernissi's *The Veil and the Male Elite* (1991) emerges as a shifting yet situated signifier. Locating the "veil" in its sociohistorical context, Mernissi explains that the "veil" or *hijab* is a three-dimensional word in Arabic:

> The three dimensions often blend into one another. The first dimension is a visual one: to hide something from sight. The root of the verb *hajaba* means "to hide." The second dimension is spatial: to separate, to mark a border, to establish a threshold. And finally, the third dimension is ethical: it belongs to the realm of the forbidden. A space hidden by a hijab is a forbidden space.[7]

In Al Ahzab Sura (33: 53), the *hijab* designates the House of the Prophet as a space visually and morally forbidden:

> O you who believe, do not enter the Prophet's homes unless you are given permission to eat, nor shall you force such an invitation in any manner. If you are invited, you may enter. When you finish eating, you shall leave; do not engage him in lengthy conversations. This used to hurt the Prophet, and he was too shy to tell you. But God does not shy away from the truth. If you have to ask his wives for something, ask them from behind a barrier. This is purer for your hearts and their hearts. You are not to hurt the messenger of God. You shall not

marry his wives after him, for this would be a gross offense in the sight of God.[8]

In Sufi philosophy, the *hijab* is a negative signifier that prevents the believer from perceiving his Creator.[9] In contrast with Muhammad's life where there was a "spatial intimacy between the mosque"[10] and Aïsha's apartment and therefore between women and politics, during the reign of the Ummayad Caliph Mu'awiya a *hijab* was erected to separate women from politics and the Caliph from his people. The *hijab* of the Prince, according to Mernissi, is the veil or "curtain" that separates the ruler from the "gaze" of the Muslim masses.[11] Contrasting the common view that Islam is incompatible with democracy, Mernissi argues that the early Islamic period was democratic because of its inclusion of women and because of the absence of barriers (*hijab*) between the Prophet and his community.

Mernissi's reformist feminism lies especially in her strategic reexamination of the hadith. Her analysis of the hadith is subversive because *al-fiqh* ("the science of explaining religion") is a male field that traditionally excludes women. Following Benazir Bhutto's election as a prime minister in Pakistan in 1988, the Islamist groups argued that a woman leader is a *bida'*, that is to say, an innovation that is alien to Islam. To support their claim, they brandished al-Bukhari's hadith, according to which Abu Bakra heard the Prophet say: "Those who entrust their affairs to a woman will never know prosperity."[12] Using the same methodology as the male recorders, notably al-Bukhari, al-Tirmidhi, Ibn Saad, and al-Baghdadi, Mernissi makes a distinction between the *sahih* and *mawdhu'* ("true" and "false") hadith by investigating the credibility of everyone listed in the hadith's chain of transmitters. She then proceeds to investigate Abu Bakra's biography as well as the historical context when the hadith was recorded. According to Mernissi, Abu Bakra opportunistically remembered that hadith—twenty-five years after Muhammad's death—after the Battle of the Camel where Aïsha was defeated by Alî, the Prophet's cousin and son-in-law. Because he "had refused to take part in the civil war"[13] against Aïsha, Abu Bakra fabricated that hadith after the war to protect himself against Alî's clan. Digging into Abu Bakra's biography, she discovers that al-Bukhari should have rejected that hadith, because of Abu Bakra's involvement in a story of perjury: he was convicted and flogged for providing a false testimony in an adultery trial during the reign of 'Umar Ibn al Khattab.[14] In using "the principles of Malik for *fiqh*,"[15] Mernissi simultaneously shows how the sacred has been manipulated by Muslim patriarchy and endorses, through the example she provides, women's active participation in the project of reforming the Shari'a laws.

Whereas in the Orientalist narrative of Lord Cromer "Islam degraded"[16] women through "veiling" and "segregation," in Mernissi's feminist narrative, Islam improved women's lives, by banishing the *Jahiliya* practice of female infanticide and underscoring women's right to inheritance. Under Muhammad's new faith, a woman can no longer be inherited like "camels and palm trees." She is now a free subject who is entitled to inheritance like men. According to Mernissi, Islam's endorsement of a woman's right to inheritance created a "bombshell" or a "conflict"[17] of interest between the male population of Medina and the Prophet of the new religion.

In contrast with Ahmed[18] who claims that the veiling of Muhammad's wives is a logical continuity to the pattern of male domination that started to emerge in Arabia during the rise of Islam, Mernissi asserts that Muhammad's ideal of social and gender equality constitutes a break with the *Jahiliya* pre-Islamic practices. Women's participation in war, their right to "gain booty," and "to have a say with regard to the sex act" overthrew "the pre-Islamic—relations between men and women."[19] However, the strong male opposition to Islam's ideal of gender equality—as exemplified by 'Umar Ibn al-Khattab and the Medinese Hypocrites[20]—pushed Muhammad to abandon these ideals in order to guarantee the survival of the new religion. Digging into Muhammad's biography, Mernissi also shows how his wives participated in war, entered the mosque, asked him for marriage (like his first wife Khadija), and even repudiated him as in the cases of Mulaika Bint Ka'ab and Fatima Bint al-Dahhak.[21] In her effort to bring about legislation that is favorable to women, Mernissi strategically invents a Muhammad who has neither the divinelike status he is given in Orthodox Islam, nor is marred by the sensuality and pedophilia of Mahound, the protagonist of Salman Rushdie's *The Satanic Verses*. In her reconstruction of Muhammad's biography, Mernissi shows that his strength lies in his love, not aggression, toward women. Commenting on the split between Muhammad's teaching[22] and his fatal attraction to women's beauty, she writes:

> It should be noted here that the Muslim Prophet's heroism does not lie in any relation of aggression, conquest, or exercise of brute force against women, but on the contrary in his vulnerability. . . . It is because he is vulnerable, and therefore human, that his example has exerted such power over generations of believers.[23]

MERNISSI'S ISLAMIC FEMINISM: BETWEEN CONFORMITY AND RESISTANCE

A closer examination of Mernissi's writings reveals not only resistance to but also conformity with the Orientalist and Islamic discourses on the "Muslim woman." Mernissi's feminist reinvention of the "Muslim woman" illustrates what de Lauretis calls the feminist subject's double position "inside and outside the ideology of gender, and conscious of being so."[24] Even though it is presented as a multiple signifier, the veil in Mernissi's writings is quite often associated with the perpetuation of gender inequality. Reversing the equation of the veil with Islamic identity maintained today by right-wing Islamic groups and in the past by Arab nationalists, Mernissi reinvents the *hijab* as an obstacle to democracy and to the "true" meaning of Islam. According to Mernissi, Islam's egalitarian project was compromised when Muhammad, because of his military difficulties, complied with the wishes of the hypocrites and secluded his wives. Rather than being the symbol of Islamic identity, the veil is rewritten thus as the symbol of Muhammad's submission to his enemies and "retreat from the principle of equality."[25]

In responding to the Islamic right, Mernissi falls within the modernist view that associates the veil with oppression and links women's emancipation with unveiling. Echoing Qassim Amin and other Arab nationalists, Mernissi associates unveiling with cultural survival and progress. Examining the history of Moroccan women's emancipation, she writes that King Muhammad V "puzzled the entire country in 1943 when he presented his daughter, Princess Aïsha, unveiled before the nation."[26] Unlike Mernissi, who holds an uncritical attitude toward Qassim Amin, the father of Egyptian feminism, Ahmed argues that Amin's advocacy of women's liberation through unveiling, rather than higher education, derives from the Western construction of the veil as a symbol of Islam's inferiority.[27] Echoing Fanon's discourse on the cultural alienation of the national bourgeoisie, Ahmed writes that it is the upper-class status and the French education of Qassim Amin, Doria Shafik, Mai Ziada, and Huda Sha'rawi that make them conceive of Muslim women's emancipation only through the unveiling of their bodies. The Arabic narrative of resistance, whereby the veil becomes the symbol of Arab Islamic identity, is written by feminists who did not have a Western education. For example, even though she is a member of the upper middle class, Malak Hifni Nassef's traditional education made her oppose the emancipation of Egyptian women after the Western model.[28] Ahmed shows that the current Islamic dress, *al-ziyy al-Islami*, is not a fixed code of dressing, but a pastiche of modern and old dress codes.[29]

Armed with recent sociological studies, Ahmed demonstrates that most of the women who wear the Islamic dress today are from families where other women are already veiled[30]; belong to the new middle classes who recently migrated to the urban areas[31]; and are the first generation of women in their family to enter a "sexually integrated world."[32] In contrast with Mernissi's feminist construction of the *hijab* as a negative signifier, Ahmed argues that

Islamic dress has to be reconceived as a sign of "educational and professional upward mobility" and "a practical coping strategy, enabling women to nego-tiate in the new world while affirming the traditional values of their upbring-ing."[33] Whereas colonial feminism views Muslim women's return to Islam as detrimental to their interests in the long run, the "activities being pursued by some veiled women, such as reclaiming of the right to attend prayer in mosques," suggest that these women are in fact challenging "the practices of establishment Islam with respect to women."[34] Ahmed concludes that the dichotomy between secular and Islamic feminism reflects deeper social divi-sions between an elitist urban feminism and a "grass-root"[35] movement an-chored in rural Egypt.

Thus, it is the double privilege of class and Western education that allows Mernissi to speak on behalf of all Moroccan women and equate women's emancipation with unveiling. As in Western colonial feminism, the veil in Mernissi's writings is seen as a symbol of female oppression. Even though she talks about the history of the veil in Sufi philosophy, she does not exam-ine the wearing of the veil in Morocco as a class issue. In her recent visit to Morocco, the American feminist Elizabeth Warnock Fernea[36] observes that the issue of women's emancipation in Morocco is primarily a question of class and social status. In Morocco Fernea discovered, in contrast with what she hears about Moroccan women in Western mass media, that there are Mo-roccan women judges, university professors, and others elected in Parliament, yet most of them come from the upper and middle classes of Moroccan soci-ety.[37]

In Mernissi's autobiographical work, *Dreams of Trespass*, women's seclu-sion is presented as both anachronistic and alien to Islam. As Mernissi's cousin Chama explains, the harems were adopted from the Byzantines in the Middle Ages. At that time power meant the conquest of territory and women, but the rules of the game have changed today:

> While the Arabs were busy locking women behind doors, the Romans and the other Christians got together and decided to change the rules of the power game in the Mediterranean. Collecting women, they declared, was not relevant any-more. From now on, the sultan would be the one who could build the most pow-erful weapons and machines, including firearms and big ships. But the Romans and other Christians decided not to tell the Arabs about the change; they would keep it a secret so as to surprise them. So the Arabs went to sleep, thinking that they knew the rules of the power game.[38]

Mernissi's concept of "chronopolitics" which she uses to describe "Islamic fundamentalism's" attempt to turn the clocks into Harun al Rachid's time seems objectionable on two grounds. First, because in reducing the problem of

"Islamic fundamentalism" to a clash between the Middle Ages and modernity, Mernissi falls not only within the binarism characterizing Islamic monologic thought, but also the Eurocentric evolutionary understanding of time. Indeed, Mernissi's concept of "chronopolitics" is based on the same dichotomy between tradition and modernity that we find in the writings of Amin, the Western-educated Egyptian feminist who equates the wearing of the veil with the backwardness of Islamic tradition. In *Maps of Englishness*, Simon Gikandi traces the dichotomy between tradition and modernity to the European modernist discourse, when "the invocation of colonial alterity,"[39] the dismantling of the old social fabric, combined with the racial anxieties "about what constitutes Englishness" led to the invention of a pure European tradition. As Gikandi argues, the concept of tradition that African nationalist leaders like Nkrumah or Kenyatta have deployed to assert African identity derives "its moral authority from its association with [the] bourgeois civility"[40] exemplified in the writings of T. S. Eliot. As a parallel, Mernissi's perception of the veil does not seem locally generated, but imposed by her elite status and acquaintance with Western culture.

The second objection to Mernissi's concept of "chronopolitics" is that Islamic tradition, to use Amselle's words, is "an exclusively contemporary conflict, that of fundamentalists speaking in the name of tradition while simultaneously projecting current ideological models into the past."[41] Mernissi herself explains the problem of "Islamic fundamentalism" and the oppression of women by the lack of democracy and the increasing rate of poverty,[42] unemployment, and neocolonialism in countries like Morocco.[43]

Two related problems arise here: First, how can Mernissi reduce the problem of "fundamentalism" to a clash between tradition and modernity while claiming that "fundamentalism" is caused by the contemporary problems of poverty, unemployment, and neocolonialism? Second, how can she attack Islamic tradition while relying on that same patriarchal concept to defend women's rights in Morocco? Mernissi's reauthentication of Islamic tradition ought to be conceived along the lines of Bhabha's view that tradition is an ongoing process of negotiation, subjected to the current hegemonic configurations of power. In "restaging the past," Mernissi's contradictions illustrate what Bhabha calls "the power of tradition to be reinscribed through the conditions of contingency and contradictoriness that attend upon the lives of those who are 'in the minority.'"[44]

Quite problematic indeed is Mernissi's criticism of Islamic tradition and reliance on the authority of the hadith to bring about women's rights in Moroccan society. In her reauthentication of the hadith, Mernissi ascribes to herself the authority of the Muslim male elite who has the power to distinguish between the false and true hadith. Rather than deconstructing or destabilizing the religious authority of the hadith, Mernissi reinforces the Law of the Muslim Father she is criticizing. She does nothing but reverse the terms of that Muslim symbolic: to the Law of the Muslim Father, she substitutes the Law of the Muslim Mother.

Not least significant is Mernissi's ambivalence toward the notion of "truth." In *Beyond the Veil*—written in French even before Said's *Orientalism*—Mernissi reiterates the Foucauldian suspicion toward truth and certainty:

> I leave the truth to those who seek certainty. My own feeling is that we move forward faster and live better when we seek doubt. . . . The qualitative analysis is not intended to flood the reader with statistical truths, which are in any case at anyone's disposal at the offices of the census department in Rabat. No, qualitative analysis ought to have the opposite effect: not to fortify your certitudes but to destroy them. It is understandable that a good number of walking dead may not appreciate that.[45]

Whether her reinvention of the "Muslim woman" is truthful or not, Mernissi could care less; as she puts it herself, she left truth for "those who seek certainty." However, throughout her writings, Mernissi presents her reinvention of early Muslim society and the ideal of gender equality in Muhammad's time as the truth that has been hidden or "veiled" by the Muslim male elite. Mernissi's reauthentication of the hadith—a strategy within the very system she opposes—paradoxically endorses the notion of truth from which the hadith derives its authority and hence reinforces the power of tradition to reinscribe and perpetuate itself.

Even though her distinction between true and false hadith is phallocentric, Mernissi's feminist revision of Islamic tradition is strategically deployed to provide a common basis for feminist mobilization in Moroccan society. The contradictions in the Islamic feminism of Mernissi also stem from the double bind to protect the rights of "Muslim women" against the rising Islamist or "internal" threat and to respond to the increasingly anti-Islamic feeling in the West (the external threat). To use Spivak's words, Mernissi's feminist construction of the "Muslim woman" is subjected to "two levels of articulation": a "comparison/competition" on the "internal" level, and a "comparison/competition at the international level."[46]

Even though Mernissi emphasizes the diversity of Moroccan women's experiences, this diversity is still based on the exclusion of illiterate men and women and the Berber-speaking population of Morocco, who are denied not only access to ancient Arabic sources, but, more importantly, a position from which to speak and legislate laws on behalf of Muslim women. The rhetoric of diversity, as Scott Michaelsen puts it, is thus "a theory of assimilation grounded upon a fundamental exclusion, an exclusion so thoroughly buried it goes virtually unnoticed, almost unread."[47] Thus, it is the privileges of class, race, and education that give Mernissi the power to reauthenticate the hadith, compete with male religious authorities like al Bukhari, and speak on behalf of the Moroccan "Muslim woman."

A NORTH AFRICAN OEDIPUS?
BEYOND THE REIFICATION OF CULTURE

Another problem in Mernissi's feminist reinvention of the "Muslim woman" is her assumption of a homogeneous oppressive Islamic culture. Comparing the Western and Islamic perceptions of female sexuality, Mernissi claims that in contrast with the model of passive female sexuality in Freud's theory, the entire Muslim social structure is an attack on, and a defense against, the disruptive power of female sexuality. For instance, the eleventh-century theologian al-Ghazali (1058–1111) sees civilization as a struggle to contain women's destructive power or *fitna* ("chaos").[48] Societies, he says, prosper only if we create institutions that foster male dominance through sexual segregation. Mernissi's claim that the teachings of al-Ghazali determine the male-female dynamics in contemporary Muslim society is problematic for many reasons. First, Mernissi ignores those teachings in al-Ghazali's *Ihya' Ulum al Din* or *The Revivication of Islam*[49] that are not detrimental to women. Despite his obvious and undeniable misogyny, al-Ghazali's recommendation for the Muslim man to engage in foreplay and be preoccupied with his wife's sexual pleasure is very advanced for his century:

> Let him proceed with gentle words and kisses. The Prophet said, "Let none of you come upon his wife like an animal, and let there be an emissary between them." He was asked, "What is this emissary, O Messenger of God?" He said, "The kiss and [sweet] words."
>   Once the husband has attained his fulfillment, let him tarry until his wife also attains hers. Her orgasm (inzāl) may be delayed, thus exciting her desire; to withdraw quickly is harmful to the woman. Difference in the nature of [their] reaching a climax causes discord whenever the husband ejaculates first. Congruence in attaining a climax is more gratifying to her because the man is not preoccupied with his own pleasure, but rather with hers; for it is likely that the woman might be shy.[50]

The second problem with Mernissi's analysis is her "cultural mummification"[51] of Moroccan society and of the Islamic world in general. Unlike Ahmed, who focuses on the heterogeneity of Islamic tradition, its constant change through time, and its affinities with the Judeo-Christian traditions,

Mernissi's construction of Islamic tradition seems based on a closed and localized notion of culture. By positing a total cultural break between *Jahiliya* and Islam, Mernissi reproduces the Islamist originary narrative locating the origin of culture and civilization in the early years of Islam. As Harrow puts it, culture is to be viewed as a process of "contestation,"[52] rather than something confined within some established geographical borders. Mernissi never questions the paradigm from which this so-called Moroccan Islamic culture is assumed to be present and already operating. Rather than positing an originary Islamic Moroccan culture that is oppressive to women, women's condition in Morocco has to be examined in view of a syncretic[53] Mediterranean[54] patriarchal culture, for the boundaries between the crescent and the cross, between the southern Muslim shore of the Mediterranean and the northern Christian side have constantly been fluid and shifting. For instance, the history of the renegade population in North Africa points not simply to the cultural exchange that must have inevitably occurred between the northern and southern bank of the Mediterranean, but more importantly, to the invention of North Africa as Europe's Muslim Other.

Mernissi's view on love in Muslim society raises another theoretical problem: how solid is any claim that bases social practice on an authoritative text, especially a text from the eleventh century? To claim that al-Ghazali's teachings have determined women's condition and rights in Morocco presumes that Moroccan society is culturally reified and frozen. Also, Mernissi's claim that the entire Muslim order condemns love between a man and a woman, and a husband and his wife, presupposes a homogeneous misogynistic Islamic tradition with no internal antagonistic or contradictory elements. Ibn Hazm's (994–1064) *The Ring of the Dove: A Treatise on the Art and Practice of Arab Love*,[55] for instance, undermines Mernissi's claim that Islamic tradition condemns love between a man and a woman. Just as Montaigne's and de Courtois's defense of the arranged marriage serves to protect the aristocratic blood line, the "Muslim order's" attack on love needs to be historicized as a defense of the practice of endogamy that existed not just in Morocco, but in southern Europe, especially in Italy, Greece, and France.[56]

Throughout her writings, Mernissi presents "Islamic fundamentalism" and Islamic patriarchy as essentially male. The two women's marches, which took place in Morocco on 12 March 2000, show that the Islamist movement is not always male. Whereas the Rabat demonstration was led by the feminists who supported the plan of Saïd Saadi, the Moroccan secretary of state, who wanted to reform *al Mudawana* (the Moroccan family/Shari'a laws), the Casablanca march was led on the same day by the Islamist sisters, who believed that the abolition of polygamy, the banning of unilateral divorce,

and women's right to get married without their parents' consent were inno-
vations alien and contrary to the teachings of Islam.[57] Mernissi's reading of
the veil as a universal symbol of female oppression reveals how her upper-
class social background separates her from the lower-class Moroccan
women, who wear the veil to engage in public activities they would otherwise be denied. Furthermore, Mernissi's distinction between the Muslim exploitation of the female body through seclusion and veiling and the
exploitation of women through the commodification of their bodies in the
West does not apply to all the classes and all the Muslim countries.[58] In postcolonial Tunisia, for instance, the veil is rejected as an imported "sectarian"
garment, which is alien to Tunisia's authentic traditions. Similarly, brand
name Jeans, T-shirts, navel rings, and tattoos are not an uncommon sight
among the middle- and upper-class young women in Arab/Islamic countries
like Syria, Lebanon, Tunisia, Morocco, and Egypt. With globalization and
infiltration of Western capitalism in the "third world," the exploitation of the
female body is not restricted to the Western world.

Mernissi's use of Freudian theory as a universal model to analyze the psyche
of Muslim societies is quite problematic. Ignoring the revisions of Freud's theory done by Lacan and Julia Kristeva, Mernissi reads Freud in literal rather than
symbolic terms. Mernissi makes the claim that all Muslim men display symp-
toms of the Oedipus complex, that is, obsession with the mother and hatred for
the wife: "In Muslim societies not only is the marital bond weakened and love
for the wife discouraged, but his mother is the only woman a man is allowed to
love at all, and this love is encouraged to take the form of life-long gratitude."[59]
She also ignores the implications of applying the European construct of the
Name of the Father to non-Western societies where the Name of the Father does
not necessarily involve the biological father. In *Oedipe Africain*, Marie Cécile
and Edmond Ortigues write that the Oedipus complex, rather than being universal, is always mediated through local culture. During their clinical practice
in Dakar from 1962–1966, these two French psychoanalysts "found out that the
mental illnesses of their patients are related to certain aspects of Western
African culture and basic tenets."[60] In the West African context, the Oedipus
myth is "a structure of relations" where the Father appears as "a function"
rather than a "progenitor." In contrast with the Greek myth, "the [African]
youth . . . does not imagine killing the father but must be referred to the ancestors through him." Mernissi's claim that all men in Muslim societies suffer from
the Oedipus complex is not only totalizing—as it assumes "a singular patriarchal kinship system [common to all Arab and Muslim societies, that is, over
twenty different countries]"[61]—but also recalls the reductionist tendency in
Western feminist scholarship to analyze the "Muslim woman" as victim of a
homogeneous Islamic patriarchal family system in the Middle East. Moreover,

Mernissi's statement that the Muslim order perceives the "Muslim woman" as the enemy within and the Christian West as the enemy without is not relevant solely to Islamic culture, but to all said patriarchal cultures.[62] Once again, because of the double privilege of class and education, Mernissi was able to combine the authority of the Muslim theologian with that of the Western psychoanalyst, to unlock the mysteries of "Islamic memory" and investigate "the consciousness of Muslims" over the last "fifteen centuries."[63]

As demonstrated in this chapter, the Islamic feminism of Mernissi, far from being ethnocentric, uses Freudian, historicist, and poststructuralist approaches to her feminist reconstruction of Islam. Despite her essentialist construction of the West and the Muslim world, her reinvention of the early Muslim women is strategic in that it destabilizes the authority of legalistic Islam and reforms the Shari'a laws. Subverting Islamic patriarchy's claim that "women are deficient in mind and faith," Mernissi uses the Islamic concept of *ijtihad* (independent juristic reasoning) to revise and historicize the misogynistic hadith held as insurmountable obstacles to Muslim women's emancipation. Unlike Butler,[64] who locates political agency in subverting the dominant phallocentric discourse, "Third World" feminists like Mernissi are committed to effect social and economic change through the intermediary of the state; that is, they want to involve the government in enacting laws that guarantee women's education and their equal access to economic and social privileges.

Mernissi is one of the Arab feminists who, to use Ahmed's words, "hears the voice of ethical Islam," and for whom there is no contradiction between Islam and democracy or Islam and secularism.[65] As Mernissi puts it: "The democratic glorification of the human individual, regardless of sex, race, or status, is the kernel of the Muslim message."[66] This is why she argues later in the book that democracy starts in the "non-political" space of the "household"[67] not the chambers of parliaments.

Finally, both Mernissi's reliance on the Shari'a law and defensive claims that there is no discrepancy between Islam and democracy, and that Islam elevated women's status far more than any other religion, could be co-opted by conservative Islamic groups to preclude further demands for women's rights. The real challenge for Muslim feminists today is not simply to prove Islam's compatibility with women's rights, but how to empower and include women in the political apparatus of the postcolonial Islamic state, which remains for the time being (with few exceptions) inaccessible to the Muslim masses, male and female alike.

NOTES

1. See Fatima Mernissi's autobiographical novel, *Dreams of Trespass: Tales of a Harem Girlhood* (Reading, Mass.: Addison-Wesley, 1994).

2. Bhabha, *The Location of Culture*, 155.

3. Mohanty, "Under Western Eyes," in Williams, *Colonial Discourse and Post-colonial Theory*, 201.

4. I shall discuss later in this chapter the division between tradition and modernity in the writings of Mernissi and Ahmed.

5. Mernissi, *Beyond the Veil: Male Female Dynamics in Muslim Society* (London: Al Saqi Books, 1985), 90.

6. Mernissi, *Chahrazad n'est pas Marocaine: autrement, elle serait salariée!* (Casablanca: Le Fennec, 1991), 40–41.

7. Mernissi, *The Veil and the Male Elite: A Feminist Interpretation of Women's Rights in Islam*, trans. Mary Jo Lakeland (Reading, Mass.: Addison-Wesley, 1991), 93.

8. Rashad Khalifa, trans., *The Quran: The Final Testament* (Tucson: Islamic Productions, 1989).

9. Mernissi, *The Veil and the Male Elite*, 96.

10. Mernissi, *The Veil and the Male Elite*, 111.

11. Mernissi, *The Veil and the Male Elite*, 94.

12. Mernissi, *The Veil and the Male Elite*, 49.

13. Mernissi, *The Veil and the Male Elite*, 53.

14. Mernissi, *The Veil and the Male Elite*, 60–61.

15. Mernissi, *The Veil and the Male Elite*, 61.

16. Leila Ahmed, *Women and Gender in Islam: Historical Roots of a Modern Debate* (New Haven, Conn.: Yale University Press, 1992), 153.

17. Mernissi, *The Veil and the Male Elite*, 120.

18. Ahmed, *Women and Gender in Islam*, 33.

19. Mernissi, *The Veil and the Male Elite*, 130.

20. According to Mernissi, the hypocrites are a powerful group of Medinese, who, threatened by Muhammad's egalitarian project—such as his stand on slavery and prostitution, women's right to inheritance and booty (*The Veil and the Male Elite* 131)—had invented the story of Aïsha's affair with Safwan (178), and harassed Muhammad's wives in public (180). As a result, Muhammad was pushed to comply with their wishes by veiling his wives. This demarcation between the veiled and the unveiled woman sanctioned the harassment of the "unveiled woman," and protected thus the hypocrites' lucrative trade in slave-prostitution. Even though Mernissi explains Muhammad's failure to abolish slavery by the strong male opposition to Islam's ideal of gender and racial equality, she never tackles the problem of non-Muslim slaves in early Islam.

21. Mernissi, *Beyond the Veil*, 52–53.

22. Even though he says women should be married for their religion, the women Muhammad married were chosen for their beauty rather than their faith. See Fatima Mernissi, *Beyond the Veil: Male Female Dynamics in Muslim Society* (London: Al Saqi books, 1985) 54.

23. Mernissi, *Beyond the Veil*, 57.

24. De Lauretis, *Technologies of Gender*, 10.

25. Mernissi, *The Veil and the Male Elite*, 179.

26. Mernissi, *Beyond the Veil*, 155.

27. Ahmed, *Women and Gender in Islam*, 160–61.

28. Ahmed, *Women and Gender in Islam*, 179.

29. Ahmed, *Women and Gender in Islam*, 220–21.

30. Ahmed, *Women and Gender in Islam*, 222.

31. Ahmed, *Women and Gender in Islam*, 221.

32. Ahmed, *Women and Gender in Islam*, 223.

33. Ahmed, *Women and Gender in Islam*, 223.

34. Ahmed, *Women and Gender in Islam*, 228.

35. Ahmed, *Women and Gender in Islam*, 225.

36. Elizabeth Fernea Warnock, *In Search of Islamic Feminism: One Woman's Global Journey* (New York: Doublday, 1998), 88.

37. Fernea, *In Search of Islamic Feminism*, 72.

38. Mernissi, *Dreams of Trespass*, 44–45.

39. Simon Gikandi, *Maps of Englishness: Writing, Identity in the Culture of Colonialism* (New York: Columbia University Press, 1996), 228.

40. Gikandi, *Maps of Englishness*, 227.

41. Amselle, *Mestizo Logics*, 3.

42. Mernissi, *Beyond the Veil*, 149.

43. Mernissi, *Beyond the Veil*, 163.

44. Bhabha, *The Location of Culture*, 2.

45. Mernissi, *Beyond the Veil*, 94.

46. Gayatri Chakravorty Spivak, *A Critique of Postcolonial Studies: Toward a History of the Vanishing Present* (Cambridge, Mass.: Harvard University Press, 1999), 159.

47. Scott Michaelson and David E. Johnson, ed., *Border Theory: The Limits of Cultural Politics* (Minneapolis: University of Minnesota Press, 1997), 23.

48. Mernissi, *Beyond the Veil*, 31.

49. I am using here Mernissi's translation of the Arabic title *Ihya' 'Ulum al Din*. The exact date when al Ghazali wrote this monumental work is unknown. Subsequent quotations from al Ghazali are from Madelain Farah's translation of some essays in *Ihya*, published under *Marriage and Sexuality in Islam* (Salt Lake City: University of Utah Press, 1984).

50. Farah, *Marriage and Sexuality in Islam*, 106–7.

51. Bhabha, *The Location of Culture*, 78.

52. Harrow, "Shibboleths in the Production of Culture," n.p.

53. Amselle, *Mestizo Logics*, 161.

54. Ann-Louise Shapiro suggests that the patriarchies on both sides of the Mediterranean seem to have reached a consensus as to what a woman's role and place in society should be. "Blaming the fall of Rome on women's emancipation," Camille Ducreux, a Parisian lawyer, argued that a woman's natural place is home, not politics: "The Greek hid his wife in the gynécée, the Roman placed her under the guard of two *lares* (domestic spirits), the Moslem enclosed her in his harem, our society shelters her under the protective roof of the home." Dr. Toulouse, another French expert in "*la science intersexuelle*" made the claim that in mental institutions women sought "soli-

tude more than men did." They "naturally" want to be left alone, "a bit as a recluse in the home." See Shapiro's *Breaking the Codes: Female Criminality in Fin-de-Siècle Paris* (Stanford: Stanford University Press, 1996), 187.

As a matter of fact al-Ghazali's *The Revivication of Islam* bears many similarities with the medieval moral treaties like *The Goodman of Paris* (1393), which urged women to seek the safety of the home. The early church fathers and the Catholic Church also warned men against what al-Ghazali calls *fitna*, that is, "chaos" or "women's power of seduction." The Abbè de Gibergues cautioned his male congregation that "the devil makes use of women to ruin men by seducing them." See James F. McMillan, *Housewife or Harlot: The Place of Women in French Society 1870–1940* (New York: St. Martin's Press, 1981), 9–10.

Jean Jacques Rousseau—the father of French humanism—has also recommended women's seclusion in harems similar to those created by the "Persians," the "Greeks," the "Romans," and "the Egyptians." See Rousseau, *Politics and the Arts: Letter to D'Alembert on the Theatre*, trans. Allan Bloom (Ithaca, N.Y.: Cornell University Press, 1989), 8: 89.

55. Ibn Hazm, *The Ring of the Dove: A Treatise on the Art and Practice of Arab Love*, trans. A. J. Arberry (London: Luzac, 1953).

56. Moreover, in sixteenth- and seventeenth-century France, many writers warned people against the dangers of marrying for love. For instance, Michel de Montaigne (1533–1592) wrote that one must marry not for love, but for the sake of family line. In *Le Livre de famille*, Antoine de Courtois (1762–1828) defended arranged marriages because parents knew what was best for their children's interests. It would be very naïve, indeed, to conclude based on the authority of the two above texts that French society condemns love between a man and a woman, and a husband and his wife. The very fact that Montaigne and de Courtois attacked love, proves that romantic love did exist in their time. Mentioned by McMillan, *Housewife or Harlot*, 31.

57. Ahmed R. Benchemsi, "Maroc: minijupes contre tchadors," *Jeune Afrique* 21–27 March 2000: 34–37.

58. Mernissi, *Beyond the Veil*, 167.

59. Mernissi, *Beyond the Veil*, 121.

60. Mentioned by Hortense Spillers, "All the Things You Could Be by Now: If Sigmund Freud's Wife Was Your Mother: Psychoanalysis and Race," *Boundary 2* 23, no 3 (Autumn 1996): 75–141.

61. Mohanty, "Under Western Eyes," 204.

62. Rick Lazio's attack on Hillary Rodham Clinton in the 2000 New York senate election as an agent of Islamic terrorism for receiving a $50,000 campaign donation from a Muslim group, and Hillary's subsequent return of this "tainted money" after conceding that all Muslims are terrorists, ironically reveals how Christian patriarchy, despite its claim that Western women's emancipation is a model for the "Muslim woman," still perceives the "Christian woman" as the enemy within and Islam as the enemy without.

63. Mernissi, *The Veil and the Male Elite*, 179.

64. Butler opposes pushing the state to legislate hate crime laws, because in depending on the government to protect them, gays, lesbians and bisexuals risk being

overpowered by the state, undermining thus their own authority and political agency. See *Excitable Speech: A Politics of the Performative* (New York: Routledge, 1997).

65. In *Women and Gender in Islam*, Ahmed does not discuss thoroughly the issue of Islam and democracy as Mernissi does in *Islam and Democracy* and *Beyond the Veil*.

66. Mernissi, *Beyond the Veil*, 19.

67. Mernissi, *Beyond the Veil*, 95–96.

Chapter Two

Isabelle Eberhardt, ou *"La Roumia Convertie"*: A Case Study in Female Orientalism

ISABELLE EBERHARDT: AN INTRODUCTION

Isabelle Eberhardt (1877–1904) was a European woman who traveled throughout the Maghreb disguised as an Arab man at the turn of the nineteenth century. She was the daughter of Nathalie Eberhardt, wife of General Paul de Moerder, a Russian of noble birth and officer of the Tsar's imperial army. Mme de Moerder eloped to Switzerland with her children's tutor, Alexander Trophimowsky, a Russian priest who later became an anarchist. He is believed to be Eberhardt's father, even though he never acknowledged she was his daughter.[1] Because of her upbringing, Eberhardt mastered both Russian and French. Later on, Trophimowsky taught her Arabic, which paved the way for her fascination with Islamic mysticism. In 1897, she sailed with her mother to Annaba (Algeria), where they officially converted to Islam. After her mother's death, she shocked the French colonial authorities in Tunisia and Algeria by her addiction to kif and alleged sexual promiscuity with both Arab men and the French soldiers stationed in North Africa. Her masquerade as Si Mahmoud Essaadi as well as her "scandalous" marriage with an Arab man, Slimène Ehnni, threatened the racial hierarchy underlying French North Africa. In 1901, she was expelled from North Africa by the French authorities after a fanatic member of the Tijaniya tried to assassinate her, partly because of her male disguise and partly because of her affiliation with another rival religious brotherhood, the Qadiriya. The French authorities deemed her presence to be dangerous for the colonial law and order.[2] In October 1901, her husband was transferred to Marseilles where he and his wife Eberhardt married this time in a French civil ceremony. Once a French citizen, Eberhardt was able to return to North Africa. This time, however, she was recruited as an informant by the French General Hubert

31

Lyautey. Her journey to Kenadsa and her meeting with the Qadiriya leaders gave her invaluable information that she would later submit to the French authorities.[3] Eberhardt's career came to an end when she tragically died during the floods that struck Ain Sefra (Algeria) in 1904. General Lyautey found the manuscripts she was working on in an urn. He sent them to Victor Barrucand,[4] who revised Eberhardt's "*Sud-Oranais*" stories and published them in 1920 under the title of *In the Shadow of Islam*.[5]

Eberhardt's writings cannot be understood without being located in the context of the French presence in North Africa, the prevalent nineteenth-century gender ideology in France, and Eberhardt's personal history. This chapter examines Eberhardt's oeuvre—namely, *Écrits intimes* (1991), *In the Shadow of Islam*, *Écrits sur le sable* (1988), *Departures* (1994), *The Passionate Nomad* (1987), *The Oblivion Seekers* (1972), and *Rakhil* (1990)—as a case of female Orientalism. My objective here is not just to provide a corrective to Said's silence on female Orientalism but, more important, to determine whether occidental women share the biases of their countrymen during the colonial encounter.

In *Women's Orients*,[6] Billie Melman argues that unlike the uniform and authoritative discourse on the "Muslim woman" in Said's discussion of male Orientalism, the representation of the Oriental woman was not unified in female Orientalism. Melman argues "that the discourse about things Oriental was polyphonic and that the experience of the eastern Mediterranean was heterogeneous and [not only] political," as Said claims. Along the lines of Melman's criticism, this chapter contends that Eberhardt's construction of the "Muslim woman" as a prostitute/Saint reveals a split within "the subject of colonial enunciation."[7] One major claim in this chapter is that the production of the "Muslim woman" in Eberhardt's writings depends on the location of the author within the apparatus of power, which informs both her colonial subjectivity and her ideological construction of the Other Without. I will be using Eberhardt's own expression, "*la roumia convertie*" ("the converted non-Muslim woman"), to discuss the antagonistic sites of enunciation she occupies while negotiating her social, sexual, and racial identity. In contrast with Bhabha's presentation of the hybrid as androcentric, my analysis of "*la roumia convertie*" as a metaphor for the articulation of identity and difference shows that the hybrid is always gendered. This chapter also argues that the Third Republic's views on women's roles and Eberhardt's double allegiance to the bourgeois feminism of Maria Deraismes and the radical feminism of the Saint Simonians and Hubertine Auclert have a strong bearing on her reinvention of the "Muslim woman" as a prostitute/Saint. This chapter also makes the claim that Eberhardt, while reproducing the male Orientalist stereotypes about the "Muslim woman," transforms them to criticize the ideal of domesticity in fin de siècle European society. In relocating the harem on the road, Eberhardt not only redefines the seraglio genre found in male Orientalism, but also subverts the domestication and desexualization of the harem by nineteenth-century women travelers in the Middle East.

Eberhardt's writings are both complicit with and resistant to the French imperial ideology. Eberhardt is not unique, however, in presenting the colonial female subject's position as inside/outside the hegemonic discourse of empire. In *Imperial Eyes*, Mary Louise Pratt shows how Flora Tristan, the French socialist feminist, while relying on the "linear emplotment of conquest narrative,"[8] created in Peru a "feminotopia," that is, "an idealized world of female autonomy, empowerment and pleasure."[9] In *Maps of Englishness*, Gikandi also examines the "ambivalent interpellation"[10] in Mary Seacole's *Wonderful Adventures* (West Indies) and Mary Kingsley's *Travels in West Africa* toward the British imperial project. Joining Pratt, Gikandi argues that "because it seems free of the gender ideologies that constrain white women in the metropolis, the imperial field was construed as a social space for freedom and fulfillment."[11] In opposition to Pratt and Gikandi, in her analysis of Olive Schreiner's writings about South Africa, Anne McClintock[12] focuses on Schreiner's rebellious feminism and deemphasizes her racist attitudes toward blacks.

In *Women's Orients*, Melman notes that Western women's writing about the Middle East is essentially "a middle class activity"[13] that coincides with the rise of the European colonial powers and collapse of the Ottoman Empire. In the Maghreb, the Turkish Empire encompassed Tunisia and Algeria, but did not extend to Morocco. In the nineteenth century, the ties of these colonies with Turkey became quite loose, as Algeria and Tunisia gradually overthrew the indirect rule of Istanbul and placed themselves under the direct rule of the native Deys (Algeria) and the Beys (Tunisia). Eberhardt's peregrinations in the Maghreb could not have been possible if "the Old Sick Man" hadn't lost its grip on North Africa, paving the way for the French capture of Algiers in 1830 and Tunisia in 1881.

THE FEMALE IMPERIAL SUBJECT UNDER THE THIRD REPUBLIC: AN OVERVIEW OF COLONIAL HISTORY AND GENDER IDEOLOGY IN NINETEENTH-CENTURY FRANCE

In colonial Algeria, the French pursued two policies: association and assimilation. Given the fact that the French and the Algerian population belonged to two different racial stocks in the colonial view, the antiassimilationists argued that the cultural gap between the two societies could never be bridged.[14] Even though the policy of assimilation depended on the complicity of the native rulers and administrators, it was based on a notion of partnership, which did not exist given the inequality[15] inherent in any relation between a colonizer and a colonized society. The associationist policy was first put into practice by Napoleon III, who stated in an 1860 speech in Algiers that France "will take care of the happiness of these millions of Arabs, improve their existence, elevate them to the dignity of free men, spread education among them while respecting their religion." "France," he insisted, "[did] not have the right to transform the indigenous population of North Africa into French."[16]

This associationist policy was also championed by General Hubert Lyautey, who sponsored Eberhardt's journey to Kenadsa and recruited her as an informant on the rebellious tribes in the south. Complicit with Lyautey's policy, as early as 1902, *L'Akhbar*, the weekly newspaper of Victor Barrucand and Isabelle Eberhardt, held the slogan: "Neither exploitation, nor assimilation, association."[17] Instead of direct rule, Lyautey championed the protectorate system, which the French imposed on Tunisia in 1881 and Morocco in 1912. "Instead of getting rid of the old native administrators," Lyautey once explained, "We must use them to govern with the [native] ruler, and not against"[18] him. But the colonial divide and rule policy was at the heart of Lyautey's policy of association. In his own words:

> Running a protectorate means to maintain as often as possible the indigenous fights, to give them the direct power of the police, administration, justice itself, tax collection, under the supervision of one agent who resides near the native chief. It is through this agent that the eyes of the indigenous chief and his people will be opened to our ideas about justice.[19]

This divide and rule policy is best illustrated in the doctrine of "pacification" Lyautey introduced to Algeria. This policy consisted of winning one tribe after another, and with the cooperation of the tribes he had already rallied to the side of France, he would exert an economic boycott against those tribes hostile to French rule. In 1892, Eugène Etienne, a member of the French Colonial Party wrote: "The question of Morocco is capital for the security of Algeria. . . . We cannot admit that another power settles there before us."[20] Paul Bourde, the brain of the French Colonial Party, also suggested the necessity of a treaty with England, whereby Morocco would be exchanged for Egypt.[21] Eberhardt's participation in the pacification of these hostile tribes who lived near the Algerian-Moroccan border led in the long run to the colonization of Morocco. Eberhardt's journey to Kenadsa as a liaison agent between Lyautey and her Muslim brothers shows her complicity with the French colonial project. Including herself in the masculine world of empire, she writes:

Very soon *we* [my emphasis] can hope to see accomplished, thanks to the actions of the General and his collaborators who are as intelligent as they are dedicated, not—as our colleague from la Dépêche coloniale called it—"the moral conquest of the Berbers," but rather the pacification and economic conquest of the region.[22]

The use of the collective relative pronoun "we" not only allows this Russian woman to inscribe herself as French, but also to re-redefine French empire in nonexclusive gendered terms. Eberhardt's description of Lyautey's collaborators as "intelligent" and "dedicated" is a self-congratulatory statement that simultaneously underscores European women's active participation in the project of colonialism and Western patriarchy's reluctance to recognize them as equal partners in the imperial field.

In contrast with association, the French policy of assimilation was based on the principle that Algeria, being an extension of France, must have institutions similar to those in the homeland. The French who immigrated to the colonies enjoyed their full rights as French citizens, including "the right to be represented by an elect deputy in the metropolitan Parliament."[23] The theory of assimilation, by extension applied both to the foreign settlers of European origin (mainly Spanish, Italians, Maltese, and Sicilians) and the native Algerian population, who could theoretically be naturalized French citizens if they were to demonstrate their love and allegiance to France. For instance Eberhardt's Algerian husband, Slimène, obtained French citizenship after serving in the French army for many years as a Spahi.

In 1870, assimilation became the official colonial policy of the Third Republic. It was championed by Jules Ferry, the Prime Minister of the Third Republic, and one of the founding fathers of the French colonial education. Despite the constant bickering between the Royalists and the Republicans in the Ferry period, both sides seemed to agree that "'the inferior races' could only bend down to the civilization coming from the [North]."[24] In an 1885 speech, Ferry, deputy of the Vosges then, gave three reasons for the French conquest of Tunisia, Annam, Tonkin, Congo, and part of Madagascar: (1) to guarantee France's control of the world's markets and natural resources; (2) to bring civilization to the rest of the world, because "an occidental society like France, which has reached an elevated degree of scientific, technical, and cultural development, has rights and duties vis à vis 'the inferior races' which have remained on the margins of progress"; (3) and last, "to maintain France's rank in the world,"[25] especially after France's defeat in the Franco-Prussian War (1870) and the loss of the Alsace and the Lorraine.

Many people in France opposed the French "civilizing mission." The pacifist economist Frédéric Passy argued that it "was a waste of French blood while Germany was getting stronger."[26] The nationalists also disapproved of

Ferry's new conquests. Paul Déroulède for instance, shouted at Ferry: "I lost two sisters (Alsace and Lorraine) and you offer me twenty servants!" The French intellectual circles were also divided toward Ferry's imperialist policy: Whereas Alphonse Daudet, Pierre Loti, Guy de Maupassant, Jules Vallès, Lèon Bloy, Sèverine, and Henri Rochefort took a stand against the project of colonization,[27] Emile Zola, Louis Bertrand, and George Sand endorsed the Republic's imperialist policy and claimed that France would be regenerated by its colonies.[28] Sharing the revolutionary idealism of the Third Republic, Robert Randau, Eberhardt's friend in Algeria, also prophesized in his fiction that France would create "an immense colonial empire in Africa without brutalizing the population, with the simple peaceful propaganda of our kindness, without betraying the pure traditions of our Revolution."[29]

Eberhardt's frequent battles with the French colonial authorities have to be contextualized within the nineteenth-century gender ideology at home and in the colonies. Even though French women had been working in the factories since the beginning of the nineteenth century, both the Republicans and the Royalists in fin de siècle France agreed that a woman's role was to be a mother and wife. If the ideal of the angel in the house gained strength in late-nineteenth-century and early-twentieth-century France, it was because of the ideological rivalry between the Catholic Church—which lost most of its privileges after the French Revolution—and the anticlericals who supported the laic Republic. According to Ferry, the Church created barriers between husbands and wives by its tight control of girls' education. In a famous speech, he called for the "necessity of rescuing women from the Church in order to win them to science."[30] In the law of 9 August 1879, Ferry made girls' primary education compulsory and announced the creation of a training school for elementary school women teachers.

The Third Republic's preoccupation with women's roles as mothers was also caused by the decline in France's population after the Franco-Russian War. Women were urged to stay at home and raise republican *citoyens* ("male citizens") till "the corrupt, clerical, infertile Empire would be replaced by a morally regenerate, secular, and fecund republic."[31] In Algeria, "it was the job of the [colonial] woman 'to create France' wherever she went."[32] Because of the threat of racial decline, the French women, whether at home or in the imperial field, were taught courses in child-rearing, housework, and the new science of puériculture (infant hygiene).[33] Because of the national anxieties about depopulation, there was naturally an increasing fear of the lesbian and the autonomous bourgeois feminist woman, who refused to get married and have children.[34] Eberhardt's male disguise, sexual freedom, and use of the neo-Malthusian method of contraception[35] did certainly make her a dangerous nonreproductive *hommesse* ("masculine woman") in the eyes of the Third Republic.

In the nineteenth century, some of the rights Muslim women enjoyed, especially inheritance and control of their own property in case of divorce, were still denied the French women. Decreed by Napoleon in 1804, Article 213 of the Civil Code placed the married woman's property under the tutelage of her husband. She could not open a business or dispose of her property without his consent.[36] By institutionalizing the "crime de passion," the Napoleonic Code allowed only the French male to get away with the murder of his adulterous wife. Only in 1881, did French women obtain the right to open a savings bank account without the assistance of their husbands. Unlike the British Suffragettes, French women obtained the right to vote only after World War II, because of the strong male opposition to the female vote. Reflecting the laws in the mother country, colonial Algeria declared that only the Muslim men had the right to vote if they were naturalized French citizens.

BETWEEN COMPLICITY AND RESISTANCE: EBERHARDT'S AMBIVALENCE TOWARD THE "MUSLIM WOMAN" AND THE FRENCH CIVILIZING MISSION

Even though she supported Lyautey's policy of pacification, Eberhardt was also a firm believer in the principle of assimilation. Defending the French civilizing mission, she tells her husband Slimène that the best way to serve Islam and the Arab nation is by serving France:

> Imagine that in working for the goal that I set out for you here that you are working for all your Arab brothers, for all our Muslim brothers. You will provide for the French gentlemen—disdainful and Arabophobe—the example of an Arab who, having begun as Spahi of the second order, has raised himself to a rank envied and respected, by his intelligence and work. If there were many such Arabs in Algeria, the French would have been obliged to change their minds on the subject of "dirty Arabs." That is how you must serve Islam and the Arab nation, and not by fomenting useless and bloody revolts which serve only as ammunition for the enemies of all that is Arab, and not by discouraging those honest French who would like to be brothers.[37]

This is contradictory not just with her support for Lyautey's policy of pacification, but also with her defense of the Marguerite rebels and her participation in the 1899 Bône riots.[38] In her diaries, Eberhardt mentioned that she would write an article in defense of the Marguerite rebels who attacked a French garrison, but she never kept her promise:

> I may have to go to France this winter to see about writing a piece in defense of the Marguerite rebels. O! if I could only say everything I know, speak my mind

and come out with the whole truth! What a good deed that would be! In due course it would have positive results and establish my reputation too! Brieux was certainly right about that: I must start my career by coming out openly in defense of my Algerian Muslim brethren.[39]

As the above passage suggests, Eberhardt's project of writing this article can be read not only as a career move but also as a sign of her genuine care for her Muslim brothers. Because of her participation in the Bône riots, however, Eberhardt was duly recorded in the colonial records at Constantine as a dangerous Russian woman conniving with the natives.[40]

In a letter to Victor Barrucand, Eberhardt's friend and editor of *L'Akhbar*, Rosalia Balaban Bentami[41] wrote:

> You cannot imagine how this Isabelle Eberhardt awakened forgotten feelings in me—my unrealized dreams! I understand very well why she idealizes the Arab and Islam so much because it's very characteristic of the Russian soul to get carried away about anything that's surrounded by mystery. But there is one thing that touched me profoundly and that she passes over as if it were unimportant— that's the life of the Arab women . . . she, the Russian woman . . . the woman who's free as a bird, who's Bohemian, she doesn't see a whole people, millions of women—prisoners, deprived of the most elementary rights in the world, the right to live, to think, to see the sun . . . to have respect for their personality. If you knew, dear Sir, how I study them and how I want to cry.

Bentami's criticism of Eberhardt's silence on the "Muslim woman's" condition is not only inaccurate but also Eurocentric. Eberhardt did in fact criticize the seclusion of Muslim women in North Africa. She once wrote: "I am not bound at all as a Muslim woman to wear a *gandoura* and a *mléya* and to be cloistered. These measures have been imposed on Muslim women to prevent their possible fall and preserve their chastity." True purity, she argued, was one that was "free and not imposed."[42] Bentami's own marriage to an Arab[43] man did not deprive her of "the right to live," "to see the sun," and to write about the oppression of the "Muslim woman."[44] Also, her statement that the Russian woman was "as free as a bird" is inaccurate given the evidence to the contrary in Eberhardt's own family background. Her adoptive father Trophimowsky not only controlled Mme de Moerder's money, but also used it to purchase Villa Tropicale under his own name,[45] an estate that Eberhardt and her brothers could not inherit later because it was claimed by Trophimosky's heirs in Russia. All of Mme de Moerder's children suffered from Trophimowsky's patriarchal tyranny: Nicolas[46] left home in 1885, Nathalie[47] eloped in 1887, Augustin[48] in 1888, Isabelle in 1897, and Vladimir[49] put his head in a gas oven in 1898.

In the colonies, it was as a helpmate—and not as a "free bird"—that the French colonial order defined the French woman's role. As early as 1831,

Marshall Soult, the French minister of war, declared that the colonization of Algeria must be led "by married peasant soldiers who will work on their land, while serving in the military." As for their wives, they "will be employed as farm workers or laundresses."[50] Even at the time of Eberhardt's peregrinations in North Africa, the imperial field was not a suitable place for single European women. In view of the debate about the dangerous implications of hypnosis, the medical discourse in fin de siècle France "urged women not to travel alone and never to meet the eyes of male strangers."[51]

Also, the order of expulsion against Eberhardt did not come solely from the French authorities, but also with the benediction of the Russian consulate, who without hesitation supported the eviction of the Russian woman from the French territories of North Africa.[52] The reason why the French Arab Bureaux offered protection and tolerated Eberhardt's "eccentric" behavior was not because the French, like the Russians, allow women to be "free birds," but because Eberhardt was a subject of the Russian tsar, a friend of the Third Republic, England's archenemy, and the guarantor of a durable peace with Germany.[53]

In the early years of the French conquest of Algeria (1840s–1850s), the stereotype of the "Muslim woman" as victim of Islamic laws hardly appeared in the writings of French writers. It was in the period between 1870–1900, that this stereotype was produced. Once the military conquest was over and the hostile tribes pacified, "Islam," as Clancy Smith and Gouda put it, "was moved from the battlefield into the bedroom."[54] The new interest in the "Muslim woman" was kindled by the debate over the Algerian man's right to vote.[55] In the discourse of antiassimilation, the stereotype of the "Muslim woman's" oppression was deployed as a political pawn to deny the Algerian man the right to vote, on the ground of his anti-French culture that degraded and oppressed women. In French terms, the Algerian "Muslim woman" is oppressed not because she is denied equal access to political, social, and economic opportunities, but because she is subjected to the "primitive" practices of veiling, seclusion, and polygamy. Thus, both patriarchies on the opposite sides of the Mediterranean agreed on denying the "Muslim woman" her political rights such as the right to vote.

Eberhardt's criticism of the French women's movement and bourgeois women in general subverts the project of colonial feminism. Eberhardt states that she deliberately exiled herself in the Maghreb from the Paris "where the newspapers' lip-service to feminism [is] even more repugnant than the Parisian coquettes."[56] Eberhardt seems alienated from the French feminist movement, which she dubs as a bourgeois world of "salons"[57] and dance balls. In 1900, the year of the Great Exhibition in Paris, Eberhardt recalls only a sense of disgust from her visit to Paris. In *"L'Âge du néant"*

("The Age of the Void"), a short story decrying the "tragi-comedy of modern life," Eberhardt feels alienated from "the narrow-minded life" of those bourgeois "insipid women," with "no big minds, dwarfed and strangely looking alike." They are nothing but "slaves to appearances at the detriment of the real" and vulgar "courtisanes" with no "esthetic grace."[58] Penniless and still unknown despite her talent, Eberhardt reported all her anger against French bourgeois women.

During her visit to Paris, the Russian explorer Lydia Paschkoff introduced her to the famous French lesbian feminist Sèverine,[59] and to the famous literary salon of Marie Laetizia Bonaparte-Wyse[60]—grandniece of Bonaparte I—where George Sand, Victor Hugo, Alexander Dumas, and Saint-Beuve often appeared.[61] In one of her letters to Eberhardt, Paschkoff gives her the following advice:

> In France one must be French to live from journalism and have—as I was told but refused to do—a lover in the Press. A husband is more difficult, but those who have a husband manage to make a career for themselves. . . . Never! I prefer to tell you all this brutally. I am told that even George Sand could have got nowhere without Sandeau, Musset, etc. Sèverine got on because of her lovers Va . . . and Puy . . . and they are Frenchwomen.
>
> My Job on the Figaro was a miracle. I had the whole staff against me, except one, who was in love with me, and he let me down when he saw that there was no hope. All the Russians were against me, and when the Ambassador invited me to the Embassy it did me more harm than anything else.[62]

As Paschkoff's letter indicates, it was not easy for French women to achieve literary fame in nineteenth-century France. To succeed, they have to be either someone's wife or someone's lover. Eberhardt's Russian origin and modest social background could only add more hurdles on the path of her literary career.

Even though she dissociates herself from nineteenth-century French feminism, Eberhardt's writings both reflect and resist the bourgeois feminism[63] of Maria Deraismes and the radical feminism of the Saint Simonians and Hubertine Auclert. Given her upper-class background, Deraismes's feminism focused primarily on the centrality of the family. In her writings, "free love" was condemned because it entailed "the annihilation of the family."[64] To save the family, women must receive the same education as their husbands.[65] Even though she championed girls' education and the termination of the Napoleonic Civic Code, Deraismes saw that it was too soon for the issue of the woman's vote.

Recalling Deraismes's emphasis on women's education, Eberhardt wanted to create a school for Muslim girls. Despite the "constant intrigues" of the

"Moorish women"[66] and the feelings of "hatred and disgust"[67] they inspired in her, Eberhardt wanted to create a "[Qur'anic] school for little girls with an elementary French course, writing and reading in Arabic, the essentials of Islamic history, and everything in the most ardent Islamic spirit."[68] In contrast with the principle of assimilation underlying Ferry's colonial education, and Hubertine Auclert's[69] call for French women to conquer the domestic space of the "Muslim woman" and to teach her the principles of French civilization,[70] Eberhardt wanted to turn the Muslim little girls into better Muslims:

> If we can at least find at least forty five little girls to start with, then, the parents, noticing the good results and observing that instead of Europeanizing their daughters, I would have made them more Muslims, maybe then, they will be encouraged to send their daughters, and we will expand our business.[71]

Echoing Deraismes, Eberhardt argues that marital relationships should be based on love and friendship, not power and gender inequality:

> Our modern world is so distorted and warped that in marriage the husband is hardly ever the one to do the initiating into sensuality. Stupid and revolting as it is, young girls are hitched to a husband for life, and he is a ridiculous figure in the end. The woman's physical virginity is all his. She is then expected to spend the rest of her life with him, usually in disgust, and suffer what is known as her "marital duty," until the day that someone comes along to teach her, in a web of lies, the existence of a whole universe of thrills, thoughts and sensations that will regenerate her from head to toe. That is where our marriage is so different from any other—and shocks so many solid citizens: Slimène means two things to me—he is both friend and lover.[72]

In presenting her marriage to an Algerian man as an ideal to be pursued by Europeans, Eberhardt subverts the Eurocentrism at the heart of Auclert's attack on women's oppression under Islam. Eberhardt's indictment of the young girls' predicament in Europe to marry men they do not love and to suffer for the rest of their lives from "what is known as their marital duty," shows that what Auclert denounced as the Islamic practices of "bride sales"[73] and "child rape"[74] were not unheard of on the Northern shore of the Mediterranean. However, Eberhardt's intention[75] to hire a Russian woman to teach Muslim girls the gendered-vocation of needlework[76] shows how she has embraced the ethics of domesticity at the heart of the very bourgeois culture that she is criticizing.

Eberhardt's emphasis on women's sexual fulfillment is to be examined in view of the tradition of male Orientalism, the Saint Simonians' doctrine of free love, and the patriarchal concept of the family in the first half of nineteenth-century France.[77] Like the French male Orientalists Eugène Delacroix's

(*Women of Algiers*) and André Gide (*L'Immoraliste*), Eberhardt reconstructs the Maghreb as a place of sexual freedom even though the southern shore of the Mediterranean had the same oppressive sexual mores as its northern side. As a technology of space, the Maghreb becomes the locale where European identity projects itself. Putting on Arab male clothes constitutes an act of transvestism/minstrelsy, which allows her to express and liberate her sexuality. Like her fellow male Orientalist Massignon, Eberhardt's colonial "penetration" of the world of the *zawiya*[78] and fascination with Islamic mysticism—especially with the Sufi concepts of love, passion, and spiritual ecstasy—allow her to sublimate and legitimate her sexual drives. Eberhardt's rewriting of physical love along the spiritual transcendence of sex in Sufi philosophy allows her to overcome the "feeling of shame" about her sexuality. In her diaries, Eberhardt wrote that she used to "beat her breasts" because she felt her sexuality made her "debauched' and "depraved."[79]

Explaining to her Tunisian correspondent Alî Abdelwahab why she does not want to marry El Khoudja, she writes: "Knowing the despotic character of the moors and the cloistered life of Moorish women, [she] refused his proposal, preferring an illegal union to the loss of all freedom and all future."[80] Eberhardt's emphasis on being the mistress and not the wife of her rich and powerful lovers—namely, the Turkish diplomat Ahmed Rachid and the Algerian El Khoudja Ben Abdullah—and subsequent marriage to a poor Spahi in the French army, underscore a view that defines patriarchy in terms of money. Eberhardt's marriage to Slimène subverts her own stereotypes about Moorish violence and despotism. In a letter to her husband, Eberhardt apologizes for beating him up: "[She] felt ashamed of [herself] because he didn't defend himself and smiled at [her] blind anger."[81] And she promises to be an obedient and submissive wife from then on. Eberhardt's power over her husband can also be explained by his inferior status as a colonized subject. In marrying the inferior Muslim Other, both Eberhardt and Bentami—the Russian woman who was charged by Barrucand to translate Eberhardt's work from Russian into French—entered marital unions where they had more freedom than they could ever have dreamed of if they had been married to someone from their own societies. In these marital contracts between European women and native men, racial superiority seems to redress the balance of gender inferiority.

Probably because of his social and racial status, Sliméne accepted Eberhardt's lifestyle and did not object to her peregrinations in the Algerian South. Indeed, she traveled alone to Figuig, Beni Ounif and Colomb-Bechar, and Kenadsa. When her friend, the novelist Robert Randau, expressed "his astonishment at her frequent absences and Slimène's patient acceptance of them, she protested that her husband knew very well that her heart remained with him, but that she could not do otherwise than follow her own destiny."[82] In their first encounter with Randau, Slimène introduced his wife as a man: "May I introduce you to Si Mahmoud Saâdi, this is his battle name, in reality, it is Mrs. Ehnni, my wife."[83]

Because of her Russian origin, her gender, and conversion to Islam, Eberhardt occupies a double position inside/outside the French and the Muslim patriarchal order. Eberhardt's ambivalence toward the "French civilizing mission" in general and the "Muslim woman" in particular derives from the different sites of enunciation[84] she occupies while negotiating her social, racial, and sexual identity. However, unlike Bhabha's androcentric view of hybridity and colonial mimicry, Eberhardt's double belonging to French and Muslim society shows that the hybrid is always gendered.[85] This gendered hybridity is best illustrated in her frequent clashes with the French colonial authorities. Responding to the decree of her expulsion, Eberhardt strategically calls France "her adoptive country,"[86] others her Muslim brothers as "natives," and writes herself off as an agent of French imperialism. Just as she tries to include herself in the imperial field on the basis of her racial and national background—as a fellow European and "Russian citizen"—the French colonial order tries to exclude her on the basis of her gender. Throughout her stay in the Algerian desert, Eberhardt's movements were restricted by the French military. Vexed by Eberhardt's reluctance to travel with him, the head of the military Arab Bureau at Biskra, Captain Adolphe-Roger de Susbielle, forbade her to stay at Chegga for more than twenty-four hours.[87] Captain Gaston Cauvet, head of the Arab Bureau at El Oued, also put her under surveillance. In a report to his superiors, he wrote: "Physically she is neurotic and unhinged, and I'm inclined to think that she has come to El Oued principally to satisfy unhindered her dissolute tastes and her penchant for natives in a place where there are few Europeans."[88] An anonymous letter sent to General Dechizelle at Batna, also presented her as the enemy within. The writer of the letter wrote that she was the subject of an investigation by the Russian and Swiss police for poisoning and stealing the money of her adoptive father Trophimowsky. She was also accused of harboring "a profound hatred for France and would like nothing better than to excite France's Arab subjects against her."[89]

"LA ROUMIA CONVERTIE"

I would like to use here Eberhardt's description of her mother as "*la roumia convertie*"[90] ("the converted non-Muslim woman") to discuss Eberhardt's dual position as insider/outsider with respect to Muslim society. In her personal diary, published after her death as *The Passionate Nomad*, Eberhardt describes how she felt embarrassed with her *roumi* cap[91] while sitting in a Constantine café. In Arabic, the word *roumi* (masculine) or *roumia* (feminine) means a non-Muslim of European origin, usually Christian. Derived from *al-roum*, the Arabic plural for "Romans," this word is loaded with connotations of cultural, racial, and religious otherness. Eberhardt's embarrassment at the café was caused by her display of a sign of alterity that sets her apart from the Algerian men sitting in the café. This feeling of unease disappears only when she starts performing what she constructs as native male behavior, that is, smoking kif.

In her diaries, Eberhardt makes a cross before those passages in Russian and a crescent before those in Arabic.[92] In locating the (()—the sign of Islam's alterity—and the Russian Orthodox Church (†) in a French text, not only does she subvert the binarism in male Orientalism between the Christian West and the Muslim East, she also deconstructs the production by Western Europe of Russia and the Orthodox Church as Oriental Others.

As a cultural hybrid, "*la roumia convertie*" occupies different sites of enunciation. In a letter to her brother Augustin, Eberhardt writes: "My body is in the West/And my soul is in the Orient/My body is in infidel country/And my heart is in Istanbul."[93] In another letter, she advises Slimène to beware the "examples of the unbelieving, the pseudo-Muslims around [him] who are blind, degenerate and the last of the infidels."[94] The two above examples reveal an internal dislocation in the subject of enunciation.[95] Whereas in the first passage, Eberhardt seems split because of her double belonging to an infidel Europe and a regenerate Orient, in the second, "*la roumia convertie*" creates pseudo-Muslims and excludes them to write herself as a true Muslim. However, in referring to those fake Muslims as infidels, she is simultaneously othering the "*roumia*" in her, and therefore excluding herself from what she calls the society of "true Muslims."

As a mimic woman and a gendered hybrid, "*la roumia convertie*" is both free and subjected to the Law of the Muslim Father. Abdullah, the Tijaniya fanatic who tried to assassinate her, said at his trial that he attacked Eberhardt because she dressed as a man:

> I received a mission from God, who ordered me to go to the Djrid, passing by Behima, where I was to meet Mademoiselle Eberhardt, who created disorder in the Moslem religion . . . [she] wore masculine dress, which is contrary to our customs, and thus made trouble in our religion.[96]

Indeed, it is her masquerade as an Arab man—a violation of the Islamic "sexual division of gender" and therefore of "*hudud Allah*"[97]—that provoked the attack by Abdullah. At other times, however, both her male disguise and racial Otherness turn paradoxically into a blessing that allows her to pray[98] with men, and to sleep outdoors with Khelifa and Rezki, while Hennia and her son slept indoors in the larger room.[99]

As a white person, however, Eberhardt enjoys the preferential treatment due to the members of her race in North Africa.[100] Because he tried to assassinate a white woman, Abdullah was initially sentenced to the death penalty, but with Eberhardt's intercession his sentence was commuted to a life in prison.[101] The murder of Arab subjects, however, incurred no such serious legal penalties. A week after Abdullah's trial, Maître Laffont, Eberhardt's attorney, easily obtained the release of three Arabs who robbed and killed a Touggourt shopkeeper.[102]

As a colonial subject, "*la roumia convertie*" is in collusion with the French imperialist discourse. Reflecting the French distortion of Algerian history, she writes "that Old Algiers is medieval, Turkish, Moorish, or what have you, but not Arabic and certainly not African."[103] Eberhardt's statement is in accordance with French colonial historiography, which obscures the Arab period and presents the Romans as the ancestors of the French in North Africa.[104]

As a colonial accomplice, Eberhardt, the explorer, records everything that could be useful to the French imperial project: topographic information, religious and cultural beliefs, customs, and her own views on the Algerian leaders she encounters. For instance, Eberhardt's information on Sheikh Embarek is clearly addressed to the French colonial powers. Eberhardt warns the colonial authorities that even though Sheikh Embarek might be helpful in subduing the rebellious tribes, the French have to pay attention to his greed and ambitions, for he is nothing but a "highwayman" who just gave up "traditional pillaging"[105] to make profit of the newly contracted peace. She also provides the colonial government with information about the nature of the local government and the vulnerability of the native leaders. At Kenadsa, the Berber republican confederacy was slowly substituted by an Arab "theocratic" system. Whereas the cadi settles "civil" disputes, the marabout handles not only religious affairs, but also political and judicial matters such as the appointment of military chiefs or the "appeal" of the "cadi's decisions."[106] Because of his friendship with the French, Sidi Brahim is losing his "moral authority" over his "lower"[107] subjects even though no one yet dares openly criticize him.

It is true that Eberdardt is providing information to the French colonial authorities, but at the same time, while endorsing the French colonial policy of pacification, she is trying to save the lives of her Algerian coreligionists by preventing a more brutal form of colonization as previously seen in Colonel Pélissier's[108] mass extermination of the Ouled Riah tribe in 1845.

Just as the French troops are trying to penetrate the Algerian desert and tame its inhabitants, in her romantic quest, Eberhardt wants "the sun to be still

[hers]."[109] After her fever has left her, she admits that she "wanted to possess this country, and this country has instead possessed [her]."[110] As an imperial subject, Eberhardt is in the masculinist position to "possess" the country however. Her claim to the contrary—she is possessed by the country—serves the anticonquest rhetoric of the imperial project. According to Pratt, the anticonquest trope whereby the European traveler appears feminized and innocent serves to hide his/her complicity with the colonial enterprise.[111] Suddenly, the Maghreb becomes a threat that risks to engulf and destroy the Western traveler: "Sometimes, I wonder if this land won't take over all her conquerors, with their new dreams of power and freedom, just as she has distorted all the old dreams."[112]

In those passages where the Maghreb is not a threat to the European imperial subject, it becomes the locus of degeneration and decadence. In a rhetoric, which mixes nineteenth century racial ideology and the "mal du siècle" feeling of the decadent French poets, Eberhardt constructs the absence of European people as the direct cause of racial degeneration in Sfissifa. In this little town where neither Europeans nor even Jews can be seen, the villagers "exude decay" with their pale, sick, and effeminate looks, the natural outcome of centuries of "inbreeding and sedentary lives."[113]

Even though she is married to an Algerian, Eberhardt shows at times a condescending attitude toward Arabs. In a letter to the "Dépêche Algérienne," she writes that unlike other women's interest in beautiful clothes,

> All I want is a good horse as a mute and loyal companion, a handful of servants hardly more complex than my mount, and a life as far away as possible from the hustle and bustle I happened to find so sterile in the civilized world where I feel so deeply out of place.[114]

What is significant here is the split within her colonial subjectivity. On the one hand, the "native"—because of his racial inferiority—can be conceived only as her servant, regardless of his/her class. In *Écrits intimes*, for instance, she urges Alî Abdelwahab, a member of the Tunisian bourgeoisie, to do different things for her, such as babysitting her brother Alexander or selling Trophimowsky's botanical garden to the Bey of Tunis. On the other hand, by exposing the hollowness and sterility of the "civilized world," Eberhardt undermines the very basis of her authority as a colonial subject. In "*L'Âge du néant,*" too, Eberhardt subverts the project of the French civilizing mission by denouncing modern civilization as the "great fraud of our time."[115] She has even promised to write a book about the "harmful" effects of "Europeanization" on Arab society.[116]

Eberhardt also rejects Tunisian Muslim women as some Arab "*gueuses*" who "[inspire] her with an unbearable feeling of disgust and hatred."[117] According to *Le Grand Robert de la langue Française,*[118] the word *gueux* has a variety of meanings ranging from *mendiant* ("beggar"), *fripon/coquin* ("rascal"), *va-nu-pied* ("nobody"/"low life"), *débauche* ("debauched person"), and *femme de mauvaise vie* ("prostitute"). In fin de siècle France, *la gueuse* became a slur that designates the Republic in the discourse of the Far Right. According to Charles-Roux, the only Tunisian women—in fact woman—Eberhardt fought with was the mother-in-law of Alî Abdelwahab,[119] a man with whom Eberhardt was having an affair[120] and a regular correspondence. The Arab women she was calling "gueuses" were in fact wealthy women from the Tunisian elite.[121] Because Abdelwahab's wife Aïcha and her mother were neither beggars nor prostitutes, the noun *"gueuses"* probably meant in this context "nobodies." What Eberhardt's condescending attitude reveals is not simply her antibourgeois feelings, but also her deployment of race as a sign of social inscription, to compensate for her social subordination. It is as the "Arab woman" that now Eberhardt refers to Alî's wife, formerly her friend[122] and sister[123] "Aïcha."

Eberhardt's identification with or differentiation from the "Muslim woman" depends on the power position she occupies. In a fight with her husband Slimène, she distances herself from the "Muslim woman" and demands that she be given the respect and equality due to a Muslim brother:

> Yes, indeed, I am your wife before God and Islam. But I am not a vulgar Fathma or an ordinary Aïcha. I am your brother Mahmoud, the servant of God and Djilani, rather than the servant of her husband that every Arab woman is according to the law of Shari'a. And I don't want, do you hear, that you show yourself to be unworthy of the beautiful dreams that I have made for both of us, and of which I have only told you a part, in the letter of last Tuesday.[124]

As the above quotation shows, Eberhardt's identification with the Other and not the Other Without[125] expresses a relation of power. This subordination of the Algerian "Muslim woman" is expressed in Eberhardt's reliance on the French colonial discourse, which dismisses all Muslim women as Aïsha, Fatima, or Zohra, names usually given to Algerian maids[126] working for the French settlers. Just as the vulgar Aïcha and Fathma function as metaphors for gender inequality and oppression, they can also be metaphors for financial security and happiness depending on Eberhardt's financial situation. Broke and starving, Eberhardt writes:

> Here is complete destitution . . . no food, no money, no heat . . . Nothing!" Now, how little would the real misery and the cloistered life of Arab women be. . . . Even blessed would be my absolute dependence vis à vis Rouh [Slimène].[127]

In her writings, Eberhardt not only reproduces the stereotypes of the Muslim woman as prostitute in the discourse of male Orientalism, but more importantly she reinvents them to negotiate her social and sexual identity. In *The Oblivion*

Seekers, there is a fetishistic mode of representation that fixes the "Muslim woman" as a prostitute and victim of her *"mektoub."* The story of Achoura Ben Said, who becomes a prostitute after being abandoned by her husband, derives from the stories of Ouled Nail, the Algerian dancers/prostitutes who caught the imagination of the Western travelers in North Africa. In the opening passage of *"Achoura,"* we see a postcard of an "Ouled Nail"[128] prostitute, who seemed in her "bizarre garments" like a mysterious "ancient oriental idol."[129] In this short story, Achoura's victimization is produced as a cultural trope to discuss Islam's inferiority. Indeed, her marriage at a very young age, seclusion, and repudiation[130] conform to the Eurocentric view that Islam is a barbaric religion that condones polygamy and the sale of brides. In the above example, the production of Achoura as a prostitute results from the colonial subject's constitution through what Bhabha calls a "fixed" ideological construction of the Other, which circulates as stereotype.[131]

More interesting, however, are those passages where she collaborates with and resists the discourse of male Orientalism. Describing the impact of the French civilizing mission in Algeria, she observes: "Despite the riff-raff French civilization has brought over here, whore and whoremaster that it is, Algiers is still a place full of grace and charm."[132] Even though Algeria is still feminized as a graceful and charming woman, by turning France into a pimp, Eberhardt strips French imperialism of its moral justification for the colonization of Algeria.

There is no doubt that Eberhardt shares a lot of cultural narcissism and racial prejudice with her fellow European male Orientalists. Blacks, in particular, seem to be the first target of her racist attack: They were "wild, eager for childlike games and barbarous frenzy, very near, now, to our animal origins."[133] Her views about Maghrebian women, whether Muslims or Jews, blacks or Arabs, seem to derive from the nineteenth-century racial ideology in Europe. Just as sensuality is Arab, greed is Jewish,[134] and savagery is black, intellectual pursuits like Eberhardt's romantic quest in North Africa are Aryan characteristics. Eberhardt's racial and cultural self-complacency separates her from the "Maghrebian woman" who does not see further than cooking. While the native Algerian woman removes the pot to add more wood to the fire, Eberhardt's "Aryan weakness" makes her interpret this cooking scene in a spiritual and intellectual way: "All that mattered to [her is] the flame shooting up, straight and free, towards peacefulness of the stars."[135]

Eberhardt's racism prevents her from identifying in particular with the black Muslim women she meets in the Maghreb. Eberhardt's presentation of white skin as a marker of civilization and intellect and blackness as a symbol of savagery recalls the nineteenth-century racial doctrine of Le Comte de Gobineau, who claimed that the Aryans created the civilizations of Egypt, India, and China.[136] Throughout her travelogue, blacks emerge as "repulsive" apelike men, with "ferret's eyes," "tics and grimaces."[137] If condescendingly and reluctantly Eberhardt refers to black men like Salem, Sidi Brahim, and Ba Mahmadou as her brothers in Islam, the possibility of identifying with her black Muslim sisters is unthinkable. The black "Muslim woman" has no name; sexual promiscuity seems to be the generic name for "black woman-hood." The colored woman, she says, has no control over her sexual "in-stinct[s]," and "for a few sous," she would give herself up for any man, "Arab or negro."[138]

What is important here is that Eberhardt not only reproduces the male Ori-entalist stereotype of the "Muslim woman" as prostitute, but also transforms it to negotiate her own social, sexual, and gender identity. Eberhardt's con-struction of the black "Muslim woman" as harlot and the Arab "Muslim woman" as independent reflects the rigid boundaries of class, race, and gen-der in nineteenth-century Europe. Even though she does not openly identify with the black "Muslim woman" as she does with the Arab, Eberhardt's con-struction of black womanhood as sexually promiscuous mirrors her own lifestyle in North Africa, where she took many Algerian, Tunisian, and French lovers.[139] What is significant here is that the black "Muslim woman" functions like an alter ego onto which Eberhardt projects her fears of social and economic destitution.

Despite her contempt for the Republican feminism of Maria Deraismes, Eberhardt shares the Third Republic's contempt for the working-class woman. It is as "*Jenny l'ouvrière*" ("working-girl"), that Eberhardt disparag-ingly refers to her sister-in-law. In *Écrits intimes* she writes that her brother "got engaged to a commoner, daughter and sister of sailors."[140] In fin de siè-cle France, the bourgeois establishment analyzed "the perceived pathology of the city in terms of the condition of working-class women."[141] Because of her autonomy and independence, the working girl occupied a central place in those scientific and social discussions on female sexuality and criminal be-havior.[142] Eberhardt's construction of the lower-class black "Muslim woman" as a "harlot" parallels the bourgeois contempt for the working-class "French woman," who is "no woman" at all in the eyes of the Republican politician Jules Simon.[143]

At the same time, the projection of her sexual fantasies onto the enslaved black woman betrays Eberhardt's desire to liberate herself from the sexual oppression imposed by bourgeois morality. This process of inclusion and ex-clusion of the "Other Without" (Arab Muslim woman and the black Muslim woman) is an integral part of the mechanisms involved in the formation of identity. The sexuality of the black "Muslim woman" and "the autonomy" of the Arab upper-class "Muslim woman"/Saint are therefore foils to define

Eberhardt's own position in Europe. If on the other hand, the Arab "Muslim woman" or female marabout has earned the admiration of this female impe-rial subject, it is not because this special category of Muslim women conforms to the bourgeois ideal of the angel in the house, but because in her reinvention of the Maghreb, Eberhardt constructs this non-European space as a feminotopia, that is, "an idealized [world] of female autonomy, empower-ment, and pleasure."[144] The invention of the upper-class Arab woman as au-tonomous reflects Eberhardt's inner desire to reconstruct a European woman-hood that is free from the prison-house of gender.

Unlike the black "Muslim woman," the Arab "Muslim woman" often functions as a surrogate self for this European woman traveler. Even though Eberhardt displays at times a condescending attitude toward the Arab "Mus-lim woman," she does not dehumanize her like the black or the Mulatto "Muslim woman." The Arab "Muslim woman" is referred to by her colonial name "Aïsha" or "Fathma," her title as "wife" or *Lella* (lady), and sometimes her real name. As she tells the story of Embarka, the "Muslim woman" who committed suicide to escape her abusive husband, Eberhardt cannot but identify with her lot. In this instance, Embarka functions as Eberhardt's rec-ognizable imago in the mirror: she is a "rebel"[145] who put an end to her "suf-fering" and "servitude" by taking her own life. A victim of spousal violence, "the little bedouin" escapes her slavelike condition by hanging herself with a "long silk belt."[146] Eberhardt's perception of Embarka as a "slave" is framed by her views on women's bondage in Europe. Hammou Hassine is not different from the European male, who desires the European woman to remain "a slave or an idol."[147] Eberhardt's account of Embarka's suicide not only illustrates a rare example of feminine solidarity in this narrative, but also the self-dissipation and nihilism underlying Eberhardt's romantic phi-losophy. Echoing the decadent poets, she writes: "A people for whom sui-cide is still possible is a strong people. Animals never kill themselves; nor negroes unless, that is, they are stimulated by alcohol. Suicide is a kind of drunkenness, but a deliberate drunkenness."[148]

Just as she celebrates Embarka's suicide as a brave rebellion against native patriarchy, Eberhardt sanctions female maraboutism and mystical Islam in general for liberating the "Muslim woman" from the constraints of gender. Ali Behdad's argument that Eberhardt's encounter with the famous female marabout, Lella Zaynab, is instigated by her "search for Islamic spirituality" and the French army's need for "information to be used for a complete takeover"[149] might be true, but his analysis overlooks the interplay of class and gender in Eberhardt's fascination with this mystical woman. Indeed, many female marabouts traveled in the desert dressed as men like Eberhardt herself. Lella Fatma for example, "organized the resistance against the French in the Djurdjura mountains in 1857."[150] Eberhardt's wearing of an Arab male attire is consistent with her identification with these independent female marabouts who, liberated from the constraints of motherhood and wifehood, rode in the desert wearing male garments. Mackworth points to Eberhardt's acquaintance with the tradition of female maraboutism. In 1899, the year Eberhardt visited El Oued, a "little saint" affiliated with the Qadiriya was "riding in the desert of Southern Oran." Even though the "eighteen-year-old Dehbiya"[151] used to dress in a traditional male costume, she was "highly venerated" by the people living in her *zawiya*.

Eberhardt's friendship with Lella Zaynab, the Rahmaniya marabout at the *zawiya* of El Hamil[152] seemed like a dangerous alliance for the French colonial authorities who put both of them under surveillance.[153] According to Hamdy,[154] Lella Zaynab stood against both the French and the Muslim patriarchy to become her father's successor as the marabout of El Hamil. Even though the French forced Lella Zaynab's father to appoint his nephew as his successor, Lella Zaynab after his death pleaded her case in front of all the Rahmaniya brothers and became her father's successor.

Eberhardt's admiration of female autonomy in mystical Islam is clear in her appreciation of Lella Khaddoudja, an upper-class Arab woman, whose pursuit of Islamic spirituality allowed her to escape the drudgery of domestic life.[155] As she decides to go on a pilgrimage, Lella Khaddoudja, Sidi Brahim's relative, leaves behind her wifely and motherly duties and finds "in the sacred soil"[156] of Mecca a new home. Identifying herself with this upper-class Muslim woman, Eberhardt observes:

> I, too, begin musing about Lella Khaddoudja, who must have a rather adventurous soul, to break so willingly with the sleepy routine, the cloistered life she was born to, to go off and start a new life under another sky.[157]

Eberhardt's construction of the Arab "Muslim woman" reverses the ideal of femininity in Victorian gender ideology. Eberhardt's rejection of the cult of domesticity is illustrated not only in her solitary journey to the Maghreb but also in her escape from the constraints of motherhood. In contrast with the bourgeois feminism of Deraismes, which reduced marriage to "the propagation"[158] of the human species, Eberhardt did not want to have children. When asked by her friend Robert Randau whether she wanted to have children, Eberhardt said that "if [she] "had a child [she] should not give up [her] wanderings." She would "carry him with [her], strapped to [her] saddle, wherever [she] went."[159] But for the moment, she had no wish to become a mother. The romantic diction used to describe Lella Khaddoudja's spiritual journey reinforces Eberhardt's identification with the "Other Without." The two women are brought together by a common destiny: a rejection of domesticity, an "adventurous soul," a fascination with Islamic spirituality, and an attempt to reconfigure the patriarchal concept of home.

In *Marginales en Terre d'Islam* (1992), Dalenda and Abdelhamid Largueche[160] explain that the *zawiya* is a liminal and subversive space, where the sacred is reunited with the profane. Indeed, these Sufi sanctuaries have always been an asylum for the social outcasts: ex-prostitutes, the mentally ill, divorcées, runaway wives, homosexuals, and so forth. In the mystical world of Sufi brotherhood, Eberhardt uses the subversive space of the *zawiya* to legitimate her homoerotic desire. Right after the passage where she states that a good Muslim is he who "can unite without sin Faith with Sensuality,"[161] she describes a brown young woman in homoerotic terms. Sitting with her "Muslim brothers" and their "1001 cigarettes" in a place of wanton sensuality," she gazes at an "Oriental beauty who could smile at us and display herself to advantage."

In *Colonial Desire* (1995), Robert J. C. Young claims that "the repulsion that [Western] writers commonly express when describing other races, particularly Africans," is accompanied "with an equal emphasis, sometimes apparently inadvertent, on the beauty, attractiveness or desirability of the racial other."[162] Eberhardt's description of black women and mulattos falls within this ambivalent axis of attraction and repulsion toward the racial other. Despite her racist comments on blacks in general, Eberhardt's text betrays a voyeuristic trajectory of desire that transpires from her exotic description of the jewels and *mlahfa* (veil) that the black women are wearing. The first black woman she perceives is a "tall" and "thin" Sudanese "negress" wearing a "citron-yellow mlahfa," with "silver snakes fastened [to] the two long mats of her "jet black hair that spread across the chest." The second is an "alluring" mulatta dressed in a "*mlahfa* of red wool" that "fell" around her "arching loins" and round "hip[s]." She is a striking "strange beauty" with her "dark and fine" body, "voluptuous" lips, and "lovely nude arm."[163] Eberhardt's attraction to blackness reflects what Gobineau calls "the tragic flaw" of the Aryan races. As "the elite races" are compelled by their civilizing instincts to mix their blood with the "inferior" races, in the long run, this process of hybridization will bring about their demise.[164] Whereas for Gobineau civilization is white and male,[165] Eberhardt's narrative, while retaining Gobineau's ethnocentrism, includes the white woman in the Eurocentric concept of civilization though her articulation of an active economy of female desire.

Eberhardt's travelogue subverts not only the phallocentrism of the nineteenth-century imperial ideology, but also the bourgeois heterosexual matrix. Eberhardt's disguise as an Arab man becomes instrumental in expressing her desire for other women. As a she/he, Isabelle/Mahmoud becomes a "nondifferentiated oneness,"[166] that is, a subject who is simultaneously a he, a she, and a she/he. In Eberhardt's own words, she "[has] lived already in all men and in all women."[167] In her personal writings, Eberhardt seems shifting between various forms of Otherness. In *Écrits intimes*, she uses both the male[168] and female[169] inflection of French grammar. In a letter to Alî Abdel-wahab, she genders herself as female in those passages in Arabic and signs herself as Podo, the short form for Nicolas Podolinsky, the male pseudonym under which she published her short story "Infernalia."[170] At other times, her letters are signed Meriem in Arabic and Podolinsky in French.[171] This double signature allows her to criss-cross the boundaries of gender, race, and religion. In the Maghreb, Si Mahmoud Essaadi/Isabelle passes for a Turk in Tunisia[172] and a Tunisian in Algeria.[173] Before she became Mrs. Ehnni, Si Mahmoud also corresponded with a French officer posted in Algeria under the pseudonym of Nadia.[174] Eberhardt also writes herself as "daughter of Nicolas,"[175] meaning a daughter of an unknown father in Russian. In Sardaignes, she passed for the wife of her lover Abdel Aziz Osman, and received letters under the false name of "Mme Mereina Aziz Bey."[176]

In *Belated Travelers*, Behdad claims that Eberhardt's male Arab disguise, rather than challenging the "categories of race and gender, as Garber claims," is a "phallocentric appropriation"[177] of an oriental signifier that reinforces the differences between the colonizer and the colonized. This chapter argues that the disguise of "*la roumia convertie*" serves multiple functions: Eberhardt not only appropriates an oriental signifier as Behdad claims but also disrupts European ideologies of race, gender, and class. Even though she has "gone native," Eberhardt has always remained the *roumia*; hence, the attempt upon her life by Abdullah. Even though he is right in reading Eberhardt's Arab male disguise as a colonial gesture, Behdad seems to ignore how Eberhardt's wearing of an Arab male attire allows her to negotiate the antagonistic claims of her sexual and social identity in Europe. Just as they are constitutive of gender identity, clothes are also markers of social identity: Eberhardt's wearing of Arab male attire is significant not just because it subverts European gender and racial ideology, but more important, because it allows her to negotiate her social position in Europe, that is, to define herself as a middle-class woman, rather than a member of the destitute classes. Because she cannot afford the garments of European middle-class women, Eberhardt cross-dresses to reenter through the door of exoticism those same circles from which she has been excluded. During the prosecution of the Sufi fanatic who has tried to assassinate her, Eberhardt writes to her husband Slimène, informing him of her worries that her Arab male clothes might be too provocative to wear during the trial. She gives her husband two reasons why she wants to wear a European male attire: the first is the exorbitant costs of the "hat, underwear, corset, petticoats, skirts, stockings, shoes, gloves" that respectable French women wear, and the second reason she provides is her scorn for the "cheap" and "ridiculous" clothes of the lower-class French woman.[178] Even though the possibility that she might be using her poverty as an excuse to cross-dress is not ruled out, the importance of class and economic independence in defining the position of women in Europe can be adduced from Eberhardt's adamant refusal—whether genuine or not—to wear the cheap clothes of working-class women. Bearing in mind Eberhardt's aristocratic background, her willingness to wear the clothes of the European working men, rather than the "cheap" clothes that poor women wear, reveals the precariousness of her economic situation as well as her fear of falling to a lower level, of being contaminated by the European working-class women.

To avoid problems with the French authorities at the trial, Eberhardt appears not in European men's clothes as she said to her husband, but in Arab women's attire. Her choice of Arab women's clothes both conforms to and transgresses the Law of the Colonial Father: in wearing female attire, she subscribes herself to the clear-cut bourgeois distinction between the sexes, yet, her masquerade as an Arab woman, that is, her use of an Oriental signifier allows her to cross the class boundaries characterizing French society.

Just as the Arab male attire is a means of social escapism as seen in her determination not to wear the cheap clothes of poor French women, her refusal to act upon Paschcoff's[179] advice to wear Arab clothes during her first encounter with the lesbian feminist Sèverine reveals Eberhardt's effort to rewrite herself as an active desiring subject. As a voyeuristic colonial subject, Eberhardt objectifies the colonized female subject, but resists being turned into Sèverine's object of desire. Eberhardt's objectification of the "Muslim woman" is also illustrated in her visit to the brothel with Brigadier Smain to "watch the lascivious dancing and preliminaries to love-making."[180] On her way back from El-Hamel (Algeria), Eberhardt did perform some *fantasias* in honor of some prostitutes she met on the road:

> I did some galloping along the road with Si Abbès, under the paternal gaze of Si Ahmed Mokrani. Some women from the brothel were on their way back from El-Hamel (Algeria). Painted and bedecked, they were rather pretty, and came to have a cigarette with us. Did fantasias in their honor all along the way. Laughed a lot.[181]

The "us" that Eberhardt uses to include herself in the male group of Muslim men, does not just separate her from the "Other Without," but more important, it translates a voyeuristic desire to see herself desired by the object of her own desire, that is, "the Muslim woman," under the watchful eye of Islamic patriarchy. In Arabic *fantasia* means "ostentation." In North Africa, the *fan-*

tasia is a male sport involving a set of acrobatic movements on horseback, with loud cries, music, and rifle shots. Eberhardt's involvement in this male sport is transgressive because she engages in a male gendered sport and displays herself as an androgynous object of desire; one that is desired by both the prostitutes and the men she is traveling with.

Eberhardt's male disguise seems to be a double-edged sword: while it gives vent to her homoerotic desire, it disallows the possibility of her interaction with her upper-class Muslim sister, like Sidi Brahim's mother, "whose presence [she] can never enter as Si Mahmoud, the man whom everyone treats [her] as being."[182]

REDEFINING THE SERAGLIO

In contrast with the nineteenth-century European and American women travelers, who have been able to penetrate where no Western man has ever been before—the Bastille[183] of the Muslim household—Eberhardt's disguise as an Arab man forecloses for her the possibility of knowing and interacting with the upper-class "Muslim woman." Her description of the "little world of women" in Kenadsa is based on hearsay, not on an actual eyewitness account. She herself admits that she has never seen Sidi Brahim's mother. Even though this "elderly Muslim queen-mother" is in "charge of all interior administration expenses, receipts, alms," no one ever "sees her" except when she goes out "veiled" to "visit the tombs of Sidi Bou-Ziane, and of Sidi Mohammed, her husband."[184]

Invented as a place of exoticism and abundant sexuality by male Orientalists in the Renaissance, the harem was transformed by nineteenth-century Western women travelers into a desexualized space that conforms to the Victorian ideal of domesticity.[185] Standing against both male and female Orientalism, Eberhardt resexualizes the North African "harem woman" and moves the Seraglio from the enclosed space of the home into the open space of the desert. In *Western Representations of the Muslim Woman* (1999), Mohja Kahf[186] argues that the subjugation of the Muslim woman was barely present in the literature of the Renaissance. The cultural trope of the oppressed "Muslim woman" appeared only in the nineteenth century with the establishment of the French and British empires. In contrast with the British traveler Katherine Ann Elwood, who constructed the harem as a "retreat," a "shrine," and an "abode of the sacred,"[187] Eberhardt invents a "bohemian" harem, where the "Muslim woman" is unveiled and on the road: either meeting a secret lover;[188] near a fountain;[189] or going to a marabout.[190] Eberhardt's redefinition of the harem genre challenges not only the tradition of male Orientalism, but also the middle-class gender ideology in Europe. In contrast with the desexualized "Muslim woman" in the writings of Victorian women travelers in the Middle East, Eberhardt's North African "Muslim woman" is primarily a sexual being, whether she is a female marabout (through the Sufi notion of transgressive love) or a black slave. Thus, Eberhardt uses the ethnographic authority and the very aesthetics of the dominant bourgeois culture to subvert its gender ideology.

Eberhardt's subversion of the bourgeois ideal of the angel in the hearth is also illustrated in her reconfiguration of the patriarchal concept of home. A social outcast in Europe, Eberhardt tries to escape European patriarchy by finding a home elsewhere—in Islam and the Maghreb. Her conversion to Islam, the rival faith to Christianity, and her marriage to an Arab constitute a challenge to the French civilizing mission in Africa. Eberhardt's incurable romantic "malaise"[191] makes her seek freedom in the desert. Following the steps of Arthur Rimbaud and Paul Valéry, she writes: "To be alone is to be free, and freedom has been the sole happiness required by my restless impatient nature—an arrogant nature."[192] Crossing the boundary between the domestic and public space, she "rediscover[s] in the village's only Arab street calm impressions of 'home.'"[193] In her new home, she sleeps on the road, "on a mat in front of the Moorish café," under the roof of "the great sky," and "the moonlit night."[194]

As this chapter demonstrates, there is a split in Eberhardt's attitude toward the North African "Muslim woman." Despite her racial prejudices and complicity with the French colonial authorities, Eberhardt at times does not see the "Muslim woman" as the absolute Other, but rather as a mirror or imago in which she could contemplate herself. As an alter ego, the "Muslim woman" becomes Eberhardt's metaphor to discuss European identity. The function of the "Muslim woman" in Eberhardt's narrative goes beyond the metaphor of colonial penetration in male Orientalism (France's "male/active" penetration of "female/passive" North Africa) to assist in the establishment of Eberhardt's own identity and place in European society. Eberhardt might have inherited her emphasis on the "Muslim woman's" sexuality from the Enlightenment's fascination with Oriental sexuality,[195] but what is more fundamentally significant is her use of the "Muslim woman's" sexuality as a trope to criticize European bourgeois morality and gender ideology.

Although ethnocentric and overtly racist at times, Eberhardt's narrative seems to deconstruct its own discourse of racial and ethnic superiority by emphasizing the similarities between the position of the "Occidental" and "Oriental woman." Rather than subverting the value system underlying French colonial ideology, in identifying with the "Other Without" and converting to Islamic mysticism, Eberhardt reverses the concept of "cultural difference," which is central in the discourse of French imperialism. In contrast with the paternalistic discourse of the French establishment, which appropriated the language of feminism to attack Arabo-Islamic culture, Eberhardt not only attacks the shallowness of Parisian feminism but also creates the mystical "Muslim woman" as more independent and autonomous than her French sister, stripping thus French imperialism from the cloak of morality with which it hides and justifies its colonial project.

However, as in the discourse of male Orientalism, "the Muslim woman" is not allowed to speak in Eberhardt's writings and is ignored as a historically resistant subject. Eberhardt said nothing about the Algerian women's resistance to French colonialism and their sexual and economic oppression at the hands of the French colonial Father. Eberhardt's subversion of Western patriarchy has been recuperated by the colonial order when Barrucand published her book under the Orientalist title *Dans L'Ombre Chaude de L'Islam*. Whereas in Eberhardt's narrative, "l'ombre chaude de l'Islam" means "a new understanding of love,"[196] in decontextualizing the book's title from this subversive meaning, Barrucand relocates this narrative in medieval Christianity's perception of Islam as a religion of sensuality and spiritual darkness. In doing so, Barrucand markets the radical difference of Islam and silences the dissenting voice of this European woman.

NOTES

1. According to Pierre Arnoult, Isabelle Eberhardt's father was Arthur Rimbaud. Besides their physical resemblance, both of them had a "common destiny" that brought them to the Maghreb (Hedi Abdel-Jaouad, "Isabelle Eberhardt: Portrait of the Artist as a Young Nomad," *Yale French Studies* 83 [1993]: 93). Eberhardt also claimed that she was the daughter of a Turkish Muslim doctor who raped her mother. See *Écrits intimes*, 116–17.

2. Information collected from Isabelle Eberhardt, *In the Shadow of Islam*, trans. Sharon Bangart (London: Peter Owen, 1993), 8.

3. Eberhardt, *In the Shadow of Islam*, 10.

4. According to Abdel-Jaouad, one reason why Eberhardt's work remained to some extent unknown was Barrucand's claim that he coauthored her work. Recent research on Eberhardt, however, has demonstrated that Barrucand did not make serious changes to Eberhardt's text. See "Isabelle Eberhardt: Portrait of the Artist as a Young Nomad," 94.

5. Eberhardt, *In the Shadow of Islam*, 13.

6. Billie Melman, *Women's Orients: English Women and the Middle East, 1718–1918: Sexuality, Religion and Work* (Ann Arbor: University of Michigan Press, 1992), 3.

7. Bhabha, *The Location of Culture*, 72.

8. Mary Louise Pratt, *Imperial Eyes: Travel Writing and Transculturation* (London: Routledge, 1992), 157.

9. Pratt, *Imperial Eyes*, 166–67.

10. Gikandi, *Maps of Englishness*, 47.

11. Gikandi, *Maps of Englishness*, 144.

12. Anne McClintock, *Imperial Leather: Race, Gender and Sexuality in the Colonial Contest* (New York: Routledge, 1995), 258–95.

13. Melman, *Women's Orients*, 32.

14. Unless otherwise indicated, all translations from the French are mine in this chapter. Jean-Pierre Biondi, *Les Anticolonialistes 1881–1962* (Paris: Robert Laffont), 31.

15. Elizabeth Ezra, *The Colonial Unconscious: Race and Culture in Interwar France* (Ithaca, N.Y.: Cornell University Press, 2000), 6.

16. Charles-Robert Ageron, *France coloniale ou parti colonial?* (Paris: Presse universitaire de France), 192.

17. Ageron, *France coloniale ou parti colonial?* 224–25.

18. Ageron, *France coloniale ou parti colonial?* 211.

19. Quoted by Ageron, *France coloniale ou parti colonial?* 213.

20. Ageron, *France coloniale ou parti colonial?* 144.

21. Ageron, *France coloniale ou parti colonial?* 145.

22. Eberhardt, *Departures: Selected Writings*, trans. and ed. Karim Hamdy and Laura Rice (San Francisco: City Lights Books, 1994), 182.

23. Ageron, *France coloniale ou parti colonial?* 190.

24. Biondi, *Les Anticolonialistes 1881–1962*, 31.

25. Biondi, *Les Anticolonialistes 1881–1962*, 28.

26. Biondi, *Les Anticolonialistes 1881–1962*, 29.

27. Biondi, *Les Anticolonialistes 1881–1962*, 31–33.

28. Ageron, *France coloniale ou parti colonial?* 96–97.

29. Ageron, *France coloniale ou parti colonial?* 69.

30. McMillan, *Housewife or Harlot*, 50.

31. Anne Louise Shapiro, *Breaking the Codes: Female Criminality in Fin de Siècle Paris* (Stanford: Stanford University Press, 1996), 179.

32. Julia Clancy Smith and Frances Gouda, *Domesticating the Empire: Race, Gender, and Family Life in French and Dutch Colonialism* (Charlottesville: University of Virginia Press, 1998), 81.

33. Clancy Smith and Gouda, *Domesticating the Empire*, 81.

34. Shapiro, *Breaking the Codes*, 181.

35. Annette Kobak, *Isabelle: The Life of Isabelle Eberhardt* (London: Chatto & Windus, 1988), 99.

36. Shapiro, *Breaking the Codes*, 182–83.

37. I am using Laura Rice's translation in "Eberhardt's Journey from Anarchy to Complicity," in Eberhardt's *Departures*, 195.

38. Kobak, *Isabelle*, 64–65.

39. Eberhardt, *The Passionate Nomad: The Diary of Isabelle Eberhardt*, trans. Nina de Voogd, ed. Rana Kabbani (London: Virago), 100.

40. Kobak, *Isabelle*, 65.

41. The Russian woman Barrucand charged with translating Eberhardt's entries in Russian into French. Quoted in Edmonde Charles-Roux, *Nomade j'étais: les années Africaines d'Isabelle Eberhardt 1899–1904* (Paris: Bernard Grasset, 1995), 247–48.

42. *Écrits intimes: lettres aux trois hommes les plus aimés*, eds. Marie-Odile Delacour et Jean-René Huleu (Paris: Payot, 1991), 79.

43. Kobak, *Isabelle*, 247.

44. Eberhardt's and Bentami's marriage to an Arab man gave them privileges they could not have had if they had married a Russian man. The marriage to an "inferior" Other allowed them to enter marital unions where they had the upper hand as wives on account of their racial "superiority."

45. Kobak, *Isabelle*, 15.

46. Kobak, *Isabelle*, 19.

47. Kobak, *Isabelle*, 20.

48. Kobak, *Isabelle*, 25.

49. Kobak, *Isabelle*, 67.

50. Ageron, *France coloniale ou parti colonial?* 16.

51. Shapiro, *Breaking the Codes*, 134–35.

52. Kobak, *Isabelle*, 163.

53. Charles-Roux, *Nomade j'étais*, 266.

54. Clancy Smith and Gouda, *Domesticating the Empire*, 154.

55. Clancy Smith and Gouda, *Domesticating the Empire*, 155.

56. Eberhardt, *In the Shadow of Islam*, 70.

57. Eberhardt, *In the Shadow of Islam*, 69–70.

58. Eberhardt, *Écrits sur le sable*, 531–32.

59. Her real name is Caroline Rémy. Better known as the radical feminist Séverine. See McMillan, *Housewife or Harlot*, 20.

60. Charles-Roux, *Nomade j'étais*, 205.

61. Charles-Roux, *Nomade j'étais*, 211.

62. Cecily Mackworth, *The Destiny of Isabelle Eberhardt* (New York: The Ecco Press, 1975), 71.

63. The word "feminism" here refers to women's movements and writings in nineteenth-century France.

64. Claire Goldberg Moses, *Feminism in the 19th Century* (Albany: State University of New York Press, 1984), 181.

65. Moses, *Feminism in the 19th Century*, 183.

66. Eberhardt, *The Passionate Nomad*, 88.

67. Eberhardt, *Écrits intimes*, 317.

68. Eberhardt, *Écrits intimes*, 127.

69. In contrast with Deraismes, the radical feminist Hubertine Auclert was a strong supporter of women's right to vote and tried to keep a strong alliance between Republicanism and socialism. At sixteen, she was expelled from a convent because the nuns saw her as demented. Mentioned in Clancy Smith and Gouda, 167. She was also "written off" by the French police as "suffering from madness or hysterics" because she thought of men as her equals. Quoted in McMillan, *Housewife or Harlot*, 80.

Auclert's feminism is also closely tied with the Saint Simonian socialism of the 1840s, which attacked the patriarchal institution of the family. See Moses, *Feminism in the 19th Century,* 230.

70. Hubertine Auclert, *Les Femmes Arabes en Algérie* (Paris: n.p., 1900), 49.

71. Eberhardt, *Écrits intimes,* 134.

72. Eberhardt, *The Passionate Nomad,* 79–80.

73. Auclert, *Les Femmes,* 3.

74. Auclert, *Les Femmes,* 42–59.

75. Eberhardt's project to open a Qur'anic school for Muslim girls was never carried out.

76. Eberhardt, *Écrits Intimes,* 135.

77. McMillan, *Housewife or Harlot,* 78.

78. Eberhardt, *In the Shadow of Islam,* 116.

79. Kobak, *Isabelle,* 99.

80. Eberhardt, *Écrits intimes,* 72.

81. Eberhardt, *Écrits intimes,* 386.

82. Kobak, *Isabelle,* 169.

83. Kobak, *Isabelle,* 195.

84. Bhabha, *The Location of Culture,* 28.

85. In "Of Mimicry and Man," Bhabha leaves out gender in his discussion of colonial mimicry in the works of "Kipling, Forster, Orwell, [and] Naipaul," in *The Location of Culture,* 87.

86. Quoted by Kobak, *Isabelle,* 62.

87. Kobak, *Isabelle,* 90–91.

88. Kobak, *Isabelle,* 130–31.

89. Kobak, *Isabelle,* 142–43.

90. Eberhardt, *Écrits intimes,* 382.

91. Eberhardt, *The Passionate Nomad,* 63.

92. Eberhardt, *The Passionate Nomad,* 71.

93. Kobak, *Isabelle,* 35.

94. Eberhardt, *Écrits intimes,* 336.

95. Bhabha, *The Location of Culture,* 30.

96. Mackworth, *The Destiny of Isabelle Eberhardt,* 128.

97. Abdelwahab Bouhdiba, *Sexuality in Islam,* trans. Alan Sheridan (London: Routledge), 30–32.

98. Eberhardt, *Écrits intimes,* 92.

99. Eberhardt, *The Passionate Nomad,* 40–41.

100. To tighten their grip over North Africa, the "French colonial policies" played Berbers against Arabs and "resurrected the Romans as imperial progenitors of the French [and Berbers] in Africa," in David Prochaska, *Making Algeria French: Colonialism in Bône, 1870–1920* (Paris: Editions de la maison des sciences de l'homme, 1990), 213.

101. Kobak, *Isabelle,* 174.

102. Kobak, *Isabelle,* 176.

103. Eberhardt, *The Passionate Nomad,* 92.

104. Prochaska, *Making Algeria French*, 213.

105. Eberhardt, *In the Shadow of Islam*, 63.

106. Eberhardt, *In the Shadow of Islam*, 67.

107. Eberhardt, *In the Shadow of Islam*, 68–69.

108. For more information about this massacre, see Djebar, *Fantasia: An Algerian Cavalcade*, trans. Dorothy S. Blair (Portsmouth: Routledge, 1993), 64–79.

109. Eberhardt, *In the Shadow of Islam*, 16.

110. Eberhardt, *In the Shadow of Islam*, 111.

111. Pratt, *Imperial Eyes*, 82–84.

112. Eberhardt, *In the Shadow of Islam*, 111.

113. Eberhardt, *In the Shadow of Islam*, 21.

114. Eberhardt, *The Passionate Nomad*, 59.

115. Eberhardt, *Écrits sur le sable*, 531.

116. Eberhardt, *Écrits intimes*, 218.

117. Eberhardt, *Écrits intimes*, 312.

118. *Le Grand Robert de la langue Française*, 2nd ed., s.v. *"Gueux"* and *"Gueuses."*

119. Alî Abdelwahab is in fact the brother of the famous Tunisian scholar Hassan Hosni Abdelwahab who called for Tunisian women's education in *Most Famous Tunisian Women*, a book he dedicated in 1917 to his daughter Naïla Abdelwahab. The book was not published, however, till 1934.

120. Charles-Roux hints at the possibility of an affair between Eberhardt and her Tunisian correspondent in *Nomade j'étais*, 99. Charles-Roux also reports that Alî's mother-in-law showed Isabelle the door after it was rumored in Tunis that Alî was taking money from her numerous lovers. In front of a witness, Alî did return to Isabelle the money he borrowed from her to go to Istanbul, and their correspondence gradually ended after that, 108.

121. Charles-Roux, *Nomade j'étais*, 107.

122. Eberhardt, *Écrits intimes*, 132.

123. Eberhardt, *Écrits intimes*, 174.

124. Eberhardt, *Écrits intimes*, 336–37. I am using here Cecily Mackworth's translation, in *The Destiny of Isabelle Eberhardt* (New York: The Ecco Press), 142.

125. The "Other Without" refers here to the "Muslim woman" as the gendered subaltern.

126. Fanon, "Algeria Unveiled," 52.

127. Eberhardt, *Écrits intimes*, 286.

128. Eberhardt, *The Oblivion Seekers*, trans. Paul Bowles (San Francisco: City Lights, 1972), 31.

129. Malek Alloula argues that the production of the "Muslim woman" as prostitute provided an aesthetic and moral justification for the colonization of Algeria. See *The Colonial Harem*, trans. Myrna Godzich and Wlad Godzich (Minneapolis: University of Minnesota Press, 1986), 120.

130. Eberhardt, *The Oblivion Seekers*, 32.

131. Bhabha, *The Location of Culture*, 66.

132. Eberhardt, *The Passionate Nomad*, 91.

133. Eberhardt, *In the Shadow of Islam*, 77.

134. Eberhardt, *In the Shadow of Islam*, 101–2.

135. Eberhardt, *In the Shadow of Islam*, 102.

136. Arthur de Gobineau, *Essai sur l'inégalité des races humaines* (Paris: Librairie de Jacob, 1933), 347–48.

137. Eberhardt, *In the Shadow of Islam*, 46.

138. Eberhardt, *In the Shadow of Islam*, 48.

139. See Eberhardt's biography in *In the Shadow of Islam*, 6.

140. Eberhardt, *Écrits intimes*, 69.

141. Shapiro, *Breaking the Codes*, 21.

142. Shapiro, *Breaking the Codes*, 22.

143. McMillan, *Housewife or Harlot*, 37.

144. Pratt, *Imperial Eyes*, 166–67.

145. Eberhardt, *In the Shadow of Islam*, 74.

146. Eberhardt, *In the Shadow of Islam*, 74.

147. Eberhardt, *In the Shadow of Islam*, 70.

148. Eberhardt, *In the Shadow of Islam*, 74.

149. Behdad, *Belated Travelers: Orientalism in the Age of Colonial Dissolution* (Durham, N.C.: Duke University Press, 1994), 129.

150. Mackworth, *The Destiny of Isabelle Eberhardt*, 116.

151. Mackworth, *TheDestiny of Isabelle Eberhardt*, 116.

152. Eberhardt, *The Passionate Nomad*, 107.

153. Eberhardt, *Departures*, 239.

154. Eberhardt, *Departures*, 239–40.

155. Lella Khaddoudja is the only woman from the native elite toward whom Eberhardt feels connected. This is probably because Lella Khaddoudja's frequent pilgrimages to Mecca made her break away from her patriarchal role as mother and wife and live on the road like Eberhardt herself.

156. Eberhardt, *In the Shadow of Islam*, 61.

157. Eberhardt, *In the Shadow of Islam*, 62.

158. Moses, *French Feminism in the 19th Century*, 181.

159. Quoted by Mackworth, *The Destiny of Isabelle Eberhardt*, 169.

160. Dalenda Largueche and Abdelhamid Largueche, *Marginales en terre d'Islam* (Tunis: Cérès, 1992).

161. Eberhardt, *In the Shadow of Islam*, 117.

162. Robert J. C. Young, *Colonial Desire: Hybridity in Theory, Culture and Race* (London: Routledge, 1995), 96.

163. Eberhardt, *In the Shadow of Islam*, 57.

164. De Gobineau, *Essai sur l'inégalité des races humaines*, 1: 153.

165. De Gobineau, *Essai sur l'inégalité des races humaines*, 1: 92–93.

166. Luce Irigaray, *This Sex Which Is Not One*, trans. Catherine Porter (Ithaca, N.Y.: Cornell University Press, 1985), 207.

167. Eberhardt, *In the Shadow of Islam*, 98.

168. Eberhardt, *Écrits intimes*, 18.

169. Eberhardt, *Écrits intimes*, 64.

170. Eberhardt, *Écrits intimes*, 64.

171. Eberhardt, *Écrits intimes*, 86–87.

172. Kobak, *Isabelle*, 97.

173. Charles-Roux, *Nomade j'étais*, 103.

174. Kobak, *Isabelle*, 47.

175. Eberhardt, *Écrits intimes*, 111.

176. Charles-Roux, *Nomade j'étais*, 171.

177. Behdad, *Belated Travelers*, 123.

178. Katrina O'Loughlin, "The Spectre of the Veiled Dance: The Transvestic, and European Constructions of the 'East,'" *Ariel* 50 (1996): 233.

179. In a letter, Paschkoff gave Eberhardt this advice: "Wherever you go you should present yourself in elegant Oriental costume. Abou Naddara [Eberhardt's Egyptian mentor] will tell you that his clothes did a lot to make him the fashion [in Paris]," in Mackworth, *The Destiny of Isabelle Eberhardt*, 71.

180. Kobak, *Isabelle*, 92.

181. Eberhardt, *The Passionate Nomad*, 107.

182. Eberhardt, *In the Shadow of Islam*, 56.

183. In contrast with the radical feminist Hubertine Auclert and Marie Bujéga—daughter and wife of French colonial civil administrators—Eberhardt shows no interest in serving the "colonial state" by bringing "France into the domesticated space of the secluded Arab woman," in Clancy Smith and Gouda, *Domesticating the Empire*, 171.

184. Eberhardt, *In the Shadow of Islam*, 47–48.

185. Melman, *Women's Orients*, 316.

186. Mohja Kahf studies this shifting image of the Muslim woman in *Western Representations of the Muslim Woman: From Termagant to Odalisque* (Austin: University of Texas, 1999).

187. Melman, *Women's Orients*, 139.

188. Eberhardt, *In the Shadow of Islam*, 91.

189. Eberhardt, *In the Shadow of Islam*, 98.

190. Eberhardt, *In the Shadow of Islam*, 99.

191. Eberhardt, *In the Shadow of Islam*, 102.

192. Eberhardt, *In the Shadow of Islam*, 107.

193. Eberhardt, *In the Shadow of Islam*, 17.

194. Eberhardt, *In the Shadow of Islam*, 22.

195. In my discussion of Eberhardt, I am indebted to Melman's *Women's Orients* and to Kahf's analysis of the shifting image of the "Muslim woman" in *Western Representations of the Muslim Woman*.

196. Eberhardt, *In the Shadow of Islam*, 76.

Chapter Three

The "Muslim Woman" and the Iconography of the Veil in French Feminism and Psychoanalysis

In the preceding chapter, I examined the production of the Maghrebian "Muslim woman" in the writings of Eberhardt, a Russian woman traveling in French colonial Tunisia and Algeria at the turn of the nineteenth century. In this chapter, I investigate the metaphor of the veil and the production of the "Muslim woman" in those discourses situated on the French Left in the imperial and postimperial era. This chapter questions the viability of Western feminist and psychoanalytic theory in the North African context and argues that these discourses derive at times from the same Orientalist impulse we find in the male Orientalism discussed by Said. Using de Lauretis's notion of "gender" as "representation,"[1] I will examine how the metaphor of the veil in psychoanalysis and French feminism derives from earlier discourses on Muslim women and Islam. The first part of this chapter examines Fanon's discourse on the veil in his essay "Algeria Unveiled." Even though situated on the left, Fanon's discourse seems to derive from a patriarchal and sometimes an Orientalist impulse. The second section examines Lacan's notion of the "veiled phallus" in view of the primacy of the specular in Western metaphysics and the discourses on the veil generated by the Algerian Revolution. Using de Lauretis's notion that the subject of feminism speaks from a doubled position that is both inside/outside ideology, the third part of this chapter argues that in contrast with Simone de Beauvoir and Luce Irigaray, Hélène Cixous's *écriture féminine*—especially her recent work *Les Rêveries de la femme sauvage: Scènes primitives* (2000)[2]—presents a "doubled vision,"[3] which both reproduces and resists those Orientalist discourses on the veil.

In "Transparent Veils, Western Women Dis-Orient the East," Billie Melman argues that the discourse of the veil precedes the existence of Islam and the colonial situation. Used at first in the Christian East, the veil "touched on the definite status of femininity and female sexuality in Western culture."[4] In Pauline gender ideology, "a woman can prophesy only when her head is veiled, because man's head represents the spirit in Christ whereas woman's is associated with flesh and the body—that is, with sexuality."[5] In the Age of Enlightenment, the veil was "[desacralized],"[6] but "retained its association with purity and virginity." While it was increasingly being "eroticized," it became used in a metaphysical sense; "the ability to unveil" was associated with the idea of "uncovering" truth or "identity." Gradually, "the veiled woman was transformed from an ambiguous symbol of female empowerment to a site of alterity."[7] In "The Newly Veiled Woman: Irigaray, Specularity, and the Islamic Veil," Anne-Emmanuelle Berger discusses the symbol of the veil in Irigaray's text as an "instance of theoretical imperialism."[8] In contrast with Melman, who presents the veil as a Christian symbol, and Berger, who strips the veil from its Judeo-Christian background and presents it as if it were an authentic Islamic cultural icon appropriated by an imperialist Western feminist/psychoanalytic center, I would like to treat the issue of the veil from a nonoriginary point of view. Rather than presenting the problem of the veil in terms of a Western appropriation of an Oriental signifier, I would like to pose the problem differently: How can the veiled Muslim women speak in these Western discourses on the veil? And what are the implications of applying these theories of the veil to the North African context?

In *Technologies of Gender*, de Lauretis argues that the human subject is produced through discourse and that gender is a "representation" or a "construction"[9] that is produced and reproduced by various discourses. Revealing how feminism inherited Western phallocentrism, de Lauretis argues that the "construction of gender "as sexual difference" has shaped "feminist interventions in the arena of formal and abstract knowledge, in the epistemologies and cognitive fields defined by the social and physical sciences as well as the human sciences or humanities."[10] From this perspective, the metaphor of the "veiled phallus" in the psychoanalytic works of Lacan[11] and Jane Gallop[12] and the metaphor of the veil in French feminism in general derive from a preestablished Western tradition that favors visibility/presence over invisibility/absence and truth/light over concealment/darkness.

Because of the primacy of the visible in Western epistemology,[13] the veil discourse in French feminism and psychoanalysis focuses only on what is concealed/hidden, not on the specific local and social significance of the veil. In French language, the word *voile*[14] ("veil") appears as a multiple signifier. In the seventeenth century, it referred to a piece of cloth covering the statues of the gods, monuments, and so forth. Starting from the sixteenth century onward, the verb *voiler* ("to veil") was used metaphorically in the sense of "making less visible," "concealing," and "masking" light or truth.

In the nineteenth century, following the rise of French imperialism, the veil referred not only to the tchador/veil covering the face of the "Muslim woman," but also to the Arabic word *litham*, which is a veil covering the face of the male Touareg living in the Sahara Desert. Whereas in some parts of the Muslim world, both men and women wear the veil, in Europe, *le voile* ("the veil") is an exclusively feminine garment worn by brides, widows, and nuns. In the nineteenth century, the veil was invented anew as a marker of cultural difference, that is, a symbol of the "Muslim woman's" sexual oppression by Islam and Arab culture.[15]

THE "ALGERIAN WOMAN" AND THE DYNAMISM OF THE VEIL: PATRIARCHY, NATIONALISM, AND ORIENTALISM IN FRANTZ FANON'S "ALGERIA UNVEILED"

A Martinican psychiatrist appointed to work for the French army in Algeria, Frantz Fanon, a Marxist black revolutionary, soon defected to the Algerian side and joined the National Liberation Front (FLN) in its fight against the French colonial regime. Fanon's views on the veil and the "Muslim woman" in "Algeria Unveiled" come as a response to the Battle of the Veil launched by the French colonial government to weaken the ranks of the Algerian resistance during the War of Independence (1954–1962). In May 1958, the French generals in Algiers, showing their resolution to keep Algeria French, dragged Algerian women from their homes and publicly unveiled them, shouting "Vive l'Algérie française!" Hence, it is within the context of Algerian nationalism, Hegel's dialectic, and French colonial discourse that I shall examine Fanon's views on the "historic dynamism"[16] of the veil.

Throughout "Algeria Unveiled," there is a tension that arises from Fanon's ambivalent discourse about the veil, Algerian culture, and the "Algerian woman." Presenting the issue of the veil through a Hegelian dialectic, Fanon writes that the veil became a symbol of Algerian identity only because the French constructed it as a sign of cultural difference/Islamic inferiority: "It is the white man who creates the Negro. But it is the Negro who creates negritude. To the colonialist offensive against the veil, the colonized opposes the cult of the veil."[17] In his Hegelian reading of the veil, Fanon overlooks the symbolic exploitation of the "Muslim woman's" body in the patriarchal discourses of French colonialism and Algerian nationalism. Just as the French male imperial order waged its war of colonization on the female body of Algeria, the Algerian nationalist male elite turned the "Algerian woman" and the domestic space of the home into the site of the anti-colonial struggle. The French colonial image of Algeria as "a prey fought over with equal ferocity by Islam and France"[18] reveals not only the "policy" and "philosophy" of the French occupier, as Fanon says, but also the patriarchal ideology of the colonized. Because she is the symbol of Algeria, the "Muslim woman" becomes the flesh/"prey" over which both the French and Algerian men/predators are fighting.

Throughout his essay, Fanon wavers between the "historic dynamism"[19] of the veil and the fixedness of Algerian/Islamic culture. In contrast with the colonial French discourse where the veil appears as the symbol of women's oppression, Fanon presents it as an unstable semiotic icon. During the anticolonial struggle in Morocco, "the white veil was replaced with the black veil"[20] to protest the exile of King Muhammad by the French colonial authorities. In Algeria, Kabilean and Arab women in the rural areas are often unveiled. Fanon also notes that the veil was initially worn because "[Islamic] tradition demanded a rigid separation of the sexes."[21] When the French became "bent on unveiling Algeria," the veil turned into a "mechanism of resistance." During the Battle of Algiers (1958), both the removal and resumption of the *haïk* ("veil") served as a "technique of camouflage."[22] At first, the veil was strategically removed to carry weapons for the Algerian fighters. Passing for a French woman, the unveiled Algerian woman would carry in her suitcase weapons, funds, and tracts to the *fidaïs* ("suicide bombers"). When the French colonial authorities discovered the trick, the veil was once again restored "to conceal packages" for the Revolution. When the French were alerted, all women became suspect and were forced to pass through "magnetic detectors."[23] After the events of May 1958, "the veil was resumed, but stripped once and for all of its exclusively traditional dimension."[24] In contrast with the semiotic dynamism of the veil in the colonial era, Fanon constructs it as a fixed and ahistorical icon in precolonial Algeria: before the French occupation, Fanon asserts, the veil was "an undifferentiated element in a homogeneous whole."[25]

In his reading of the veil, Fanon recognizes the "power of nationalism as a scopic politics."[26] Just as the veil was constructed as the symbol of cultural difference in French colonial discourse, the veiled "Muslim woman" was produced as the visible marker of Islamic identity in Algerian nationalism. As Fanon puts it:

It is by their apparel that types of society first become known, whether through written accounts and photographic records or motion pictures. Thus, there are civilizations without hats. The fact of belonging to a given cultural group is usually revealed by clothing traditions. . . . One may remain for a long time unaware of the fact that a Moslem does not eat pork or that he denies himself daily sexual relations during the month of Ramadan but the veil worn by the women appears with such constancy that it generally suffices to characterize Arab society.[27]

Fanon's statement reveals that rather than being a given, cultures are fabricated through clothing, "motion pictures," and "photographic records." This inventedness of culture, however, is at odds with Fanon's nationalist construction of the veil as the symbol of Algeria's authentic identity. Reproducing the Arab nationalist discourse where the veil is symbolic of a precolonial Islamic identity, Fanon states that the veil stands for Algerian "society's uniqueness"[28] and "originality."[29] "French colonialism," he says, "has settled itself in the very center of the Algerian individual and has undertaken a sustained work of cleanup, of expulsion of self, of rationally pursued mutilation."[30] The French campaign against the veil epitomizes the colonial effort to "expel" or "clean up" the true "self" of Algeria. Likewise, underneath Fanon's fear that Westernization might lead to the "erosion" of Algeria's "national culture"[31] lies the assumption that cultures can be stocked/frozen and contained within a special locale. Although situated on the Left, Fanon deploys at times the discourse of French Orientalism. Even though he rejects the colonial narrative about the oppression, "confinement," "humility," and "the silent existence"[32] of the "Algerian woman," Fanon implicitly reproduces the same discourse when he states that the "Algerian woman's" life is "limited in scope" because of the "sclerosis"[33] Islamic tradition must assume during the anticolonial struggle.

In equating the violence of colonization with the rape of the Algerian woman's body,[34] Fanon is reproducing the patriarchal discourse of nationalism, where lands and women's bodies are presented as men's property. When he is pressured by his boss to "exhibit" his wife, the Algerian man feels that he is "prostituting his wife."[35] In the erotic discourse of the French conquest, "the flesh" of the Algerian woman (symbol of Algeria) is "laid bare"[36] by the "aggressive" French occupier/rapist. Unveiled and raped, the "Algerian woman" is subjected to "a double deflowering"[37] without "consent" or "acceptance." In contrast with McClintock's reading of "Algeria Unveiled," I argue here that Fanon reproduces rather than refutes the "erotics of ravishment"[38] underlying the rhetoric of the French conquest. By phallicizing the "Algerian woman" who penetrates into the heart of the European city, Fanon is reversing the colonial metaphor of sexual penetration. In the Battle of Algiers, the Algerian woman who conceals pistols and grenades under her veil becomes a "veiled phallus" that threatens to emasculate not only the Algerian men as McClintock argues,[39] but also the French male colonial order. Reversing the colonial metaphor, the "Algerian [phallic] woman penetrates a little further into the flesh of the Revolution."[40] In this nationalist narrative, the reconquest of Algeria also involves a "double deflowering":

> But after a certain period the pattern of activity that the struggle involved shifted in the direction of the European city. The *protective mantle* of the Kasbah, the

almost *organic curtain* of safety that the Arab town *weaves* round the native, withdrew, and the Algerian woman, exposed was sent forth into the conqueror's city.[41] [emphasis added]

As a "veiled phallus," the Algerian woman has to break first the "organic curtain"/hymen of the Kasbah before penetrating into the effeminized European city. In reproducing the erotics of the French conquest, Fanon remains, despite his Marxist revolutionary agenda, trapped within the phallocentric discourse of French imperialism.

Fanon's assertion that the veil "distorts the Algerian woman's corporal pattern"[42] is quite patriarchal. For "the city woman," the veil has become second nature: "accustomed to confinement, her body did not have the normal mobility before a limitless horizon of avenues, of unfolded sidewalks, of houses, of people dodged or bumped into."[43] The "Algerian woman" feels "naked" when she walks unveiled: "[T]he veil protects, reassures, isolates, [without it] the unveiled body seems to escape, to dissolve."[44] In a paternalistic tone, Fanon adds that as part of the war effort, his female comrade must not only "[relearn] her body" but also "achieve a victory" over "her childish fears."[45] Fanon also makes excuses for the sexual harassment the unveiled "Algerian woman" is subjected to in the street of Algiers while carrying weapons for the revolution. Dismissing sexual harassment as a universal male behavior, Fanon writes: "The unveiled Algerian girl who 'walks the street' is very often noticed by young men who behave like young men all over the world, but who use a special approach as the result of the idea people habitually have of one who has discarded the veil."[46]

For Fanon, only the French colonizer is frustrated by the "woman who sees without being seen."[47] The Algerian man "does not see her. There is even a permanent intention not to perceive the feminine profile, not to pay attention to women." Revisiting Fanon's discourse on the veil, Djebar asserts that the veiled woman frustrates both the colonizer and the Algerian. In *Women of Algiers*, Djebar writes:

> There's also the danger that the feminine glance, liberated to circulation outside, runs the risk at any moment of exposing the other glances of the moving body [breasts, sex, navel]. As if all of a sudden the whole body were to begin to "defy" [and threaten men's] exclusive right to stare.[48]

In *Fantasia*, Algerian women willingly participated in the Algerian Revolution: They were not entrusted[49] with direct action, nor did they need their husband's permission "to leave on an assignment."[50] Djebar's resurrection of the voices of Jennet, Zohra, and Cherifa in *Fantasia* shows that Algerian women did not participate in the nationalist struggle at the invitation of Algerian men as Fanon claims.

Because the veil was removed during the course of the revolutionary struggle, Fanon seems to imply that it will ultimately be abandoned to meet the demands of independence. In the socialist future of Algeria, Fanon's sister in the fight against imperialism seems unveiled, yet subordinated to a nationalist male leadership.

THE "VEILED PHALLUS" IN THE LAND OF VEILED WOMEN: READING JACQUES LACAN IN A NORTH AFRICAN CONTEXT[51]

Defending Lacan against his feminist critics,[52] Gallop reminds them of the nature of Lacan's text—where nothing is really what it seems—and of his assertion that the phallus "can play its role only when veiled."[53] Because "metonymic interpretations"[54] can also be phallocentric, she calls for a new kind of feminine reading that transcends the opposition between metaphor and metonymy. Using Lacan's notion of the "latent phallus," Gallop argues that there is an inevitable latency to all open, visible meanings. Unlike the unproblematic division between the hidden and the surface meaning in the conventional Freudian act of psychoanalytical interpretation, Lacan advances the thesis that every time a meaning moves to the surface, becomes open and not latent, it is simultaneously trying to hide its own reasons for making that meaning visible.

Lacan's equation of the veil with the unconscious can be traced to Freud's metaphor of the veil, in which he claims that female sexuality, in contrast with that of the male, is inaccessible to psychoanalytic research. For Freud, women's sexuality is "veiled in impenetrable darkness" not only because of cultural inhibitions, but also because of "the conventional reticence and insincerity of women."[55] Freud's Africanist construction of female sexuality as "lack" or "the dark continent"[56] has been reproduced in Gallop's perception of metonymy as "the dark continent of rhetoric," an effeminized symbolic space associated with the invisibility and "hiddenness of female genitalia."[57] In "The Agency of the Letter," Lacan deliberately plays on the ambiguity in the word *voile*[58] ("veil") in the French language. Besides the inherent duplicity between concealing and revealing in the act of veiling, the word *voile* occupies an ambiguous position between male and female in French. It means a "ship" when preceded by the feminine definite article *la*, and a "veil" when it is preceded by the masculine definite article *le*. Lacan's notion that the phallus "can play its role only when veiled"[59] and Gallop's reproduction of Lacan's metaphor (in her discussion of the interdependence between metonymy and metaphor) raise many questions as to the consequences of applying such a concept to the Algerian context, where the FIS (Islamic Salvation Front) holds that Islamic identity lies in the control of the "Muslim woman's" dangerous sexuality. Because she possesses the phallus, that is, the power of seduction or *fitna*, the "Muslim woman" must constantly be supervised; her sexuality controlled through the institutions of segregation and seclusion. From the standpoint of Muslim women activists, this metaphor could be disabling because it reinforces patriarchal fears of women's hidden powers, justifying thus women's seclusion.

Even though Lacan was not himself involved in the Algerian Revolution, his stepdaughter, Laurence Bataille, joined in 1958 a French left-wing network that collected funds for the FLN.[60] She was arrested on 10 May 1960 and sent to the Roquette prison for aiding the Algerian rebels. In prison, Lacan brought her an extract from his seminar on the "Ethics of Psychoanalysis" where he talks about "Antigone's revolt against Creon."[61] She was quickly released after her lawyer (Roland Dumas) managed to get the charges dropped. A left-wing intellectual, Lacan could only support his stepdaughter's political commitment. However, the metaphor of the "veiled phallus" disturbingly recalls the colonial French discourses produced on the Algerian woman during the Battle of the Veil in the 1950s. If the "French administration" focused their efforts on unveiling the "Algerian woman" to win the war, it was because their "sociologists" and "specialists" had argued that "beneath the patrilineal pattern of Algerian society" lay a deeper "structure of matrilineal essence."[62] To destroy Algerian resistance, "[they] must first of all conquer the women" hiding "behind the veil."[63] Lacan's metaphor embodies the colonial French argument that "behind the visible, manifest Algerian patriarchy" lies a "basic" yet invisible matriarchal system. The doubleness underlying the concept of the "veiled phallus" also recalls the doubleness of these discourses produced on the "Algerian woman" during the Battle of the Veil, where she appears both as the locus of power and victim of the Algerian man's barbarity.

Put in a Maghrebian context, the "veiled phallus" can stand for the subaltern effeminized Oriental phallic order that Said discussed in *Orientalism*. This "haremization effect"[64] raises questions as to the implications of applying Lacan's notion of the "veiled phallus" to the male Touareg, who wear veils to protect their faces from the sun of the Sahara Desert. In wearing the *litham* ("veil"), the male Touareg would seem to embody Lacan's notion of the "veiled phallus" and also acquire an ambivalent sexual identity in the eyes of those Europeans traveling in the Maghreb. The bisexuality of the male Touareg falls within the Orientalist trope that Islam's excessive sexual restrictions on women are thought to encourage the Eastern "malady of homosexuality." Lacan's metaphor recalls the ethnocentrism underlying Edouard Duchesnes's book *De la prostitution dans la ville D'Alger depuis la conquête* (1853). In this nineteenth-century French colonial narrative, Duchesnes explains homosexuality—the "Arab Muslim deviance"—by the hot African climate and the Islamic sociocultural mores. Explaining Eastern deviant sexuality by Islam's seclusion and veiling of women, Duchesnes wrote: "[Because] young Algerian men are so handsome and go about in public unveiled, side by side with veiled females, homosexuality is thereby encouraged."[65]

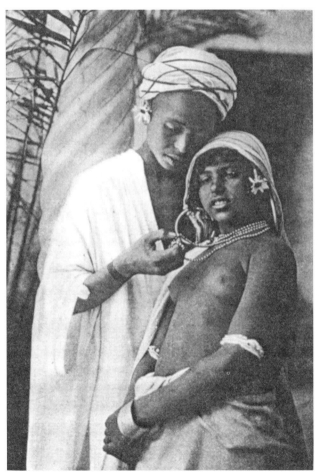

Figure 3.1.   "A Young Arab Couple." Source: Book cover of John Foster Fraser's *The Land of Veiled Women: Some Wanderings in Algeria, Tunisia and Morocco* (London: Cassell and Company, LTD, 1913).

This "haremization effect" takes shape in the picture representing "A Young Arab Couple" that appeared on the cover of Fraser's 1913 travelogue *The Land of Veiled Women: Some Wanderings in Algeria, Tunisia and Morocco*. The pubescent children are made by the Western photographer to masquerade as a modern Arab couple (see figure 3.1). Both youths are looking down avoiding the gaze or the specular power of the Western cameraman. In this child porn picture, both the body of the girl (symbol of the Tunisian nation) and the boy (symbol of a castrated native phallic order) are unveiled and eroticized by the imperial subject/photographer.[66] Because North Africa is prenarrated[67] as the "land of veiled women," the Tunisian boy can only appear as an infantilized and emasculated Other. Both the age and sensuality of these two children suggest that the autochthonous races of North Africa are too childish or immature to jump into modernity, symbolized here through the concept of the couple.[68] Lacan's metaphor of the "veiled phallus" stems thus from a Western epistemology, which derides, through effeminization of a non-Western phallic Other, both the rhetoric of the French civilization and the North African nationalist aspiration to modernity.

In "Veiling over Desire," Doane argues that Lacan's metaphor of the veiled phallus "reverses the usual terms of sexual difference in relation to the visual field."[69] In contrast with Doane, who reads Lacan's destabilization of perception outside French colonial ideology, I would like to examine Lacan's metaphor of the "veiled phallus" in view of those discourses produced on Algerian women's participation in guerilla warfare at the moment of decolonization. At first, the Algerian woman was strategically unveiled and transformed by the *fidaï* into a "woman-arsenal" carrying "automatic pistols" or "bombs"[70] in her suitcases. When the French discovered the trick, the Algerian woman reverted to a strategic wearing of the haïk "to conceal" the grenades "from the eyes of the occupier."[71] As a result, all women became suspicious: French and Algerian, veiled and unveiled. This recalls the destabilization of perception in Lacan's and Gallop's theory in which everything is indiscriminately suspect.

The notion of duplicity underlying Lacan's metaphor of the "veiled phallus" cannot be dissociated from the threat of Islamic "terrorism" in France after the Algerian war of independence. Ever since the Algerian Revolution, the image of the veil in Western mass media became linked with an increasing fear of the Islamic threat. Whereas the nineteenth-century French discourse focused on unveiling the body of the Algerian woman/nation, the discourse on the veil starting from the late 1950s onward has shifted to "hyperveiling"[72] the female Muslim body. As Neil MacMaster and Toni Lewis put it: "The Iranian Revolution of 1979, the war in Lebanon [in the 1970s], the Gulf War [1992] . . . and the spread of fundamentalism into the Maghreb, especially Algeria, have created a level of anxiety that is higher in France than for any other Western nation."[73] Lacan's image of the "veiled phallus" also recalls these Western press reports or films in the 1950s, where "heavily veiled women are shown carrying weapons, establishing an equation between the oppression of women, fanaticism and terrorism."[74] In these images, the veil becomes the symbol of Islam's medieval barbarity, fanaticism, and thus irredeemable alterity. In the discourse of the French right, *le foulard* ("scarf") has become since the 1980s associated with feelings of cultural anxiety. In "Tchadors, Excision, Cannibals," the right wing journalist Max Clos writes in the *Figaro*:

> Can we accept in our land excision and cannibalism? It seems like we are far from the issue of the veil here. But in reality we are not. It is the same problem minus the butchery and the mutilation, for the consequences are the same on what is primordial; the safeguard of our identity.[75]

My major argument here is that the scopic phallocentrism in Lacan and Freud has found its way in the discourse of some French feminists, who despite their dismantling of the workings of Western patriarchy at home, have failed to decolonize their writing from the concept of difference at the heart of the Eurocentric universalist mode of thinking.

BETWEEN COMPLICITY AND TRANSVALUATION: HÉLÈNE CIXOUS'S DOUBLE VISION OF THE "MUSLIM WOMAN" AND THE VEIL

The Iconography of the Veil and the Harem in Simone de Beauvoir and Luce Irigaray

Even though de Beauvoir, in collaboration with Gisèle Halimi, mobilized the left forces in France to bring to trial the torturers of Djamila Boupacha (an Algerian woman wrongfully sequestered and raped by her French torturers),[76] her views on Muslim women are still informed by the French Orientalist tradition. In *The Second Sex*, first published in France in 1953, de Beauvoir reiterates the Orientalist stereotype of the harem with its associated meaning of seclusion and veiling as a place of female idleness and sexual indulgence. Secluded from the outside world, the harem slave "has to kill time" by taking a "passion for rose preserves and perfumed baths."[77] Equating the harem with a "brothel," de Beauvoir states that if the harem woman "eagerly seeks sexual pleasure, it is very often because she is deprived of it." To escape "masculine ugliness," the slave woman "finds consolation in creamy sauces, heavy wines, velvets, the caress of water, of sunshine, of a woman friend, of a young lover." The linkage de Beauvoir creates between the Arab woman's sensuality and her seclusion derives from the tradition of male Orientalism, which is observed, for instance, in the comments of Fraser in 1913: "Kept in seclusion, languorous and without exercise, it is natural that the thought and life of an Arab woman should be sensuous."[78] In de Beauvoir's feminist text, the "Muslim woman," as a monolithic category, functions as a metonymy for Islam's inferiority. For de Beauvoir, the "abject condition" of the "Muslim woman" is caused not only by "the feudal structure" of her society but also by "the warlike ideals" of Islam, which "has dedicated man directly to Death and has deprived woman of her magic."[79]

In French, the expression *le voile d'une vierge* means not only "the veil of a bride," but also the hymen or "the veil of virginity." This throws light on the intimate connection between the veil, language, and the female body in French feminism. In "Veiled Lips," using the myth of Persephone, Irigaray questions the woman's position in "a system of representation which depends on the repression of her difference."[80] In the Greek myth, Persephone was abducted by her father Hades to live in his underworld against the will of her mother Demeter. With the intercession of Jupiter, Persephone was to spend the winter with her father and summer with her mother. "Triply veiled," the korè (virgin), violated, stolen, and veiled "[*Violer. Voler. Voiler*],"[81] stands for the absence and burial of women's "magic" in language. In a man's language, woman is always the "veil," "the sheath," or "the envelope" that "assist[s] him [and] support[s] him."[82] As Persephone, the daughter was "stolen away from her mother, from herself, by her father, the brother,"[83] the veil in Irigaray's essay becomes symbolic not only of women's oppression by patriarchy, but also of their alienation from the maternal. Even though Irigaray does not mention any Muslim women in her work, she has influenced many North African women writers such as Djebar. Because of the reliance of Muslim women writers on French feminist theories, one question needs to be addressed here: How can the veiled "Muslim woman" speak or be read in a system of representation where the veil—the sign of her cultural difference—is "synonymous with rape, ravishment, theft, and death"?[84]

This image of the veiled "woman" as wrapped goods in Irigaray's works can be traced to Freud, who claims that women cover themselves with clothes and "jewels in order to hide [their] organs,"[85] that is to say, their "lack." "The duplicity of the veil" for Freud serves to "cover a lesser 'value' and to overvalue the fetish."[86] Reflecting similar imagery in "Algeria Unveiled," Fanon writes that the French doctors are often disappointed to discover that Algerian women are "commonplace" and "vulgar" when "they remove their veils" during "medical consultation."[87] In contrast with the French men, who wonder why the Algerian women are veiled if they have nothing to hide, European women in Algeria read the veil as part of universal feminine coquetry. Just as "beauty treatment, hairdos, fashion"[88] in the West are used to disguise "feminine imperfections," the veil of the "Algerian woman" serves to "con-

ceal" and "cultivate the man's doubt and desire." The male "customer," however, is often misled by "the wrapping in which the 'merchandise'" has been
presented to him. The European women conclude that the wrapping in which
the "Algerian woman" comes in "does not really alter [her] nature, nor [her
value]." Despite his Marxist views, Fanon does not critique the commodification of the "Algerian woman" in the discourse of the European women. In
contrast with Fanon, Irigaray writes that the veiling of women's bodies serves
to enhance their value in a "ho(m)mosexual" system of exchange. As "fetish-
objects" exchanged between men, women "are the manifestation and the cir-
culation of a power of the Phallus."[89] Reversing[90] Freud's metaphor, Irigaray
writes that women veil themselves not because they are hiding the "defi-
ciency of [their] genitals,"[91] but in order to compete in a capitalistic economy
controlled by men.[92] Here, the veil does not hide women's lack, but enables
the commodification of the female body. Even though she critiques the capitalist commodification of the woman's body over which Fanon remains
silent, Irigaray leaves out all differences between women and reproduces the
universalist claim in Western feminism that all women are oppressed regardless of their differences of class, race, and sexual orientation.

Even though she criticizes Lacan for representing only the male subject as
he reflects and contemplates himself in the mirror, Irigaray does not reject
specularization as a constitutive condition for identity. To the flat mirror in
Lacan's analytic theory, she substitutes the speculum, a curved instrument,
which allows women to understand themselves and explore their sex.[93] Even
though the speculum emphasizes female specificity and obliterates the sym-
metrical "self-representation" of the "male mirror,"[94] it is still contingent
upon the primacy of the visible when deployed as a gynecological tool. Given
the primacy of female visibility in Irigaray's feminist project, the veiled
woman can only be read as a silent and "submissive slave."[95] The strategic
shift in Djebar's writings, from using French feminist aesthetics in the 1980s
to the deployment of Islamic feminism on the eve of the Algerian Civil War,
indicates her search for a more empowering feminist framework; one that responds to the particularities of the local patriarchy. In advocating Muslim
women's rights from an Islamic point of view, Djebar is acknowledging the
limits of applying French feminist theory to the Maghreb. This is why in *Loin
de Médine*, Djebar reinvents the House of the Prophet through the lens of both
Islamic feminism and écriture féminine.

The Decree Crémieux and the Aryanization of the Algerian Jews

In *Les Rêveries*, Cixous's perception of the "Muslim woman" and the veil
seems less Eurocentric than that of de Beauvoir or Irigaray. In this section, I

propose to explain the ambivalent discourse on the veil and the "Muslim woman" in Cixous's writings in view of the French colonial policy toward the Algerian Jews, the racist discourses against Jews and Arabs in France, and Cixous's self-proclaimed literary identity. In the early years of the conquest of Algeria (1830), the French colonial attitude and policy toward Algeria's Jews and Arabs was the same. In 1837, Maréchal Bugeaud called for the expulsion of all the Jews from Algeria. In 1847, Doctor Bodichon proposed to settle the native question by "[exterminating] all Arabs."[96] This changed however, with the Crémieux Decree of 1870, which automatically granted the Algerian Jews French citizenship provided that they abandon Rabbinic laws. In France and colonial Algeria, the right-wing circles opposed the Crémieux Decree as it gave the Algerian Jews too much power in the municipal elections[97] and "public administration."[98] The Crémieux Decree was not extended however to the rest of North Africa. The Tunisian Jews had to wait for the Morinaud Law of 1923 to be granted French citizenship, but still "on an individual basis."[99] In Morocco, because France refused to grant them French citizenship, the Jews remained under the jurisdiction of Islamic law as *ahl dhimma* ("People of the Book").[100]

In Algeria, the Westernization and integration of the Jews in French society depends on their "abnegation" of the Rabbinic laws such as the *yboum* or ("*levirate*"), whereby a brother-in-law marries his brother's widow.[101] The Crémieux Decree made it illegal for a Rabbi to marry a couple without them having first a civil marriage. As early as 1873, the Rabbi L. Isidor wrote to his coreligionists: "In order to be French, you have to abandon your dear customs, and the practices which seem sacred to you. Look at our brothers in France and behave like them. We honor our faith by showing it is compatible with civilization."[102]

As Ayoun and Cohen put it: "It is not the alliance with the Zionist Jewish Nationalist project which isolated the Algerian Judaism from the indigenous society, but its acceptance without any hesitation of *la Francité* ("Frenchness").[103] As early as 1871, French colonial policy played Arabs and Jews against each other.[104] For the Jewish intelligentsia, the Arab anticolonial struggle was constructed as a misunderstanding of "the virtues of occidental democracy."[105] After the Balfour Declaration of 1917, very few Algerian Jews immigrated to Israel. Because Algeria's Jews were very attached to "French culture,"[106] most of them immigrated to France. The *'aliya* to Israel attracted only the poor Jews from Constantine and the M'zab.

During the Algerian Revolution (1954–1962), with few exceptions like Albert Memmi, the Jews of Algeria and Tunisia generally did not participate in the anticolonial struggle. Whereas the Arab population perceived them as collaborating with the colonial French order, the French warned them against collaborating with the FLN in Algeria and the Neo-Destour Party in Tunisia.[107] In Algeria, because the Jewish leaders as French citizens were reluctant to join the nationalist struggle, there were bloody attacks against them in Constantine, Orléanville, and Batna.[108] Starting from May 1956, the Jews of Constantine organized themselves into organizations like the Misgeret to defend themselves, and to launch counterattacks against the FLN. Also, because they were French citizens, some Algerian Jews were "reservists in the French army." Some of them were even used in the French army headquarters as "interrogators of FLN sympathizers,"[109] because they spoke both French and Arabic.

In 1960 the FLN made an official statement in which it addressed Algeria's Jews:

> You are an integral part of the Algerian people; you are not asked to choose between France and Algeria, but to become effective citizens of your true country. Either you choose to function fully in this country where the future will inaugurate freedom and democratic principles to be enjoyed by all the nation's children; or else you accept to live under the reign of contempt and to be content with a citizenship granted by your oppressors within a context which is in contradiction even with the most elementary human rights.[110]

Even though the Comité Juif Algérien d'Études Sociales responded that they had no authority to speak on behalf of all the Jews in Algeria, they stated that they would "live in humiliation" if they "renounced a citizenship for the preservation of which [they] always fought, to which [they] remain attached with a faithfulness that deserves respect, and which inspired [them] with its dignity and honor."[111] After the Evian agreement of 1962 according Algeria its independence, there was a sharp decrease in the Algerian Jewish population. In summer 1962, only 10,000 Jews remained in Algeria, and most of them departed for France.[112] The bad socialist economy of *"autogestion"*[113] under the regime of Ahmad Ben-Bella and Houari Boumedienne drove out the rest of the Jews in the late sixties and early seventies.

Looking through the Lens of Aryan Sycorax: The "Muslim Woman" and the Veil in the Text-Lait of Hélène Cixous

In "Difference, Intersubjectivity, and Agency in the Colonial and Decolonizing Spaces of Hélène Cixous's '*Sorties*,'" Sue Thomas[114] argues that in her search for a maternal mythical symbolic, Cixous reproduces the Orientalist discourse of subduing and inhabiting Africa as a black and effeminate space. In relying on a Western masculinist universal symbolic, Cixous ends up by recolonizing the "dark continent" and inhabiting the bodies of its women,

namely, Cleopatra and Dido. Instead of the uniform Orientalist vision
Thomas finds in Cixous's discourse on Africa and its women, my own reading of Cixous's "The Laugh of the Medusa,"[115] *The Newly Born Woman*,[116]
Hélène Cixous: Photos de racines,[117] and *Les Rêveries* reveals both conformity and resistance to the French colonial discourse on the Maghrebian "Muslim woman" and the veil. I propose to read Cixous's ambivalence toward
Africa and the "North African woman" in view of de Lauretis's notion that
the feminist subject "is at the same time inside and outside the ideology of
gender, and conscious of being so, conscious of that twofold pull, of that division, that doubled vision."[118] I intend to read Cixous's ambivalence toward
Africa and the "Muslim woman" against two warring ideological systems:
first, the "Francisation" of the Algerian Jews and Cixous's internalization of
Western Orientalist discourse; and second Cixous's resistance to that process
of Aryanization through her self-proclaimed imaginary *identité littéraire*
("literary identity").[119]

In "The Laugh of the Medusa," Cixous addresses the problem of creating
a feminine language in terms of change. "The future," she writes, "must no
longer be determined by the past."[120] The question is, then, how to create a
feminine language that breaks free from earlier male colonialist discourses. In
"*Sorties*," Cixous makes the claim that her *écriture féminine* can "escape the
infernal repetition" and reproduction of the old "system," and helps "invent
new worlds."[121] However, in her search for a maternal presymbolic order,
Cixous reproduces those colonialist masculinist metaphors referring to Africa
as a woman, the "dark continent," and a primitive space that is "below" or
"before culture."[122] As she insists on writing the female body and on recu-
perating the woman's voice, the "harem" and its associated meanings of veiling and seclusion becomes a metaphor for patriarchy's repression of female
sexuality and silencing of women's voices:

> It is writing, from and toward women, and by taking up the challenge of speech
> which has been governed by the phallus, that women will confirm women in a
> place other than that which is reserved in and by the symbolic, that is, in a place
> other than silence. Women should break out of the snare of silence. They
> shouldn't be conned into accepting a domain which is the margin or the
> harem.[123]

In the above passage, the veil is produced as an unchanging signifier of female victimization. Just as "hierarchy," in the words of Arjun Appadurai, is
"associated" with "India," or "filial piety in China,"[124] the veil[125] of the "Muslim woman" has become in Western feminist writing a prenarrated space, that
is, a metaphor for a backward and repressive Muslim East. If Africa is defined

in Cixous's maternal text as preculture, the implication is that the veiled Sycorax lives outside history; that is, outside the realm of culture. In "*Sorties*," the veil functions as a metaphor for historical marginalization: "Is this me, this no-body that is dressed up, wrapped in veils, carefully kept distant, pushed to the side of History and change, nullified, kept out of the way, on the edge of the stage, on the kitchen side, the bedside?"[126] Thus, *écriture féminine* or the search for a feminine language replicates the cultural patterns, which patronize and have power over the history of Muslim women. Even though she proposes a feminine practice of writing that "will always surpass the discourse that regulates all Western "phallocentric system[s]"[127] and "speculation/specularization,"[128] Cixous's association, in the cultural context of Islam, of unveiling/visibility with freedom and veiling/invisibility with oppression and silence are reproductions of the same "phallologocentric" discourse she is criticizing.

In opposition with Cixous's earlier works, *Les Rêveries* underscores a transvaluation of the conventional discourse about Algeria in the tradition of French Orientalism. Parodying the imperial metaphor of exploring and inhabiting the body of a female exotic Algeria, Cixous puts herself in the masculinist position to "embrace"[129] and repossess Algeria by holding on to the body of her servant Aïcha who appears creamy, feminine, and maternal. Whereas she presents her German mother and grandmother as upper-class "masculine" women with "discrete virility" and small chest, she presents their servant, Aïcha as "the real woman," and her "veil" as a catalyst of her "burning"[130] sensuality. Turning the stereotype into a grotesque caricature, Cixous states that she wants to inhabit the body of the "Algerian woman": she wants to be passionate and adulterous "*à la mauresque*" ("like a Moorish woman"),[131] "she wants everything, the fine veil on the face, the linen and silk haïk, the harem pants, the hidden legs; she wants Algeria." Cixous adds that her mother's honesty is an offense or an absurdity in a country where the veil has become second nature to women—like "an organ" or "a retina"—and for others the symbol of "hypocrisy" and deceit."[132] In this passage, Cixous is responding not only to Fanon's patriarchal claim that the veil is a constitutive element of the Algerian woman's "corporal pattern,"[133] but also to the Orientalist construction of the Oriental woman and man as "duplicitous."

The most traumatic event in Cixous's life in Algeria is perhaps the accident she saw at the fair in La Place d'Armes in Oran, where a woman was cut to pieces after her veil got caught in the slats of a carousel. As she describes the veil, Cixous states: "L'Algériefrançaise sort de la scène."[134] However, in dismissing the veil as another "*histoire d'Arabes*," Cixous puts the discourse on the veil outside the French colonial situation. In "Algeria Unveiled," Fanon explains how the veil became a sign of Algerian Islamic identity only when the French decided to break the native resistance by strategically unveiling the "Algerian woman" and imbuing her in the principles of French civilization by sending her into French schools. Two questions come to the fore here: Why does the veil occupy a preeminent place in Cixous's traumatic memories? And why does she still carry inside herself the body of that unknown "veiled young woman"?[135]

In "Trauma Narratives and the Remaking of the Self," Susan J. Brison problematizes the issue of remaking the self for survivors of traumatic events:

> A further obstacle confronting trauma survivors attempting to reconstruct coherent narratives is the difficulty of regaining one's voice, one's subjectivity, after one has been reduced to silence, to the status of an object, or, worse, made into someone else's speech, the medium of another's agency?[136]

Because I believe memories to be constructed through "socially constituted forms, narratives, and relations,"[137] I intend to read Cixous's memoirs associating the veil with trauma both as a reproduction of the French narrative about the oppressed "Muslim woman" and as a mental palimpsest of the Algerian woman's participation in the anticolonial struggle. In this scene, the veil becomes a metaphor for Islam's amputation of female sexuality and repression of women's voices. Indeed, the accident in question happens when the unknown veiled woman—who stands metaphorically for all Muslim women—is embraced by another unknown Arab man. As she jumps in fright, her veil gets caught in the slats: "her body was driven in the veil, her body was seized like meat in a grinder, she couldn't get out."[138] "Her screams could be heard from the top of the Cathedral before her body dropped on the floor cut in two around the middle." Just after witnessing this terrible accident, Cixous felt a "horrible feeling of relief," for despite her death the veiled woman was able to break the silence imposed on her by Islam and Arab culture. The question that rises here is: What does it mean to read the veiled woman's howling/the sound of death as "feminine" and "humane"? My argument here is that even in death, this Algerian veiled woman is made to unspeak, as her death screams are interpreted according to the Western center (*écriture féminine*) equating visibility and voice with female freedom, and veiling and silence with female amputation and oppression. Also, how can this "veiled woman" speak when her death is reappropriated and reconstituted as a metaphor for "the tragedy of a town, a country, a history"?[139]

In presenting this veiled woman as a victim, Cixous is reading this accident along the lines of the Western narrative of the Muslim woman's victimization. In presenting this "Muslim woman" as a passive and silent victim, Cixous is erasing the history of female resistance in the anticolonial struggle. My argument here is that Cixous's recontruction of this traumatic event along the narrative of the "Muslim woman's victimization" is shaped by the 1990s Civil War in Algeria where women have become the targets of Islamic fundamentalism. By projecting the present into the past, and ignoring the strategic deployment of the *haïk* ("veil") in the Algerian Revolution, Cixous is denying the semiotic mutability of the veil.

The discourse on the veil in *Les Rêveries* is, however, ambivalent. When Cixous's mother used to go to the police commissioner as a midwife to solve "*les histoires Arabes* [*de culotte*],"[140] she would wear the veil, for she never knew whether these incidents would turn into tragedies or comedies. Thus, the veil is no longer a symbol of female oppression and amputation, but also a symbol of female freedom, as the veiled woman can travel incognito and see without being seen. It follows that the invisible is no longer synonymous with darkness and oppression, but tied with the notion of some liberty under the veil. When the FLN attacks against Jews started during the Algerian war, Cixous's mother advised her to wear the veil and travel to Morocco if she were chased by the police."[141] Rather than dismissing the veil as a universal symbol of women's oppression like Irigaray, Cixous shows that under certain constraints placed on women's movements, the veil can function as the condition for moving into the male realm.

Also, Cixous's political commitment or what she calls her "literary identity" allows her to reach out for all Muslim women regardless of their social class. Cutting across social borders, she reveals how much she longed to visit her servant's house.[142] Exposing the social disparities between Algeria's Jews and Arabs, she remembers how her mother never knew that the real names of her domestic workers were Messaouda and Barta.[143] Instead she used to call them Aïcha and Fatma, two colonial names given indiscriminately to all Algerian women. This shows to what extent Algeria's Jews got separated/cut from the Arab population and to what extent they internalized the French colonial ideology.

Pointing to the separation of Arabs and Jews in her childhood, Cixous notes how the French colonial situation and social inequities divided the Arab and Jewish population of Algeria. As she revisits the past, Cixous tries to give names to the people she loved yet called *les Arabes* ("the Arabs"),[144] *petizarabes* ("Arab children"),[145] *mauresques* ("Moorish women"),[146] or *lézarabes*.[147] She remembers Muhammad the doorman, Aïcha their servant, Barta the domestic worker at the Clinic, and Kheira the cook. Even though she "never knew their homes,"[148] she still remembers the names of her few Muslim classmates Zohra Drif, Samia, and Leila.[149] She was never allowed to visit their home, because the Algerian Jews "were filtered and rejected as

'French.'"[150] She even recuperates her Algerian Arabic-French dialect: "*Yadibonfromage, yadlavachkiri, yadizoeufs, yadinestlé.*"[151]

Unlike her earlier works, Cixous's *Les Rêveries* reflects the recent feminist debate about the veil in the West. Rather than being a sign of the "Muslim woman's" oppression, Western feminists and Muslim feminists living in the West have recently been arguing that the veil gives Muslim women access to certain freedoms they would be otherwise denied in the segregated societies of certain Islamic countries like Saudi Arabia. As Ahmed puts it:

> The strict segregation of Islamic societies has meant in fact freedoms for women and freedoms to engage in activities that their Western sisters engaged in literally at the peril of their lives. For in segregated societies, all or almost all activities performed in the world of men for men and by men must also be performed in the world of women for women by women. The woman saint, the woman sooth-sayer, the witch, the seances held for women by women to exorcise or empower are a common and accepted part of the Middle Eastern folk life.[152]

Because these Western discourses on the veil and the Muslim women focus on what is concealed, they fail to understand the significance of the veil in its specific local context. In *Gender Trouble*, Judith Butler warns against the "universalization"[153] of the notion of patriarchy, for it erases and elides the "distinct articulations of gender asymmetry in different cultural contexts."[154] In a 1998 interview, Butler challenges the notion in Eurocentric feminism, that the "veiled body" when "she/it enters public space, counts as an example of the abject."[155] In some Islamic countries like Iran, women have access to some form of power "facilitated by the veil, precisely because that power is deflected and made less easily identifiable."[156] Similarly, in "The Veil in their Minds and on Our Heads," Homa Hoodfar argues against the naïve association of de-veiling with female emancipation. When the Shah's father passed a law in 1936 to modernize Iran, "without any legal and socioeconomic adjustments,"[157] those women who refused to take off the veil because of their religious beliefs became dependent on their male relatives. Before the law, the veil allowed women to perform "public tasks" and to negotiate their wages as they sold their carpets directly to the customers. With the new law, some of them stopped "going to the carpet weaving workshops," and became increasingly dependent on "their male relatives"[158] and carpet traders to sell their goods.

In Remembrance of Algeria Past: Hélène Cixous and the Search for Arabitude

In "Difference," Thomas's analysis ignores how Cixous's frequent discourse on the "dark continent" and the "African woman" serves to embrace and reclaim a denigrated Oriental Jewish/Arab identity. In 1963, the diatribe "in vogue" among the Ashkenazi Jews of Marseilles was the "Jew of Tizi Ouzou."[159] In "Sephardim in Israel: Zionism from the Standpoint of its Jewish Victims," Ella Shohat explains how the Arab Jew/Sephardi/Mizrahi voice was muffled and silenced by the discourse of European Zionism."[160] In "the Zionist master narrative, European Zionism 'saved' Sephardi Jews from the harsh rule of their Arab 'captors,' and 'rushed' them into modernity . . . democracy . . . and humane values."[161] Sephardim[162] were often referred to as schwartze chaies ("black animals")[163] in European Jewish circles. Even Ben Gurion referred to the Moroccan Jews as "savages."[164] In the 1970s, finding inspiration in the revolt of black America, the children of Arab Jewish immigrants formed the Black Panthers, a radical Arab Jewish organization in Israel.[165] The amputated veiled Muslim woman Cixous still "carries inside her" functions as a symbol for an Arab identity from which she has been "cut off" or "separated."[166]

In "*Sorties*," Cixous claims à la Césaire that "we are black and we are beautiful."[167] Claiming a nonoriginary Jewish identity, she observes:

I was born in Algeria, and my ancestors lived in Spain, Morocco, Austria, Hungary, Czechoslovakia, Germany; my brothers by birth are Arab. So where are we in history? I side with those who are injured, trespassed upon, colonized. I am (not) Arab. Who am I? I am "doing" French history. I am a Jewish woman. . . . Who is this "I"? Where is my place? . . . Which language is mine? French? German? Arabic?[168]

In putting in parentheses her denial of her Arab identity, she is putting under erasure her own statement that she is Jewish, not Arab. In *Les Rêveries*, Cixous states that her father, besides being "Jewish," is "a real Arab under the false appearances of a young and handsome French doctor."[169] She also makes the claim that her sickness/thirst for Algeria—*la désalgérie*—is also a sickness for *l'arabité* and l'arabitude (Arabness and Arabitude).[170]

In *Hélène Cixous*, Cixous draws only her Ashkenazi family tree. The missing Sephardic branch of her family tree stands for what de Lauretis calls the "space-off" representation, which, even though outside representation, does "still exist concurrently and alongside the represented space."[171] In Cixous's own words, "the omissions as well the acts of forgetting"[172] in her autobiographical narrative are still a constitutive part of her *écriture féminine*. In contrast with the Eurocentric image of woman as the dark continent in "The laugh of the Medusa," in *Les Rêveries*, Cixous not only breaks the silence over her Sephardic roots, but also overturns the racist values on which her earlier metaphors were based. As a cartography of remembrance and forgetting, Cixous's Algeria, with its exotic veils, its "dark continent," the "Abyss of the Savage Woman"[173] rather than being a "themed" or "prenarrated space"[174] as in *"Sorties"* and "The Laugh of the Medusa," becomes instrumental in retrieving Cixous's Arab/Jewish/African identity.

As a childhood narrative, *Les Rêveries* constitutes an act of "cultural memory" to resurrect a Jewish Algeria and to understand and destigmatize her Oriental roots. According to Mieke Bal, cultural memory is a social and individual memory that links "the past to the present and future."[175] All acts of remembering involve the reenactment of "traumatic events."[176] The act of memory is "potentially healing,"[177] as it "calls for political and cultural solidarity." However, the subject of a traumatic event can heal only if he/she interacts with the others. In *Les Rêveries*, she explains that she is writing her childhood memories to quench her *désalgérie*[178] and to "cure herself from her "incurable"[179] love for Algeria, which uncured might lead to her self-destruction.[180]

Cixous's *Les Rêveries* could be seen as a feminist attempt to open a dialogue with Algerian intellectuals and feminists like Djebar who wrote about the current events in Algeria in *Vaste est la prison* (1995) and *Le Blanc de l'Algérie* (1996). Just as Shohat tries to open a dialogue in Israel between Palestinians and Sephardim and to show them how they "have been played against each other"[181] by a Eurocentric Zionist ideology, Cixous is also trying to show how Muslims and Jews in Algeria have been played against each other by the French colonial establishment. In French colonial Algeria, anti-Semitism was directed at all Jews regardless of their origin: "French Jews from both France and Algeria, Spain, Arabs, or Corsican."[182] When Vichy was in Oran, Cixous's father lost his job as a Jewish doctor.[183] Cixous's family suffered a double exclusion, from the Arab circles because they were French, and from the French circles because they were Jewish Arabs. "After the War," Cixous's family was "no longer admitted to the Red Cross swimming pools."[184] As a child, Cixous could not visit her French friend Françoise at home because she was Jewish.[185] Thus, Cixous's autobiography could be located within the recent mobilization on the part of Jewish and Muslim intellectuals on the left (notably, Edward W. Said and Noam Chomsky) to put an end to the increasing violence against women in Algeria and Palestinians in Israel.

In this autobiography, the issue is not whether Cixous is creating an idealized homogeneous past, "the question" is rather, as Shohat puts it, "who is mobilizing what in the articulation of the past, deploying what identities, identifications, and representations, and in the name of what political vision and goals?"[186] Cixous's identification with Muslim women and writing about Algeria after forty-five years of silence is prompted by her "literary identity,"[187] that is to say, by her political engagement as a feminist facing the

FIS's increasing violence against women in 1990s Algeria. Cixous states that she thought about writing this book[188] since 1994, that is, two years after the break out of the Civil War in Algeria. Given the fact that as a Jew, Cixous is no longer an Algerian citizen, her "literary nationality" does not simply give her the license to write about the current events in Algeria, but more important, it becomes a form of self-reterritorialization beyond the boundaries of nation. This imaginary "international"[189] identity becomes not only a passport for border crossing, for speaking and writing about Algeria and the Algerian women, but also for claiming a nonoriginary Jewish identity.

NOTES

1. De Lauretis, *Technologies of Gender*, 3.
2. Cixous, *Les Rêveries de la femme sauvage: Scènes primitives* (Paris: Galilée, 2000). All subsequent English translations from this book are mine.
3. De Lauretis, *Technologies of Gender*, 10.
4. Melman, "Transparent Veils, Western Women Dis-Orient the East," in *The Geography of Identity*, ed. Patricia Yaeger (Ann Arbor: University of Michigan Press, 1996), 461.
5. Melman, "Transparent Veils," 461–62.
6. Melman, "Transparent Veils," 462.
7. Melman, "Transparent Veils," 463.
8. Anne-Emmanuelle Berger, "The Newly Veiled Woman: Irigaray, Specularity and the Islamic Veil," *Diatrics* 28, no. 1 (1998): 94.
9. De Lauretis, *Technologies of Gender*, 3.
10. De Lauretis, *Technologies of Gender*, 1.
11. Lacan, *Écrits*, 288.
12. Gallop, *Reading Lacan* (Ithaca, N.Y.: Cornell University Press, 1985): 130.
13. This scopophilic drive in Western metaphysics can be traced back to the symposium between Socrates and Glaucon in Plato's *Republic*. In Book 7, there is a "screen" or a "wall" (220), separating the prisoners from the light of a fire burning outside the cave. The prisoners know neither themselves nor one another, the only thing they can see are "the shadows cast by the fire on the wall of the cave" (20). Just as the act of concealing/veiling in the story of the cave is synonymous with obstruction and darkness, the act of seeing/unveiling is conversely associated with "the truth of what is beautiful and just and good" (226). Plato, *The Republic*, ed. G. R. F. Ferrari, trans. Tom Griffith (Cambridge: Cambridge University Press, 2000).
Even though he has retained this phallocentrism, Friedrich Nietzsche departs in *The Gay Sciences* from Western metaphysics by undermining the idea of any truth lying behind the veil. Dissociating himself from the Orient of "the Egyptian youths," who, looking for truth, "endanger temples," "embrace statues, and want by all means to unveil . . . whatever is kept concealed for good reasons" (38), Nietzsche allies him-

self with the Greeks, who "are superficial out of profundity," and who know when "to stop courageously at the surface, the fold, [and] the skin." In Nietzsche's text, the veil becomes the symbol of an Oriental/Egyptian Otherness that is effeminate and duplicitous. See *The Gay Sciences*, trans. Walter Kaufmann (New York: Vintage Books, 1974). After stripping the courageous Greeks of their previously constructed cultural ties with the Orient and reinventing them as part of Western tradition, Nietzsche goes on to re-create the veil as a symbol of the "deception" of women who often conceal the fact that there is nothing behind the veil, that is, that their "essence is [merely] to appear." I am indebted here to Mary Anne Doane's discussion of the metaphor of the veil in Western thought in "Veiling over Desire: Close Ups of the Woman," in *Feminism and Psychoanalysis*, ed. Richard Feldstein and Judith Roof (Ithaca, N.Y.: Cornell University Press, 1989), 121.

14. *Le Grand Robert de la langue Française*, 2nd ed., s.v. "*voile.*"

15. Ahmed argues that the practice of seclusion and veiling in Medieval Islam was borrowed from the neighboring Christian, Judaic, and Persian societies, and that the nineteenth-century European imperialist discourse invented Islamic civilization as separate from the Judeo-Christian and Greek civilizations of the Middle East. See *Women and Gender in Islam*, 33.

16. Fanon, "Algeria Unveiled," 63.

17. Fanon, "Algeria Unveiled," 47.

18. Fanon, "Algeria Unveiled," 41.

19. Fanon, "Algeria Unveiled," 63.

20. Fanon, "Algeria Unveiled," 36.

21. Fanon, "Algeria Unveiled," 63.

22. Fanon, "Algeria Unveiled," 61.

23. Fanon, "Algeria Unveiled," 61.

24. Fanon, "Algeria Unveiled," 63.

25. Fanon, "Algeria Unveiled," 47.

26. McClintock, "No Longer in a Future Heaven," *Dangerous Liaisons: Gender, Nation, & Postcolonial Perspectives*, ed. Anne McClintock, Aamir Mufti, and Ella Shohat (Minneapolis: University of Minnesota Press, 1997), 97.

27. Fanon, "Algeria Unveiled," 35.

28. Fanon, "Algeria Unveiled," 35.

29. Fanon, "Algeria Unveiled," 37.

30. Fanon, "Algeria Unveiled," 65.

31. Fanon, "Algeria Unveiled," 39.

32. Fanon, "Algeria Unveiled," 65.

33. Fanon, "Algeria Unveiled," 66.

34. Djebar revisits Fanon's patriarchal metaphor by telling the stories of women who were really raped during the process of French colonization. See *Fantasia: An Algerian Cavalcade*, trans. Dorothy S. Blair (Portsmouth: Routledge, 1993).

35. Fanon, "Algeria Unveiled," 40.

36. Fanon, "Algeria Unveiled," 42.

37. Fanon, "Algeria Unveiled," 45.

38. McClintock, "No Longer in a Future Heaven," 96.

39. McClintock, "No Longer in a Future Heaven," 98.

40. Fanon, "Algeria Unveiled," 54.

41. Fanon, "Algeria Unveiled," 51.

42. Fanon, "Algeria Unveiled," 59.

43. Fanon, "Algeria Unveiled," 49.

44. Fanon, "Algeria Unveiled," 59.

45. Fanon, "Algeria Unveiled," 52.

46. Fanon, "Algeria Unveiled," 53.

47. Fanon, "Algeria Unveiled," 44. I am indebted in my discussion of Fanon, Djebar, and the veil to Rita A. Faulkner's "Assia Djebar, Frantz Fanon, Women, Veils, and Land," *World Literature Today* 70, no. 4 (Fall 1996): 847–55.

48. Djebar, *Women of Algiers in their Apartment*, trans. Marjolin de Jager (Charlottesville: University Press of Virginia, 1992), 139.

49. Fanon, "Algeria Unveiled," 53.

50. Fanon, "Algeria Unveiled," 59.

51. I make allusion here to the title of a British travelogue by John Foster Fraser, *The Land of Veiled Women: Some Wanderings in Algeria, Tunisia & Morocco* (London: Cassell and Company, LTD, 1913).

52. Lacan's presentation of metaphor as open and masculine and metonymy as latent and feminine made many critics like Luce Irigaray accuse him of phallocentrism. See *This Sex Which Is Not One*, trans. Catherine Porter (Ithaca, N.Y.: Cornell University Press, 1985), 108.

53. Gallop, *Reading Lacan*, 130.

54. Gallop, *Reading Lacan*, 133.

55. Freud, *Three Contributions to the Theory of Sex*, trans. A. A. Brill (New York: E. P. Dutton & Co., 1962), 16.

56. Freud, *Three Contributions to the Theory of Sex*, 55.

57. Gallop, *Reading Lacan*, 127.

58. Lacan, *Écrits*, 156.

59. Lacan, "Signification of the Phallus," *Écrits*, 288.

60. Elisabeth Roudinesco, *Jacques Lacan*, trans. Barbara Bray (New York: Columbia University Press, 1997), 295.

61. Roudinesco, *Jacques Lacan*, 295.

62. Fanon, "Algeria Unveiled," 57.

63. Fanon, "Algeria Unveiled," 37–38.

64. I am using Reina Lewis's words in her analysis of Lacan's Oriental metaphor in *Gendering Orientalism: Race, Femininity and Representation* (London: Routledge, 1996), 181.

65. Quoted by Clancy Smith and Gouda, *Domesticating the Empire*, 159.

66. See Malek Alloula, *The Colonial Harem*, trans. Myrna Godzich and Wlad Godzich (Minneapolis: University of Minnesota Press, 1986).

67. Patricia Yaeger, "Introduction: Narrating Space," *The Geography of Identity*, ed. Patricia Yaeger (Ann Arbor: University of Michigan Press, 1996), 18.

68. In his discussion of the colonial postcard in *The Colonial Harem*, Alloula explains how the couple came to symbolize an advanced Western modernity while polygamy was dismissed as the sign of a primitive Islamic patriarchal order.

69. Doane, "Veiling over Desire," 132.

70. Fanon, "Algeria Unveiled," 58.

71. Fanon, "Algeria Unveiled," 61.

72. By "hyperveiling," MacMaster and Lewis refer to the French media's obsession with images of Muslim women wearing the tchador. See "Orientalism: from Unveiling to Hyperveiling," *European Studies* 82 (1998): 121–35.

73. McMaster, "Orientalism," 128. The same anxiety has struck the United States
after the 11 September 2001 attacks. In the first days following the bombing of the
Pentagon and the World Trade Center, the giant U.S. networks frequently deployed
the veil as the symbol of Oriental or Islamic barbarity. If many veiled Muslim
women became the target of retaliatory violence in the aftermath of the attacks, it
was partly because the veil had been displayed all over the American mass media as
a sign of Islamic/Arab hatred, duplicity, and barbarism. One day after the attacks,
CNN, MSNBC, and FOX 47 broadcast footage showing Palestinian children and a
veiled Muslim woman celebrating the loss of thousands of American lives. According to the Independent Media Center, this footage was shot in 1991 during the invasion of Kuwait. Even though CNN denied the manipulation charge, it never showed
this footage again. Whether or not these images were fabricated, the fact remains the
same: the horrible pictures of this Palestinian woman dressed in black, eating cakes,
and ululating over the death of American nationals were instrumental in kindling
people's fear and in turning the veil into a sign of an irrational and demonic otherness. When the U.S. engaged its troops in Afghanistan, the threatening image of the
Muslim woman ("veiled phallus") receded to the background to pave the way for the
images of the helpless Afghan "Muslim woman" unable to breathe and see from beneath her burqa.

74. McMaster, "Orientalism," 128.

75. This is my translation from McMaster, "Orientalism," 132.

76. During the Algerian Revolution, De Beauvoir and Halimi denounced this Algerian woman's torture and the sham trial of her torturers by the French Judicial authorities in Algeria. See *Djamila Boupacha*, trans. Peter Green (New York: The
Macmillan Company, 1962).

77. De Beauvoir, *The Second Sex*, trans. H. M. Parshley (New York: Alfred A.
Knopf, 1968), 603.

78. Fraser, *The Land of Veiled Women*, 9.

79. De Beauvoir, *The Second Sex*, 166.

80. Irigaray, "Veiled Lips," *Mississippi Review* 11, no. 3 (1983): 93.

81. Irigaray, "Veiled Lips," 105.

82. Irigaray, "Veiled Lips," 106.

83. Irigaray, "Veiled Lips," 112.

84. Irigaray, "Veiled Lips," 114.

85. Irigaray, *Speculum of the Other Woman*, trans. Gillian C. Gill (Ithaca, N.Y.:
Cornell University Press, 1985), 115.

86. Irigaray, *Speculum*, 16.

87. Fanon, "Algeria Unveiled," 44–45.

88. Fanon, "Algeria Unveiled," 45.

89. Irigaray, *Speculum*, 182–83.

90. In my discussion of the veil, I derive the interconnections I am making between Freud, Irigaray, and Fanon from Anne-Emmanuelle Berger's insightful essay "The Newly Veiled Woman: Irigaray, Specularity, and the Islamic Veil."

91. Irigaray, *Speculum*, 115.

92. Irigaray, *Speculum*, 114.

93. Irigaray, *Speculum*, 146.

94. Elizabeth Grosz, *Sexual Subversions: Three French Feminists* (St Leonards: Allen & Unwin, 1989), xxii.

95. Irigaray, *Speculum*, 87.

96. Richard Ayoun and Bernard Cohen, *Les Juifs d'Algérie: 2000 ans d'histoire* (Paris: Lattès, 1982), 121.

97. Ayoun, *Les Juifs d'Algérie*, 128.

98. Ayoun, *Les Juifs d'Algérie*, 134.

99. Michael M. Laskier, *North African Jewry in the Twelfth Century: The Jews of Morocco, Tunisia, and Algeria* (New York: New York University Press), 24.

100. Laskier, *North African Jewry*, 35.

101. Ayoun, *Les Juifs d'Algérie*, 142.

102. Ayoun, *Les Juifs d'Algérie*, 142.

103. Ayoun, *Les Juifs d'Algérie*, 152.

104. Ayoun, *Les Juifs d'Algérie*, 160.

105. Ayoun, *Les Juifs d'Algérie*, 164.

106. Laskier, *North African Jewry*, 315.

107. Laskier, *North African Jewry*, 261–62.

108. Laskier, *North African Jewry*, 318–19.

109. Laskier, *North African Jewry*, 321.

110. Quoted by Laskier, *North African Jewry*, 329.

111. Laskier, *North African Jewry*, 329–30.

112. Laskier, *North African Jewry*, 334.

113. Laskier, *North African Jewry*, 342–43.

114. Sue Thomas, "Difference, Intersubjectivity, and Agency in the Colonial and Decolonizing Spaces of Hélène Cixous's '*Sorties*,'" *Hypatia* 9, no. 1 (Winter 1994): 53–69.

115. Cixous, "The Laugh of the Medusa," in *New French Feminism: An Anthology*, ed. Elaine Marks and Isabelle de Courtivron (Amherst: University of Massachusetts Press, 1980), 245–64.

116. Hélène Cixous and Catherine Clément, *The Newly Born Woman*, trans. Betsy Wing (Minneapolis: University of Minnesota Press, 1986).

117. Cixous, *Hélène Cixous: Photos de racines* (Paris: Des femmes, 1994). All English translations from this book are mine.

118. De Lauretis, *Technologies of Gender*, 10.

119. Cixous, *Hélène Cixous*, 205.

120. Cixous, "The Laugh of the Medusa," 245.

121. Cixous and Clément, *The Newly Born Woman*, 72.

122. Cixous, "The Laugh of the Medusa," 247.

123. Cixous, "The Laugh of the Medusa," 251.

124. Quoted by Patricia Yaeger, "Introduction: Narrating Space," *The Geography of Identity*, 23.

125. This does not mean that the meaning of the veil is fixed in the West. In weddings and mourning, the veil does not have an Arabic or Muslim connotation.

126. Cixous and Clément, *The Newly Born Woman*, 69.

127. Cixous, "The Laugh of the Medusa," 253.

128. Cixous and Clément, *The Newly Born Woman*, 94.

129. Cixous, *Les Rêveries*, 13–14.

130. Cixous, *Les Rêveries*, 91.

131. Cixous, *Les Rêveries*, 135.

132. Cixous, *Les Rêveries*, 102.

133. Fanon, "Algeria Unveiled," 59.

134. Cixous, *Les Rêveries*, 145.

135. Cixous, *Les Rêveries*, 146.

136. Brison, "Trauma Narratives and the Remaking of the Self," *Acts of Memory: Cultural Recall in the Present*, ed. Mieke Bal, Jonathan Crew, and Leo Spitzer (Hanover, N.H.: Dartmouth College, 1999), 47.

137. From Jonathan Crewe, "Recalling Adamastor: Literature as Cultural Memory in 'White' South Africa," in *Acts of Memory,* ed. Bal, Crewe, and Spitzer, 75.

138. Cixous, *Les Rêveries*, 145.

139. Cixous, *Les Rêveries*, 146.

140. Cixous's mother is condescendingly referring here to the old wedding night sheet custom in North Africa. If the bridegroom has doubts about his wife's virginity, a midwife is called upon to check the bride's hymen. In such cases, the police intervene to either protect the bride or to prevent fights between the two families. Cixous, *Les Rêveries*, 97–98.

141. Cixous, *Les Rêveries*, 104.

142. Cixous, *Les Rêveries*, 92.

143. Cixous, *Les Rêveries*, 93.

144. Cixous, *Les Rêveries*, 35.

145. Cixous, *Les Rêveries*, 45.

146. Cixous, *Les Rêveries*, 59.

147. There is a pun/racial slur here: *Lézarabes* means not only Arabs but also *lézard* ("lizard"). Cixous, *Les Rêveries*, 72.

148. Cixous, *Les Rêveries*, 152.

149. Cixous, *Les Rêveries*, 151.

150. Cixous, *Les Rêveries*, 58.

151. *"Du bon fromage"* ("good cheese"), *"La vache qui rit,"* (cheese), *"les oeufs"* ("eggs"), and *"Nestlé."* See Cixous, *Les Rêveries*, 114.

152. Ahmed, "Western Ethnocentrism and Perceptions of the Harem," *Feminist Studies* 8, no. 3 (1982): 527–28.

153. Butler, *Gender Trouble: Feminism and the Subversion of Identity* (New York: Routledge, 1990), 35.

154. Butler, *Gender Trouble*, 35.

155. Butler, Interview, "How Bodies Come to Matter: An Interview with Judith Butler," An Interview with Irene Costera Meijer and Baukje Prins, *Signs* 23, no. 2 (Winter 1998): 281.

156. Butler, "How Bodies Come to Matter," 281–82.

157. Homa Hoodfar, "The Veil in Their Minds and on Our Heads: Veiling Practices and Muslim Women," *The Politics of Culture in the Shadow of Capital*, ed. Lisa Lowe and David Lloyd (Durham, N.C.: Duke University Press, 1997), 259.

158. Hoodfar, "The Veil in Their Minds and on Our Heads," 261.

159. Ayoun, *Les Juifs d'Algérie*, 222.

160. Shohat, "Sephardim in Israel," in *Dangerous Liaisons*, ed. Anne McClintock, 30.

161. Shohat, "Sephardim in Israel," 40.

162. Whereas Moroccan Jews used to hide Moroccan Jewish customs and holidays, now they are openly practicing their North African traditions. The election of Netanyahu to the position of prime minister shows that the Sephardim are no longer disempowered.

163. Shohat, "Sephardim in Israel," 43.

164. Shohat, "Sephardim in Israel," 42.

165. Shohat, "Sephardim in Israel," 63.

166. Shohat, "Sephardim in Israel," 146.

167. Cixous and Clément, *The Newly Born Woman*, 69.

168. Cixous and Clément, *The Newly Born Woman*, 71.

169. Cixous, *Les Rêveries*, 46.

170. Cixous, *Les Rêveries*, 57.

171. Cixous, *Hélène Cixous*, 26.

172. Cixous, *Hélène Cixous*, 206.

173. The Abyss is the name of the poor neighborhood where thousands of "wretched" Arabs lived, separated from the Clos-Salembier, a middle- and upper-class *Pieds Noirs* suburb, where Cixous's family lived. Cixous, *Les Rêveries*, 40.

174. Yaeger, "Introduction: Narrating Space," *The Geography of Identity*, 17.

175. Bal and Crewe, *Acts of Memory*, vii.

176. Bal and Crewe, *Acts of Memory*, viii.

177. Bal and Crewe, *Acts of Memory*, x.

178. Cixous, *Les Rêveries*, 68.

179. Cixous, *Les Rêveries*, 41.

180. Cixous, *Les Rêveries*, 17.

181. Cixous, *Les Rêveries*, 66.

182. Cixous, *Les Rêveries*, 43.

183. Cixous, *Les Rêveries*, 62.

184. Cixous, *Les Rêveries*, 64.

185. Cixous, *Les Rêveries*, 121–22.

186. Shohat, "Notes on the Post-Colonial," *The Pre-Occupation of Postcolonial Studies*, ed. Fawzia Afzal Khan and Kalpana Seshadri Crooks (Durham, N.C.: Duke University Press, 2000), 136.

187. Cixous, *Hélène Cixous*, 207.

188. Cixous, *Les Rêveries*, 167.

189. Cixous, *Les Rêveries*, 107.

Chapter Four

Body, Home, and Nation: The Production of the Tunisian "Muslim Woman" in the Reformist Thought of Tahar al Haddad and Habib Bourguiba

> The Tunisian women's movement is original! It is not a feminist move-
> ment. It has no demands: it has been granted everything.[1]

Whereas the previous three chapters focused on the invention of the "Muslim woman" in Islamic feminism, female Orientalism, and French psychoanalysis and feminism, this chapter examines the ideological production of the "Muslim woman" in the nationalist narratives of Tahar al Haddad (1899–1935) and Habib Bourguiba (1903–2000). Taking into consideration the debate over authenticity and modernity in colonial and postcolonial Tunisia, this chapter tries to reconceptualize the relations between gender, nation, and home in al Haddad's social treatise *Our Woman in the Shari'a Law and Society*[2] (*Imra'atuna fi al shari'a wa al mujtama'*) (1930) and Bourguiba's policy and public speeches on the veil and women's rights. These texts will be studied in conjunction with some cartoons and articles published by the Tunisian nationalist press in the colonial era and the official government press in postcolonial Tunisia. This chapter starts by introducing al Haddad and Bourguiba in view of the debate over women's emancipation in nineteenth- and early-twentieth-century Tunisia. The major objective of this first section is to demonstrate al Haddad's and Bourguiba's indebtedness and resistance to these early discourses on the "Muslim woman."

In *Nation and Narration*,[3] Bhabha presents nationalism as an ambivalent discourse and a fractured system of cultural production. Relying on Bhabha's notion that the nationalist subject is split[4] at the site of enunciation, this second section examines the ambivalence within al Haddad's and Bourguiba's nationalist reconstruction of the "Muslim woman." Despite their revolutionary ideas, al Haddad and Bourguiba often tend to reinforce Tunisian women's roles as wives, mothers, and guardians of Islamic tradition, as assigned to them within a patriarchal system.

According to Bhabha, the nation is a "modern Janus" figure "wavering between two vocabularies" and vacillating between the imperatives of authenticity and the social reality of "modernity."[5] Taking up Bhabha's notion that all nationalist discourses are ambivalent, this third section tries to examine the woman's position in the fractured discourse of nationalism, an issue hardly broached by Bhabha in *Nation and Narration*. Using the texts of al Haddad and Bourguiba, this section will examine how the Tunisian "Muslim woman"—as the "atavistic and authentic body of national tradition"—came to represent Tunisian nationalism's "conservative principle of continuity," while the "Tunisian man"—as the "progressive agent of national modernity"—came to embody "nationalism's progressive, or revolutionary, principle of discontinuity."[6] This section will focus on three key points: (1) the "Muslim woman's" construction as the body of the "*umma*"; (2) the male gendering of nationalist agency; (3) and finally the gender politics implicated in Bourguiba's concept of the "Tunisian personality."

The fourth argument of this chapter is that despite some continuity in their conception of masculinity and femininity, the nationalist ideologies of al Haddad and Bourguiba have produced two different forms of domesticity. Whereas in al Haddad's writings the "Muslim woman" is the domestic subject of the Islamic *umma*, under the paternalistic authority of Bourguiba, the "Muslim woman"—including feminist organizations like the UNFT (*Union Nationale des Femmes Tunisiennes*)—occupies a double position as a subnational subject of the Shari'a law and a citizen of the modern state.

Subsequently, this chapter will examine the power politics prevalent in colonial and postcolonial Tunisia. This part argues that it is the privileges of gender, education, and, in Bourguiba's case, class[7] that allow these two nationalist figures to speak on behalf of the "Tunisian woman" and to claim for her a traditional past and a modern future. This part will also focus on the recent laws affecting the lives of Tunisian women in the 1990s. Even though patriarchal and essentialist in nature, these laws had a positive impact on the lives of Tunisian women and granted them rights unequaled in the Arab and Islamic world.

AL HADDAD AND BOURGUIBA AND THE DEBATE OVER THE WOMAN QUESTION IN NINETEENTH- AND EARLY-TWENTIETH-CENTURY TUNISIA

Al Haddad was born in Tunis in 1899 and grew up in a very modest family that came originally from the Tunisian South (Al Hamma). His father used to sell poultry at the Marché Central of Tunis. In contrast with Bourguiba, who received a French colonial education, al Haddad attended a Qur'anic school where he learned only Arabic. He then attended the theological school of the Zaytuna Mosque[8] from 1911 till 1920, where he earned the *Tatwi'* diploma that allowed him to work as a notary. Al Haddad also attended the Khaldounia (literary club) conferences and enrolled in law school.[9] He quickly became involved in the Tunisian nationalist movement. He joined the Old Destur Party at its inception in 1920, but, disenchanted with its methods, he soon left it to found, in 1924, with Muhammad Alî al Hammi, the first union of the Tunisian workers, *La Confédération Générale Tunisienne du Travail.* In 1927, al Haddad wrote his first book, *The Tunisian Workers and the Trade Unionist Movement in Tunisia*, followed in 1930 by his controversial book *Our Woman in the Shari'a Law and Society.* Because of his call for women's emancipation, the Sheiks of the Zaytuna accused al Haddad of heresy and issued a fatwa whereby they revoked his Zaytuna degree, his notary license, and barred him from an exam room.[10] Isolated and living in poverty, he died of a heart attack on 7 December 1935 at the age of thirty-six.

Although not from the old Tunisian nobility, Bourguiba belonged to the new rising bourgeoisie. He was born in 1903 in the small town of Monastir. Despite Bourguiba's claim that he lived his childhood in utter poverty, the annals of the Tunisian Ministry of Information show that he came from an upper-middle-class background. His father was an officer in the Bey's army, owned a house, 123 olive trees, and was able to send his five sons to school.[11] Bourguiba pursued his high school education at the Collège Sadiki, where he obtained the Brevet Certificate in Arabic, and at the Lycée Carnot, where he earned his baccalaureate degree in 1924. He then went to the Sorbonne to study law. In 1927, he graduated with a dual degree in law and political science. In the same year, he married a French woman Mathilde Louvain. As soon as he returned to Tunisia, he worked as a lawyer and joined the Old Destur Party (1927–1934). He wrote articles in many nationalist newspapers such as *La Voix du Tunisien* and *L'Etendard Tunisien.* On 1 November 1932, he started running a new nationalist newspaper, *L'Action Tunisienne.* After splitting from the Old Destur Party in the aftermath of the Ksar Hlal Congress (2 March 1934), he served as the General Secretary of the Neo Destur Party. In the middle of the 1930s, under the colonial repression of the Résident Général Marcel Peyroutan, he was forced into exile, first to Kébili and then to Borj Leboeuf. He was then permitted to return, but after the bloody incidents of 9 April 1938,[12] he was arrested and sent to a prison in France. After World War II, he established contacts with the United Nations and the Arab League to campaign for Tunisia's independence. Collaborating in the early fifties with the French left government of Pierre Mendès France, he was able to obtain Tunisia's internal independence on 3 June 1955 and full independence on 20

March 1956. He remained president until 7 November 1987 and passed away on 6 April 2000.

As in Egypt, the debate over the "Muslim woman's" emancipation in Tunisia was initiated by the European colonial encounter. Having lived in the same colonial era, Bourguiba and al Haddad were heirs to the modernist and nationalist currents prevalent in Tunisia, the West, and the Middle East in the nineteenth and early twentieth centuries. Both of them were familiar with the works of Muslim and secular reformers in the Middle East like Muhammad Abdu, Jamel Addine al Afghani, Qassim Amin, and Kemal Ataturk. Even though al Haddad neither read nor spoke French like Bourguiba, he was exposed to the discourse of modernity and Western thought through translation and contact with the Tunisian literary and political circles such as la Khaldounia (literary club), the Association of the Former Students of the Sadiki College, and *Jama'at Tahta Assour*, a literary circle that included nationalist intellectuals like Abu Kacem Chebbi, Alî Dou'agi, Mustapha Khraif, and Zaine Abidine Snoussi.[13] He was also influenced by the modernist ideas of Abdelaziz al Th'aalbi, the leader of the Old Destur Party and by the socialist ideas of Said Aboubaker, Hédi La'bidi, Muhammad Noomane, Eve Nohelle, Anne el Dey, and Jules Brunet, who wrote many articles in the 1920s against the veil and polygamy in *Tunis Socialiste*. Bourguiba's dual Arabic and French education and his involvement with the nationalist press exposed him to the same modernist currents that influenced the reformist thought of al Haddad.

Started by liberal statesmen in the nineteenth century, the reformist movement in Tunisia came under the aegis of the nationalist leadership in the twentieth century; namely the Desturian nationalists (al Th'aalbi) and the Tunisian socialists (Muhammad Noomane and Eve Noelle). In the middle of the nineteenth century, Léon Roches, the French consul in Tunisia between 1853–1863, critiqued in his communication with the Tunisian political reformer Ahmed Ibn Abi Dhiaf (1802–1874) the condition of the "Muslim woman" in Tunisia. Even though he refuted the colonial premise that Islam is behind the "Muslim woman's" backward condition, Ibn Abi Dhiaf still believed in men's superiority over women because of man's exclusive powers of "rationality," "prophecy," and *"jihad."*[14] Well-known for his political reforms, Ibn Abi Dhiaf's views on the "Muslim woman" were startlingly conservative. A father, he wrote, could arrange the marriage of his minor daughter without her consent; "because he [knew] what [was] best for her."[15] In his opinion, the wife could not ask for divorce since she became the husband's "property" the day "he paid for her dowry."[16] Condoning polygamy, he stated that besides fitting the strong sexual drive of Arab men, polygamy was a natural "phenomenon" like having "four members, the four seasons, the four heavenly books, the four fundamental bases of the world—administration, commerce, agriculture, and industry—and the number of elite women—Hagar, Mariam, Khadija, and Fatma."[17] Disapproving of women's education and *sufur* ("unveiling"), he wrote that besides encouraging women to mix with men, "a woman's education" and introduction to "the sciences" made her mannish, which was something *makrouh* ("frowned upon") among Muslims.[18] Ibn Abi Dhiaf's conservatism, however, was not shared by many of his contemporaries. In 1867, the Tunisian reformist and Secretary of the Bey Ahmed Kheireddine called for women's education to make them good spouses capable of running their households and raising their children.[19]

In 1917, the man of letters Hassen Hosni Abdelwahab (1884–1968) wrote in his book *Most Famous Tunisian Women* (*Shahirat Attunisiyat)*: "We today urgently need educated Muslim young women who will take charge of our future" and "awaken the nationalist spirit." Without this "solid national education," he warned, "the remedy would be transformed into ailment, life would turn to nihilism and the consequences would be disastrous. May God protect us!"[20] The call for women's education was also endorsed by the Old Destur leader and Zaytuna Sheikh Abdelaziz al Th'aalbi (1876–1944). He too linked the Muslim woman's role as educator with the development of her country. "Woman," he wrote, "has to take her share from life and sunlight at the same level as man. Only then, will the Islamic world witness any change."[21] In his book *The Liberal Spirit of the Qur'an* (1905), Al Th'aalbi stated that the verses about the veil were about Muhammad's wives, not ordinary Muslim women.[22] In the same book, al Th'aalbi denounced the oppressive "weight of traditions and customs," and argued that "neither gender inequality" nor "veiling"[23] originated in Islam.

An overview of al Haddad's and Bourguiba's reformist thought reveals both conformity and resistance toward these earlier discourses on the "Muslim woman." Their call for the Tunisian woman's education and participation in the building of a modern Tunisia reproduces the earlier discourses of Amin, Abdelaziz al Th'aalbi, and Hassan Hosni Abdelwahab on women's roles in the project of national regeneration. Of all the above Tunisian and Arab reformers, it is al Th'aalbi who seems to have the strongest impact on the reformist and feminist thought of al Haddad and Bourguiba.[24] Echoing al Th'aalbi's antinativist views in *The Liberal Spirit of the Qur'an*, al Haddad claims that Islam has been adulterated not with Western values, as the Algerian Muslim reformist Sheikh Abd el Hamid Ibn Badis claimed, but with local Tunisian customs and traditions. In *Our Woman*, al Haddad claims that there is a discrepancy between woman in the Shari'a law and society. Whereas in the first part of his book, al Haddad examines women's rights and status in the Qur'an, in the second, he focuses on the "Muslim woman's" condition in Tunisia of the 1920s. At the end of this second section he concludes that women's oppression is caused not by Islam but by Muslims. Like al Th'aalbi, he claims that "the seclusion we impose on the woman as one of the edicts of Islam, and which takes the form of either her house imprisonment, or the wearing of the veil, is not an easy question to confirm in Islam."[25]

Reproducing al Th'aalbi's argument, al Haddad argues that the hijab was imposed only on the Prophet's wives, not on all Muslim women.[26] In contrast with Fanon's construction of the veil as a neutral or innocent signifier in precolonial Algerian society, the veil for al Haddad points to women's exclusion from social and economic life. Rather than being a symbol of Islamic identity, the hijab for al Haddad is deployed by men to "rob" women from their wealth by forcing them to "rely on the tutelage of men."[27]

Against the Maliki Sheikh Abdelaziz Djait and Ibn Abi Dhiaf, al Haddad argues that the veil encourages, male, not female, depravity:

> The hijab gave men a private life outside the home that women are not aware of. [Men] spend whatever amount of money they lay their hands on, on prostitution, drunkenness, gambling and everything that would give them fun and entertainment in this separate life from which the wives are excluded.[28]

He concludes that putting the veil on a woman's face to prevent immorality is like putting "a muzzle on a dog's mouth so that it does not bite those who pass by."[29]

As a unionist, al Haddad argues that "immorality" is caused not by "unveiling" as the proponents of the veil argue, but by "poverty, which beset us from everywhere."[30] Separating the veil from morality and religion, he discusses it in terms of national and economic survival. While Tunisians are still debating "the positive and negative consequences of unveiling," European clothes are "drowning our kingdom" and "putting an end to [our] traditional textile, wool, silk, *fouta* ['a traditional female garment'], and scarf industries."[31] Thus holding the "Tunisian woman" responsible for society's corruption is a surface reading of the real causes, which are unemployment, inadequacy of the traditional economic infrastructure to respond to the needs of the family and society in general.[32]

In 1897, Muhammad Snoussi (1851–1900) published "Breaking the Chains Over Women's Rights in Islam," a letter in which he urges the "husband to feed and clothe his wife, and to provide her with servants"[33] to spare her the burden of doing housework and breastfeeding her children. The same idea is reproduced by al Haddad when he writes in 1930 that "raising children is not an obligation [for the Muslim woman], but one of her rights, which she could give up according to Imam Shafi'i and Abu Hanifa. It is the husband's duty to find someone to take care of them unless the wife has to do so."[34]

Reflecting the early-twentieth-century European patriarchal discourse about the science of rearing children, al Haddad writes: "We need the European woman's knowledge and capacity to bear and raise children, capable of not only engaging in the battle of life, but also of winning the battle, and benefiting from the world resources and peoples."[35] Thus, the success of European imperialism according to al Haddad was possible only because of the education and emancipation of the European mother. Just as the French mother is able to create a successful imperial male subject, so should the Tunisian mother and future mothers of the nation; they must create successful nationalist male children. What is important here is not al Haddad's construction of the Tunisian and French woman alike as "creator/lactator,"[36] but his appropriation of the right-wing French imperial construction of womanhood as the basis for a Tunisian nationalist/imperialist project.

Likewise Bourguiba's defense[37] of the veil as a component of the "Tunisian personality" in 1929—one year before al Haddad published his book—reflects the nationalist debate in French colonial Tunisia. For Youssef el Mahjoub, a Tunisian nationalist and student of law and philosophy, "the hijab is our individuality and its distinctive sign." To abolish it means to "change our morality and erode our personality."[38] Following the debate on the veil at L'Essor,[39] there was a long polemic in 1929 between the anti-veil campaign of Muhammad Noomane[40] and Joachim Durel[41] in *Tunis Socialiste* and Bourguiba's pro-veil campaign in *L'Etendard Tunisien*. Although he was "educated in a French school" and "expressed himself in an elegant French style,"[42] the young Bourguiba asserted in a speech he gave at L'Essor that the veil is an important component of the "Tunisian personality."[43] In 1929, Noomane attacked Bourguiba for defending the veil while being married to an unveiled French woman. "Bourguiba's daughters," Noomane sarcastically observed, "are French citizens and enjoy all the political and social prerogatives of French women including the individual freedom and the right to throw away the "'hijab' to the devil."[44]

Even though he attacks in principle le *feminisme vestimentaire*,[45] in his fight against the French politics of assimilation, Bourguiba calls Tunisians to "hold on to all the manifestations of the Tunisian personality," even on the "level of clothing."[46] "Veiling," he says, is "a custom that has entered into our ethics centuries ago. It is now part of who we are."[47] In contrast with Durel's claim that there is no "Tunisian individuality," Bourguiba asserts that Islam, the veil, and territorial unity are quintessential elements of Tunisian identity:

Territorial unity, the Community of Believers, the unity of language, custom, past, the joys felt together, the reversal of fortunes and humiliations experienced in the same way, all of these things do not help create, for Mr. Durel, any tie, any feeling of solidarity, or any patriotic idea among the children of this country.[48]

Like al Haddad, Bourguiba links the issue of the veil and the *chechia* (traditional male turban) to the issue of economic imperialism. Even though Bourguiba used to wear Western clothes, he accuses Durel of promoting French clothing and therefore of being complicit with the French imperial project of assimilation: "Whereas [Durel] is supposed to represent the interests of the Tunisian workers, he calls for the abolition of the chechia, a major trade item in Tunisia, in favor of French products."[49] Bourguiba's discussion of male clothes in economic rather than cultural terms and his silence over his own consumption of Western products indicate how nationalism invents different roles for men and women: only the "Tunisian woman" is bound to be the visible marker of the Tunisian personality; the Tunisian man, is the protector, not the marker, of cultural identity.

In "Algeria Unveiled," Fanon writes: "It is by their apparel that types of society first become known."[50] Much earlier than Fanon, el Mahjoub and Bourguiba presented nationalism as a politics of visibility. For these two male Tunisian nationalists, the "Muslim woman" functions as the "visible marker of national homogeneity." This explains her subjection to "vigilant and violent discipline" as well as "the intense emotive politics of dress"[51] in Maghrebian nationalism.

AMBIVALENCE IN AL HADDAD'S AND BOURGUIBA'S CONSTRUCTION OF THE "MUSLIM WOMAN"

In contrast with Ibn Abi Dhiaf's conservative views on marriage and divorce and Abdelaziz Djait's[52] sanction of the triple[53] divorce formula, al Haddad claims that the "Muslim woman" is not a "man's property" or "slave" even if he paid for her dowry.[54] He calls for the establishment of divorce courts,[55] the "Muslim woman's" rights to "equal inheritance,"[56] to initiate divorce procedure,[57] to choose a husband,[58] and "to administer her wealth."[59] Perhaps, the most feminist statement in al Haddad's book is his outcry that the "Muslim woman" is not "a vessel for our penises."[60]

In his argument against polygamy, which he condemns as lust,[61] al Haddad does not hesitate to desacralize the persona of Muhammad. If the Prophet married more than one woman, it was not to encourage polygamy, but because of special circumstances, "[for] the Prophet is a human being who cannot be exempted from the influence of accidental facts which impact [ordinary] human beings; facts which are not codified by God's Revelation."[62]

Al Haddad was greatly influenced by the "discursive theological framework of the Hanafi school in which '*ijtihad*' was based on arguments, justifications, rhetoric, and approbation."[63] In *Our Woman*, al Haddad claims that the Qur'anic and Shari'a laws are not eternal, but bound to a historical context. He often investigates the causes of *tanzil* ("the Sura's descent") and examines the different explanations a verse is given by the *fuqaha* ("men of religious science").[64] Because the essence of the Islamic faith is "justice" and "equality between people,"[65] polygamy and gender inequality, like slavery, are to be abolished gradually.[66] During Muhammad's life, new laws and texts came to cancel earlier texts and laws. Because of historical progress, divine law is not eternal; it has to be compatible with modern times.

Even though he defended the veil in 1929 and remained silent over the fatwa issued against al Haddad in the early 1930s, Bourguiba did implement many of al Haddad's reforms when he enacted The Personal Status Code (PSC) on 13 August 1956. After Tunisia's independence, Bourguiba launched [à la Ataturk] a campaign to abolish the veil. In a postindependence speech delivered on 5 December 1957, the veil shifted from being a sign of Tunisian personality to being "a horrible rag (*chiffon*)" that has nothing to do with "religion."[67] Reflecting Bourguiba's anti-veiling policy, the government's official newspaper *L'Action* presented in 1958 the veil as a Persian import, which is alien to the teachings of Islam. Because the Qur'an ordered only the Prophet's wives to wear the veil, the "Muslim woman today must take off the veil."[68]

Recalling al Haddad's comparison between the issue of slavery and polygamy in Islam and his argument that the Qur'anic and Shari'a laws are subject to historical change, Bourguiba writes in 1960 that polygamy has to disappear because it is anachronistic: "No one can deny that the Qur'an has some dispositions regarding slaves: rights, obligations, trade conditions. But a century ago, social circumstances led everywhere to the abolition of slavery, which was initially legal." The Caliph Umar himself revoked the sentence of cutting the thief's hand because it was "a year of famine."[69]

Like al Haddad, who states that polygamy must be abolished because the essence of the Islamic faith is justice,[70] Bourguiba writes that the "general spirit of the Qur'an is generally directed towards monogamy as indicated in the verse 'in case you fear being unfair, you must marry one woman.'"[71] And he adds, not without a touch of sarcasm, that the supporters of polygamy must admit, "in the spirit of just equity, that a woman [must become] polyandrous in the case the husband is sterile and that it would be legitimate for her to marry many men to make sure she has progeny."

Giving voice to al Haddad's outcry against the practice of *al jabr* ("compulsion to marriage"), Article 3 of the PSC banned marriage without consent. The PSC also forbade unilateral divorce by according to both partners the right to divorce through the intermediacy of a judge. Heeding al Haddad's call for a "premarital medical screening" to prevent the passing of "genetic diseases" and "alcoholism" onto the children and the wife's entrapment with an "impotent husband,"[72] Bourguiba implemented the prenuptial medical exam in 1962 to prevent "diseases like tuberculosis and syphilis"[73] from being passed to the children and wives.

Even though he did not change the Islamic laws of inheritance whereby the male inherits twice the share of the female, Bourguiba dissolved the *habus*[74] system that al Haddad found inimical to the egalitarian spirit of Islam. In *Our Woman*, al Haddad writes that the "custom of *habus* whereby the father restricts his wealth to his sons," whereby "the daughters are provided for as long as they are in their father's house or returned to it," is a way "to break free from the Islamic law that gives women the right to inherit and a return to the *Jahiliya* practice where women could be inherited."[75]

The history of the Tunisian nationalist press and the examples provided by al Haddad and Bourguiba undermine Leila Ahmed's homogeneous claim (*Women and Gender in Islam*) that those who advocate women's emancipation in the language of unveiling and democracy are Western-educated upper- and middle-class Arab modernists, and those who call for the reform of women's condition in Islamist terms have all received a traditional Arabic education and come from a more modest social background. As a matter of fact, except for *Tunis Socialiste*, the Tunisian nationalist press in French like *L'Etendard Tunisien* and *La Voix du Tunisien* were much more adamant in their opposition to the French colonial government than the nationalist newspapers in Arabic like *Al Nahdha* (*The Renaissance*) or *Al Zuhra* (*Venus*). Even though al Haddad spoke only Arabic and attended the theological school of the Zaytuna, his ideas were more daring and threatening to the Tunisian patriarchy than those of Bourguiba who studied law at the Sorbonne. Besides calling for the abolition of the veil in 1930, he is the only Tunisian or Muslim male reformer who called for gender equality in inheritance. "In its essence," he writes, "Islam does not oppose the principle of equality in all its respects."[76] Because the Shari'a law is based on *muruna* ("leniency") and is compatible with "the developments of human life," gender inequality in inheritance has to disappear, following Islam's gradual prohibition of alcohol and slavery. Al Haddad goes so far as to show the ambivalence in the Islamic laws of inheritance. It is well known that the Qur'an gives "the male twice the share of the female," but what is less known is that women are equal to men in the case of parental inheritance: "The parents of the deceased son shall each receive ⅙ from what he left if he had a son."[77] And the same thing for the siblings' inheritance: "If the deceased leaves behind children and a wife and he has a brother or a sister, each of them shall receive ⅙ of what he left. If they were more than two, they will share the ⅓ of what remains after a will or the payment of a debt." What the Qur'an said about inheritance was compatible with the Arabs' condition in early Islamic days, not today.

An overview of al Haddad's and Bourguiba's writings reveals a split in their construction of the "Muslim woman." For them, the Tunisian "Muslim woman" exists only within the family, as a mother and a wife. To start with al Haddad, neither Zeineb Ben Said Cherni, Hédi Balegh, nor Ahmed Khaled point to the ambivalence in al Haddad's discourse about women's emancipation. Despite his criticism of violence against women, al Haddad still places the husband as the wife's teacher and head of the family. Throughout al Haddad's writings, the purpose of a woman's education is not self-fulfillment, but to be "a good spouse" and "helpmate."[78] Throughout al Haddad's writings, the "Tunisian woman" is confined to the patriarchally assigned roles of mother and wife:

> Woman is the mother of humanity, she carries [man] in her womb and arms. . . . She is also the domestic spouse who quenches the hunger of his soul, dissipates his loneliness, and sacrifices her health and peace of mind to provide him with his needs and alleviate the weight of the obstacles he encounters.[79]

The new "Tunisian woman" must be given a *tha'kafa manziliya* or "domestic culture."[80] To raise healthy nationalist subjects, she must learn hygiene, child nutrition, [and] food conservation."[81] Thus, if the hijab is to be abolished, it is for the purpose of making the "Muslim woman" a good housewife who is able to "run the household budget and every day life."[82] To be a good mother, the "Muslim woman" must also be given a *tha'kafa 'a'kliya* or "rational culture."[83] The Renaissance of Tunisia is impossible as long as the Tunisian mother believes in "ghouls" and "the benefits of talismans." For al Haddad, "these superstitions" fill the empty heads of the youth and "leave no room for rational and intellectual thinking." In despair, al Haddad exclaims: "If it is difficult to "remove these poisons from the mind of the young boy [then] let's imagine how difficult this would be for the young girl who has been barred from any educational and social environment."[84] How can she be a good mother after being inculcated with these "superstitions and customs"?

Al Haddad's views on the educated "Tunisian woman" are not flattering either. For him these educated women from the well-to-do classes have misunderstood the concept of modernity and progress: "They are better than their illiterate sisters only in conceit and the imperative to consume to excess the cosmetics [required] in their Western lifestyle, without considering their husbands' budget or what lies in the interest of their marriage."[85] Hence, if al Haddad attacks the educated "Tunisian woman," it is because of her possible challenge/escape from her patriarchal duties as mother/wife. In *Our Woman*, the "Muslim woman's" national contribution is confined to the traditional domestic space. Rather than being a prison, the "home," al Haddad says, "is a job and a dwelling for the woman." If we understand "this illuminating reality, we would realize that it is our duty to educate the girl so that she might run rightly and effectively the affairs of her kingdom."[86]

Likewise, Bourguiba's call for women's education in colonial and post-colonial Tunisia is generated by his concern with the project of national re-generation. As he puts it in a postindependence speech:

> Reform of customs and ethics is an element that cannot be dissociated from the fight against colonialism. What made us vulnerable to imperialist cov-etousness was our weak state, born out of the ignorance and superstitions to which we were holding, wrongly believing they were inseparable from reli-gion.[87]

The "Tunisian woman's" emancipation is to be viewed as a strategic nation-alist exercise to bring the Tunisian nation back on its feet after years of deca-dence. Explaining women's mission in postcolonial Tunisia, Bourguiba declares: "Our nation had reached in the past a high degree of civilization and power. Our ancestors, covered with glory, took the torch to Sicily and Egypt. Kairouan, Mahdia and Tunis were in turn a pole of attraction for the entire Muslim world." He then identifies the "inhuman conditions" of Tunisian women—who constitute "half of the Tunisian population"—as the major cause for Tunisia's present "decadence."[88]

Bourguiba's feminist agenda reinforces values of female subordination and gender inequality. During the Women's March on 1 January 1957, he made a public speech where he reminds the "Tunisian woman" of her subordinate po-sition[89] at home:

> The Woman must not exaggerate. . . . The man remains the head of the family [frenetic applause of the men], and he will always remain so. The woman can-not at any moment seek refuge under "Mr. Habib said." She must know that she has responsibilities to assume and that the man will always have the last word.[90]

In continuity with the earlier Tunisian nationalist literature, the Tunisian nation appears as a mother in Bourguiba's discourses. Just as a dutiful son shows respect and tries to please his mother, "everyone must respect law and those in charge of its application. We are all sons to the same mother, Tunisia, and every one has to contribute to her happiness."[91]

ON THE GENDERED DISCOURSE OF TUNISIAN NATIONALISM: THE FEMALE BODY OF THE NATION AND THE MALE GENDERING OF NATIONALIST AGENCY

In *Nationalism and Sexuality*, George Mosse[92] describes how the nineteenth-century bourgeois concept of "respectability" constructed men as active agents of the nation through their "self-control" and sublimation of their low passions, and invented women as shallow and frivolous creatures to be constantly watched. Whereas the former are seen as the producers of culture/ tradition, the latter are assigned the role of "guardian[s] of morality." In Tunisian nationalism, the Tunisian woman's identity also lies in her unpaid services and sacrifices to the *umma* ("nation") through her dedication to her husband and children. Whereas Tunisian men embody the political and economic agency of the *umma*, women are the keepers of Islamic tradition and the *umma*'s moral and spiritual mission. However, in contrast with Mosse's claim that only "women" embody the nation's respectability,[93] in the nationalist discourses of al Haddad and Bourguiba, men too are subjected to the ideals of respectability. As a matter of fact, al Haddad denounces the widespread sexist mentality that allows man to be adulterous in many ways and holds woman responsible for the spread of immorality.[94] Like al Haddad in his postindependence speeches, Bourguiba strips the veil of any moral significance and places the moral burden on both sexes, not just women. "By the knot around the woman's neck," he writes, "we pretend that we are avoiding shamelessness: however, for shamelessness to exist, there must be two people; but we refrain ourself from applying the same principles to the man, the second partner."[95]

Pointing to the alliance between European nationalism and bourgeois morality, Mosse explains how "homosexuality became the antithesis of respectability."[96] Hence, if French, German, and British nationalism criminalized homosexuality, it was because homosexuality constituted a challenge to the bourgeois construct of the family.[97] Like European nationalism, Tunisian nationalism is produced from a heterosexual and bourgeois point of view. In his attempt to undermine the claim that the hijab is the symbol of Islamic identity, al Haddad argues that the veil leads to "homosexuality, lesbianism, and masturbation."[98] Like al Haddad, Bourguiba conceives of gender only in heterosexual terms. Woman remains subordinate to man and exists only inside the family unit. Tunisian law recognizes only the family unit: the PSC of 1956 is silent on the status of single mothers and the Tunisian judicial system criminalizes same-sex relationships. In "Les Missions des femmes," Bourguiba shows aversion and repulsion toward the woman who does not fit into the patriarchal mold of womanhood. For him "the woman [must remain] woman, and the man a man. A woman's respect for her husband, her devotion and her softness can only make her more lovable and respectable." He is "horrified," he adds, "by the tomboyish type of women, and [he has] nothing to do with their arrogance."[99] Thus the "Tunisian woman" does not exist as a single mother, or a lesbian; she has rights only as a mother and a wife.

The "Muslim Woman" as the Body of the *Umma*

In Arabic, the word *um* ("mother") is closely tied in with the notion of identity and origin. Indeed, the words *um* and *umma* (nation) come from the same etymological root.[100] The expression *al nuskha al um* ("mother copy") means the original copy of the book. *Ummu al kitab* ("the mother of the book") is the Fatiha. *Ummu al watan* (mother of the country) is the capital. In Islam, the word *umma* refers to the followers of Muhammad. Someone who has no *umma* means she/he has no religion. As the above examples show, the function of the mother as the symbol of the nation is deeply rooted in the Arabic language. In al Haddad's reformist project, the "Muslim woman" often appears as a symbol for the Islamic nation. "She is half of humanity and half of the nation in kind, number and means of production. Were we to ignore and not care about her decline and misery that would only reflect the scorn"[101] we harbor for ourselves.

Al Haddad's writings show not only the tendency to effeminize but also to racialize the *umma*. In the Shari'a law, the "Muslim woman" cannot marry a non-Muslim man for fear her children would not be born into the Islamic faith. Al Haddad uses this same justification to condemn the Muslim man's privilege to marry Christian and Jewish women, rights that are granted to him by Islamic jurisprudence:

> The European woman is not born for us and is not prepared to be adapted to us. We can only marry women from *our race*. And if they lack the required qualities of perfection, the solution is not to marry foreign women and leave [our women] as spinsters, but to emancipate them and protect them from the dangers of this progress. *They are for us and we are for them and from us all is born the nation*. But where are those wise people who understand?[102] [emphasis added]

Al Haddad's attack on the privileges of the Muslim man is a nationalistic response to the French politics of assimilation.[103] In early Islam, the marriage to Christian and Jewish women meant an increase in the number of the *umma* and decrease in the other nations.[104] However, with the establishment of colonial authorities, these marriages do not lead to the consolidation of the *umma*, but to the loss of Arab identity. The education of the "Muslim woman" serves not only to fight French colonialism, but also to ensure the survival of the Arab race. What is subversive here is al Haddad's view that the task of preserving the nation's racial stock, even though remaining a male prerogative, involves the control of both the male and female fields of reproduction, not just the "Muslim woman's" womb.

In postindependence Tunisia, Bourguiba too tried to control male and female sexuality through his family planning campaign in the 1960s and

1970s.[105] Encouraging men to use birth control, Bourguiba reassured them that birth control does not affect a man's virility. To the general shock of the Tunisian population, he used to explain how having one testicle did not prevent him from having a son and from enjoying a healthy sexual life. Thus, in contrast with European nationalism, the Tunisian nationalism of Bourguiba and al Haddad subjects to patriarchal control both the male and female reproductive systems.

Necrophilia or the Male Gendering of Nationalist Agency

An overview of *Our Woman* reveals a constant opposition between male wisdom and discipline and female irrationality and frivolity. Condemning domestic abuse, al Haddad explains that the Qur'anic verse that gives the husband the right to educate/punish his wife for her disobedience, "is reserved [only] for the 'uneducated ignorant wife'" who is "lazy and negligent towards, herself, husband, and home."[106] Besides, "the *fuqaha* say that 'hitting' does not mean severe punishment, but a symbolic act like throwing a cloth at her so that she "comes back to her senses." He concludes that either the wife takes her case to court or we trust the ability of the "husband's wisdom" to "cure" and "discipline" his uneducated wife for the sake of "conjugal life."[107]

This opposition between female irrationality and male responsibility is extended by al Haddad to the project of national regeneration. In "The Birth and Being of the General Renaissance," an article published in the *Al Umma* newspaper on 18 April 1922, al Haddad presents civilization and progress as male, and darkness and backwardness as female: "God," he writes, "may create for the nation in adversity a man or many men who will try to rescue her from this darkness." The nation will "listen to them as a patient listens to his doctor [while] he explains to him/her the disease and shows him/her the cure."[108] In the same article, only the "Tunisian man" is presented as the producer of Tunisian history and culture:

> Oh Tunisian Man, remember that you are the son of these noble fathers who have entered history. . . . The *umma* is perfectly ready for the true renaissance. . . . It is up to her wise children now to show their good faith towards her through their "[guiding]" efforts to show her the right way where "she can safely walk, unafraid of falling in decadence."[109]

This patriarchal image of the *umma* as a mother/"minor" in need of "discipline"/"cure" by a wise husband/male children is a recurrent trope in the Tunisian nationalist cartoons of the 1930s. Consider for instance the political

الطبيب للصيدلي ـ حضرلها هذا الدواه وهي تبرا باذن الله

Figure 4.1. 'Amor al Ghrayri, "The Doctor to the Pharmacist: 'Prepare for Her This Medicine and She Will Be Cured, God Willing!'" Source: Ed. Mahmud Beyram al Tunsi. *Al Shabab*, no. 4, 19 November 1936, 1(N). Tunis: Dar al Kutub al Wataniya, 2004. 20 vols. 29 October 1936–12 March 1937.

cartoon (figure 4.1) published in Mahmud Beyram al Tunsi's (1893–1961) satirical newspaper *Al Shabab*[110] on 19 November 1936. It presents Tunisia as an unveiled bed-stricken young woman. On the forehead, she is wearing a crescent, an Islamic icon decorating Tunisia's national flag today. On her right side stand two middle-aged men in Western clothes, a doctor and a pharmacist. The doctor says to the pharmacist: "Prepare for her this medicine and she will be cured, God willing!" On the prescription, the doctor wrote: "A respectable National Parliament . . . a fully responsible Ministry." The two men in question were Mahmoud Materi (1897–1972) and Ali Bouhajeb (1888–1965), a real doctor and a real pharmacist who joined the Tunisian nationalist movement. The first became the president of the Neo Destur Party in 1934 and the second a member of its executive committee. Whereas the two wise men were wearing glasses—a symbol of male wisdom—Tunisia—as the young woman closing her eyes—seems blind and helpless. Only these two men can save her life. The belief that nationalist redemption/agency is a male prerogative can be deduced from the absence of other women at the young woman's bedside. Whereas the Tunisian woman is the embodiment of tradition, it is the Tunisian man who takes upon himself the active task of redeeming or regenerating the dead body of the nation into modernity.

Besides being gendered, the conflict between tradition and modernity in Tunisian nationalism is based upon a racialized binarism between a white progressive modernity and a black backward tradition. The caricature from *Al Shabab* entitled "The Joys of the Medina Sheikh"[111] (figure 4.2) focuses on the amusement of an Arab/white man in modern European attire by the music played by a black man in a native African costume. While the man wearing the Western suit is Mustapha Sfar, the actual Sheikh of the city of Tunis in the mid-1930s, the black man in question stands for the racist figure of Boussa'dia, who appears in Tunisian folklore as a clown, a musician, a villain, and even child kidnapper. The time reference on top, "Tunisia in the Twenty-First Century," presents the educated Zaytuna Sheikh's enjoyment of black music—"dagadi, dagadoum, dagadoum, dagada"—as anachronistic and absurd. The cartoon functions thus as a satire of the educated Tunisian men who are still attached to their native traditions. Consider now (figure 4.3) representing "Maestro Boussa'dia."[112] It is the same picture of Boussa'dia as in (figure 4.2), only the legend accompanying the political cartoon is different: "We are publishing his picture to celebrate his intent to travel to Paris to

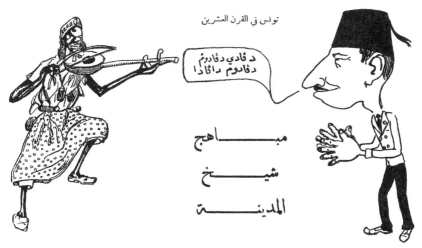

Figure 4.2. 'Amor al Ghrayri, "The Joys of the Medina Sheikh." Source: Ed. Mahmud Beyram al Tunsi. *Al Shabab*, no. 10, 1 January 1937, 3(N). Tunis: Dar al Kutub al Wataniya, 2004. 20 vols. 29 October 1936–12 March 1937.

الاستاذ بوسعدية

تنشر صورته بمناسبة عزمه على السفر الى باريس للاشتراك في معرض عام ١٩٣٧

Figure 4.3. 'Amor al Ghrayri, "Maestro Boussa'dia." Source: Ed. Mahmud Beyram al Tunsi. *Al Shabab*, no. 13, 22 January 1937, 6(N). Tunis: Dar al Kutub al Wataniya, 2004. 20 vols. 29 October 1936–12 March 1937.

participate in the fair of 1937." Mirroring France's celebration and display of its imperial wealth and possessions, the article's mock celebration of Tunisia's national wealth embodied in the figure of Boussa'dia reveals a latent cynicism that belies the Tunisian nationalist dream of resurrecting the Tunisian nation and competing with Western imperialist powers. In contrast with the productive masculinity of the Neo Destur "white"/Arab male leaders in (figure 4.1), the black figure of Boussa'dia in his native African costume symbolizes a sterile or castrated phallic order that is incapable of resurrecting the *umma*. Although Tunisian nationalism is adamant on protecting Tunisia's Arabic/Islamic identity from the threat of cultural erosion, ironically, the redemption of the *umma* is conceivable only in the garment of white modernity. This racist and stereotypical image of Boussa'dia points to the fractured discourse of Tunisian nationalism, which resorts to images of both racial and sexual Otherness to reconfigure the concept of Tunisian identity. Like the Tunisian "Muslim woman," the Tunisian "black man" in Tunisian nationalism appears biologically disqualified for politics, which suggests that nationalist agency can only be white and male.

The gendered dichotomy between the female passive body of the *umma* and the male dynamism of nationalist agency is best illustrated in figures 4.4 and 4.5. In figure 4.4, Signore Mussolini[113] is literally and metaphorically riding the body of female Lybia. If the language describing Mussolini's strategic attempt to create an alliance between Tunisia and Egypt derives from the rhetoric of upper-class bourgeois courtship, it is because colonial conquest, like the sexual conquest of women's bodies, is perceived as a male sport. Like the upper-class male seducer who abandons his sexual prey after robbing her of her chastity, Mussolini moves on to seduce Tunisia and Egypt after riding/raping their sister Lybia, who appears suffering under the chains of Italian colonialism.

In contrast with the defenseless female body of Egypt, Tunisia, and Lybia, figure 4.5[114] presents Maghrebian nationalist agency as a male sport. Like a team of male athletes, the three men representing the AFN (*l'Afrique Française du Nord*) suggest that nationalism is a competitive game that is restricted to the male sex. The three men are in fact important Maghrebian nationalist leaders who attended the Conference of Tangiers[115] held on 23–27 April 1958: on the right, the man with the beard is Muhammad Allal al Fassi, the leader of the Moroccan Istiqlal Party; in the middle, the man with the casket is Ahmed Ben Bella, an FLN leader and former president of Algeria; and on the left side, the man wearing glasses is the Tunisian statesman El Bahi Ladgham, who served in the Neo Destur Party as Bourguiba's vice president. The absence of women in this political cartoon suggests that nation-building is a male sport.

In another political cartoon (figure 4.6) from *Al Shabab*,[116] the "Tunisian woman" appears in a slightly different light. She is standing behind a cannon firing at the corrupt Tunisian *Majlis Kebir* (Supreme Council). As the female body of the nation, the Tunisian "Muslim woman" wearing the crescent rises to the masculine position of nationalist agency. "This rat hole," she says, "must be destroyed in the same way the free citizens destroyed the Bastille." The reference to the French Revolution points to the strong

Figure 4.4. 'Amor al Ghrayri,"Signore Mussolini to Tunisia—'I Introduce You to Your Sister Egypt through Tripoli.'" Source: Ed. Mahmud Beyram al Tunsi. *Al Shabab*, no. 10, 1 January 1937, 1(N). Tunis: Dar al Kutub al Wataniya, 2004. 20 vols. 29 October 1936–12 March 1937.

Figure 4.5. Hatim al Mekki, "'Dernières Nouvelles Sportives: L' AFN A L'Entrainement." [Last Minute Sport News: The AFN in Training.] Source: *L'Action*, 5 May 1958, 4(N), reproduced with the kind permission of *Le Renouveau*, Tunisia.

ideological affinities between French and Tunisian nationalism. The Roman outfit the "Tunisian woman" is wearing also reminds us of the classic costume in which the French nationalist figure of Marianne often appears. As most Tunisian nationalists have been educated in French schools, it is not surprising that they deploy icons derived from Western nationalism to defend a North African Islamic identity. What is equally interesting in this political cartoon is that the "Tunisian woman" standing behind the cannon is only the mediator not the source of this male nationalist energy, for the words engraved on the phallic bombs—"Will," "Perseverance," "Truth/Right," and "Logic"—inscribe such qualities outside the female body of the nation, which suggests that nationalist agency is male, not female.

In his 1930 article "Le Voile," Bourguiba focuses only on the male interlocutors at L'Essor and ignores the feminist intervention of Habiba Menchari, the first Tunisian woman to speak unveiled and in public on behalf of

Figure 4.6. 'Amor al Ghrayri, "This Rat Hole Must Be Destroyed like the Free Citizens Destroyed the Bastille." Source: Ed. Mahmud Beyram al Tunsi. *Al Shabab,* no. 5, 26 November 1931, 1(N). Tunis: Dar al Kutub al Wataniya, 2004. 20 vols. 29 October 1936–12 March 1937.

her secluded sisters. Bourguiba quickly dismisses Mrs. Menchari as a "charming young woman" who came to "soften us on the unfortunate lot of her sisters deprived of light" to focus only on the male allocutions of Mr. Noomane, Mr. Durel, and M. P. Laffitte. Because of her charm and softness, which Bourguiba constructs as female biology, this "Tunisian woman" is disqualified as a speaker. Mrs. Menchari can be spoken for, but she can never speak on behalf of the Tunisian women.

In Bourguiba's postindependence speeches, women are still barred from "power" politics; only *"les hommes"* or men can truly "[devote] themselves" to the business of governance.[117] "When we reestablish the woman's rights," Bourguiba announces, "we don't make her man's equal in all fields. We acknowledge, however, her equal right to dignity."[118] Bourguiba's speech shows that even though Tunisian women are being made citizens, they are not full or equal citizens. Bourguiba's "we" designates the "Muslim woman" as an object of "ho(m)mosexual exchange" (Irigaray); she is not only spoken for by the male nationalist elite but also excluded from the political process impacting her life. For Bourguiba, running the government is a male not female prerogative. In the early 1960s, the "Tunisian woman" can be a nurse, a teacher, a seamstress, a subordinate UNFT official,[119] but never Bourguiba's equal in leading the nation. The woman's role in the nationalist project is determined and conditioned by her biological function as a caring mother and wife.

In *Our Woman*, al Haddad draws a significant opposition between male activity and female passivity. Whereas the Tunisian men "toil" and "breathe life" into the family "through the woman,"[120] the latter remains dead, passive, and inanimate. This rescue fantasy is significant not just because it underscores the masculine character of nationalist agency, but also because it underscores the necrophiliac desire of the nationalist male subject to resurrect/possess the lifeless female body of the nation.

Similarly, in his frequent addresses to the "Tunisian woman," Bourguiba often presents himself as a twentieth-century Pygmalion fashioning, modeling, and bringing to life the new Tunisian woman: "Little by little, you will get used to your new rights as we get used to pure air. Little by little you will become real human beings and our Nation, God willing, an exemplary Nation."[121]

In the writings of Bourguiba and al Haddad, both the female body and the domestic space of the family appear as the site where the nationalist war of decolonization is waged. Just as the French colonizer sought to dominate its North African colonies by attacking the Bastille of the Muslim family/home, North African nationalists reappropriated the family as the site of nationalist resistance. In French colonial Tunisia, the "Muslim woman" in the nationalist discourses of Bourguiba and al Haddad served thus as a metaphor for the dislocation of home, language, and history caused by colonialism.

Bourguiba and the Invention of "La Personnalité Tunisienne" before and after Independence

Bourguiba's concept of "Tunisian personality"[122] refers to the specificity of an imagined community living within Tunisia's national borders and sharing a common set of social practices believed to derive from Islam and Arab culture. Whereas al Haddad's concept of *umma* has an Islamic etymology, Bourguiba's concept of "personality" originates in French psychoanalysis and jurisprudence. Even though this term is used sometimes by Bourguiba to signify the *umma* ("Islamic nation"), the word is deeply rooted in French semantics. The French word *personnalité* ("personality") derives from the Latin word "persona," which means the mask or the voice that a character takes on in a theatrical performance. In the field of law, *la personnalité juridique* refers to a person who "has the capacity to participate in judicial life."[123] Then the word started to be applied to the *personne morale*, who was the legal actor in French legal literature. In the field of psychology, the term refers to "a unified integrated subject constituted by a hierarchical set of biological, psychological, cultural, and social factors which give him or her 'distinctive' identity." Having studied law and psychology in Paris, Bourguiba was familiar with the legal and psychological meanings of this term. As a male lawyer, he was defending the Tunisian personality from being eroded by France's policy of assimilation. As such, Bourguiba personified the *personne juridique* or *personne morale* who spoke on behalf of Tunisia, which was itself presented as an illiterate female judicial subject. The split in Bourguiba's nationalist narrative is seen in his reliance on a French concept derived from French jurisprudence to defend the veil as a component of Tunisia's Islamic personality.[124]

After independence, however, Bourguiba launched a campaign to abolish the veil. Whereas in colonial Tunisia the veil was a symbol of Tunisia's Arab-Islamic identity for Bourguiba, in 1956 the veil became in the government's press a foreign "custom" and in Bourguiba's 15 December 1961 speech "a misunderstanding of the Qur'anic Verses."[125] Reflecting the anti-veil politics of the new government, the official newspaper *L'Action* issued on 2 August 1958 an article entitled "Pin-up d'hier et d'aujourd'hui." The article shows two pictures of Tunisian women (figure 4.7). The picture on top, "Romaine au Musée du Bardo," is a mosaic showing the Roman goddess Venus brushing her long hair while looking at herself in the mirror. The picture at the bottom, "Pin-up à la plage" displays the upper body of a modern

Tunisian woman wearing a swimming suit. The anonymous author of the article wrote:

> Our ancestors the Carthagenians had most often Phoenicians as grandmothers on the paternal side. [Our grandmothers] had a strong taste for lipstick, painted eyelashes, and indecent draperies. They had an arsenal of beauty creams and ointments that would embarrass Miss Elisabeth Arden herself, by their complexity and efficacy.[126]

The article in question mentions the debate over the veil in Tunisia and Bourguiba's fight against the backward male mentality that is intent upon possessing and controlling women. The implicit association between the draperies covering the back and legs of the Roman nude and the "indecent draperies" of our Phoenician grandmothers in the body of the text not only implies that the veil is a foreign custom brought by the Arab invaders, but more importantly, it underscores the construction of an originary Tunisian identity located halfway between the Orient (Phoenicia) and Occident (Rome). Unveiling, rather than being a European import brought about by colonization and European modernity, becomes a means of renewal with past traditions. The reinvention of the authentic "Tunisian woman" as unveiled shows not only that tradition is negotiated in the present, but also the power of the male nationalist elite to claim a past and a present for the "Tunisian woman." As a matter of fact, the location of Tunisian identity between Rome and Phoenicia reflects Bourguiba's foreign policy of "Arab fraternity and collaboration with the Occident."[127]

In another speech, Bourguiba states that Islam and Arabism are only parts of the Tunisian personality and that owing to its geography Tunisia is a bridge between East and West, "two great civilizations of which all humanity would be proud."[128] In his 1960s speeches, Bourguiba often called for the study of pre-Islamic Berber history to prove the unique character of the Tunisian personality. "The interaction between the native Berbers and the Phoenician settlers," he claimed, "created the Punic culture, a specifically Tunisian variant of the Phoenician civilization."[129] In his assertion of an originary Tunisian identity, Bourguiba claimed to retrieve a Punic patrimony that had not been sullied for more than two thousand years. This originary mythical Punic past illustrates the paradox Bhabha finds between "modern territoriality" and "the patriotic, atavistic temporality of traditionalism."[130] In postcolonial Tunisia, the unveiled body of the "Tunisian woman" serves as the visible marker of the nation's modernity. Masquerading as a past Phoenician tradition, Bourguiba's anti-veiling policy paradoxically serves to unmark or make less visible in the modern nation state the male privileges protected by the Shari'a law and Islamic tradition.

PIN-UP D'HIER ET D'AUJOURD'HUI

Romaine au Musée du Bardo

Pin-up à la plage

Figure 4.7. **"Pin-up d'Hier et d'Aujourd'hui."** Source and Permission: *L'Action*, 11 August 1958, 20(N). Courtesy of *Le Renouveau*, Tunisia.

THE "MUSLIM WOMAN" AS SUBJECT OF THE *UMMA* AND CITIZEN OF THE MODERN STATE

Whereas in al Haddad's reformism the "Tunisian woman" appears primarily as a subject of the Islamic *umma*, in Bourguiba's modernist project the "Tunisian woman" occupies a double position as a subject of the Islamic *umma* and citizen of the secular state. There is no doubt that the French colonial experience, the introduction of Western capitalism, and industrialization have in the long run destabilized the old structures and created the need for female labor, a wage system, and urbanization. After independence, the modern concept of citizenship has been substituted for the traditional family unit.[131] Because of the ethnocentrism[132] underlying the French colonial education, al Haddad constructs the Tunisian "Muslim woman" not as an individual, but as a subject of the *umma*. The Tunisian "Muslim woman" must be educated to transmit the history of her religion, country and race to her children:

She must learn the principles and history of her religion, her people's language, the history of her country and race, in a way that restores her back to life and to her past glory. . . . And from there, she will be for her children the source of the nationalist spirit that urges them to arm themselves with virtues and go forward towards the glory of life.[133]

Unlike the dichotomy Ahmed[134] observes in Egypt between the campaign for women's rights "in Islamist terms" (Zeinab al Ghazali and Hasan Ismael Hudaybi) and "the language of secularism and democracy" (Doria Shafik and Ahmed Amin), there is no clear-cut distinction between the language of secular nationalism and religious reformism in Bourguiba's modernist project. Even though he is known in the Muslim world and the West as one of the greatest secular modernists in the Arab world, Bourguiba's modernist thought is deeply steeped in Islamic theology. As a matter of fact, the PSC finds its sources in both French jurisprudence and the Shari'a law. The Napoleonic Code[135] concerning the *crime de passion* was in effect in Tunisia from 1956 until it was repealed in 1993. Also, reproducing Article 340 of the French penal code, Article 18 of the PSC states that the crime of polygamy occurs when two essential unions are contracted, that is, when one marriage is not dissolved and another is contracted even outside the legal norms.[136] Also, Tunisia is the only Islamic country to introduce adoption laws in 1956; adoption still remains illegal in other Arab-Islamic countries because it does not conform to the Shari'a law.

Rather than being a secular leader as the West and the Islamist groups perceive him, Bourguiba's feminist and reformist agenda is not free from the dictates of the Shari'a law. Bourguiba did not eliminate the Arab Islamic heritage of Tunisia, but used Islam and Arabic—the two components of the "Tunisian personality"—as a source of political legitimation. Even though Bourguiba closed the Zaytuna Mosque, forced women to unveil, and urged people to stop fasting during Ramadan—to cultivate the full energy and potential of the new modern state—many articles in the PSC are based on the Shari'a law. According to the official government newspaper *L'Action*, Bourguiba "seeks to cure and insert [Islam] into modern life"[137] rather than fight it like Ataturk. In Bourguiba's opinion, the Turkish leader's attempt to eradicate Islam was a failure: "Kemal Ataturk proclaimed his country to be laic, but the people did not change."[138] Rather than combating Islam, Bourguiba, on the contrary, tried to take into account "l'âme du peuple" in his construction of post-independence Tunisia.[139]

On 3 August 1956, the Tunisian Department of Justice issued a letter in which they stated that the PSC "is compatible with the times and does not contradict the principles of the Islamic faith."[140] The PSC was promulgated on 13 August 1956 and became effective only on 1 January 1957. The Zaytuna Sheikhs rejected the PSC for its content and social implications. In the conservative newspaper *Istiqlal*, Muhammad Moncef al Monastiri attacked in particular the creation of divorce courts: "For Muslims to be living under the same roof while waiting for the judge to pronounce divorce is living in adultery."[141] Even Muhammad al Aziz Djait (1886–1970) who participated in the drafting of the PSC asked the government to revise certain articles that do not go along with the Shari'a law; namely the prohibition of polygamy and unilateral divorce, the creation of divorce courts and adoption laws, and the new law forbidding the Muslim man the right to marry a woman he had three times divorced in the past.[142] The PSC was also criticized for not explicitly forbidding the "Muslim woman's" right to marry a non-Muslim man and for not mentioning all of the impediments to inheritance. A fatwa was published on 11 September 1956 in the *Istiqlal* condemning the PSC as inimical to the spirit of the Qur'an and the Shari'a. Tension grew between the religious institution and the government. Djait resigned. The members of the civil court also resigned and went back to teach at the Zaytuna. Following the modification of some articles in the PSC, the Minister of Justice stated in a press conference on 28 February 1964 that he was relying on Islamic, not foreign, law: "We don't need to resort to foreign judicial systems to organize marriage. We must return to the sources of Islam and the fikh."[143] This position has been retained by later judges to disallow the marriage of the "Muslim woman" to a non-Muslim man. The Ministry of Justice explicitly condemned this kind of marriage in a decree published on 5 November 1973.

The PSC dissolved the colonial confessional courts for Jewish, Hanafi, and Maliki populations, and put family law under the aegis of the state. The bifurcation of Tunisian jurisprudence into civil/Shari'a law and positive law captures the dichotomy between authenticity and modernity in Bourguiba's postindependence nationalist discourses. Whereas family law designates the "Tunisian woman" as a member of the "Muslim nation," positive law such as the right to find a job, the right to vote,[144] and the right to equal pay makes her a citizen of the modern state. As a citizen of the modern state, the Tunisian "Muslim woman" is entitled to a remunerative activity. She is encouraged to work as a nurse, teacher, and social assistant—professions deemed "consistent with [her] natural aptitudes."[145] Rather than being "consistent" with female nature as Bourguiba claims, the choice of vocations the "Tunisian woman" is offered reflects Tunisian patriarchy's construction of women as caring mothers and devoted wives. Reflecting the laws of Islamic patriarchy, the PSC of 1956 also stated that only Tunisian men could give Tunisian citizenship to their children. Even though the nation is perceived as female, citizenship is viewed as male since it is bestowed through the father, not the mother.[146]

In "Le Statut des femmes," Chekir notes that "as soon as the principle of gender equality is mentioned, resistance appears in the name of authenticity, universality, calling at times even for its negation in the name of cultural or civilizational specificity." Such specificity, she writes, is "detrimental to women's rights" as it conveys "a discrimination against women and conveys patriarchal and masculine supremacy."[147] For instance, out of the twenty-four international conventions adopted by the United Nations' General Assembly, only eighteen have been ratified by Tunisia. Tunisia ratified the international laws against gender discrimination in education (1969), but refused to ratify Article 16 of the Universal Declaration of Human Rights in the New York Convention of 10 December 1962, which stipulated women's right to marry someone outside their faith.[148] The Tunisian government also held reservations toward other international laws outlawing gender discrimination in inheritance. Tunisia refused to ratify the international laws in contradiction with the Islamic laws of the PSC. Thus, in postindependence Tunisia, Bourguiba's concept of "Tunisian personality" and its implication of cultural specificity reinforced patriarchal rule and privileges and reduced the "Tunisian woman" to an inferior legal status. Parallel to the judicial inequality founded on the Shari'a law, the dominant male order also granted the "Tunisian woman" an egalitarian judicial status in certain cases like those involving employment, wages, and education. It is this split that characterizes the construction of the "Muslim woman" in Tunisia since Bourguiba's promulgation of the PSC in 1956.

Under the centralized government of Bourguiba in postindependence Tunisia, there was a shift from family to state patriarchy. In Bourguiba's own words, "the family is no longer limited to the circle of parents. It extends to the village, the country, and beyond the frontiers, to encompass the Greater Maghreb, the Arab community, the entire continent."[149] In contrast with her function as a metaphor for the dislocation of home during the colonial period, after independence, the "Tunisian woman" became a metaphor for reterritorialization beyond the boundaries of nation, language, culture, and race. As such she is both a promise and a threat to the Tunisian nationalist male elite. As the patriarchal concept of the family is extended beyond the borders of nation to encompass the whole African continent, the body of the "Tunisian woman" with its association of home/family/*umma* poses a danger to the very concept of Tunisian identity. Like the African myth of the devouring mother[150]—the threatening figure for that which encompasses all the cultures, races, religions, and languages of Africa—the "Tunisian woman" as the body of the nation could also consume/devour what Bourguiba calls "the Tunisian personality"; hence, the need to control her destructive sexuality by preventing her from marrying non-Muslims, and denying Tunisian citizenship to her children from a foreign father.

In this era of state patriarchy, the protective power of the veil found a substitute in the *haçana* ("shield/immunity") of education. In a 1958 speech,

Bourguiba stated: "The veil does not prevent" the abuses against a woman's virtue, but education does.[151] The idea of education as a shield to protect a woman's virtue dates back to the Islamic reformism of the Egyptian man of letters Rif'at al Tahtawi (1801–1873) who, despite his defense of the veil, believed that education was the best guarantee to protect a woman's virtue.[152] Al Haddad took up the same idea when he insisted that handicraft skills were the best *hisn* ("citadel") for the married woman and her children. Families with no such skills could expose their daughters to sexual exploitation when they sent them to work as maids. The latter risk losing "their virtue"[153] by becoming prey to male predators or "wolves."

The dominant male power of the modern state is best expressed in Bourguiba's warnings to those who attempt to rob a "Tunisian woman of her virtue." In a speech delivered on 5 December 1957, Bourguiba stated that "justice [had] been done in all those cases [his government] knew of" and [warned] that "the magistrates [would] not fail to severely punish anyone who tries to violate a young girl's virtue."[154] Whether they are high school girls or members of the UNFT, all Tunisian women have been given reassurances that they could count on the protection of Bourguiba. To avoid the harassment of unveiled female students, Bourguiba passed an order "to close down the cafés, and placed police units in front of schools to intercept and arrest these young delinquents."[155] In the same speech, he promised to punish those "criminal" fathers who did not allow their daughters to go to school.

Even though the Tunisian state offers its female citizens police and legal protection, the latter must abide by the rules of Bourguiba, the Father of the Nation. As he himself put it in 1958: "Some measures have been taken to protect the *girls* when they leave their all girls' schools. On the other hand, the *woman* [my emphasis] must, by her behavior, impose respect."[156] Bourguiba's distinction between "girl" and "woman" is quite significant here. In the first part of the sentence, the word "girl" denotes female innocence and underscores a need for patriarchal protection. In the second part of the sentence, the word "woman" is used to suggest woman's sexual power or *fitna* and to remind her of her need to subject herself to patriarchal authority, not to seek its protection.

Created by Bourguiba in 1956, the UNFT[157] "counts [primarily] on the support of the governors and the delegates, on the authority of the State, and on its financial help."[158] As an extension of the state, the UNFT was created to teach the masses of Tunisian women their rights and duties in the new modern Tunisia. In "Les Missions des femmes," Bourguiba states that the purpose of the UNFT is to explain to women "their new rights," "the way in which they are to be used," and the "limits women must not trespass," to avoid a situation "as harmful as the old one."[159] The relation between Bourguiba and the

UNFT is based on a gendered division of labor. Whereas Bourguiba's government sponsors the UNFT and provides it with financial assistance, the UNFT assumes the traditional female roles of feeding and clothing the needy and inculcating hygiene, nutrition, and morality to the children of the new modern state.[160] Unlike the Moroccan and the Egyptian feminist movements, the Tunisian feminist movement in the Bourguiba era had no history of political mobilization and militancy. It had been contained from the beginning by the state. One of the responsibilities of the UNFT is to fight immorality: it must not only teach women that sexual needs cannot be satisfied outside the institution of "marriage,"[161] but also warn them against the dangers of neglecting their families that their work outside the home could incur. The UNFT must make them "aware" of their "responsibilities" as wives and mothers to prevent the breakup of the family. As Radhia Haddad, president of the UNFT once put it: her mission was to explain to the women "that the rights that [they had] obtained must not bring a revolution in the families."[162]

What does a modern "Muslim woman" mean to Bourguiba and the UNFT? A modern "Tunisian woman" is a "nationalist subject," who is "responsible" rather than "liberated." Rejecting what she perceives as "the Western model" of female emancipation, Radhia Haddad observes that "the modern woman who wakes up after midday after the tumultuous evenings she spent in salons, joking, smoking cigarettes, and playing cards to kill boredom," has no place "in our country." Similarly, the modern "Tunisian woman" must discard the "backward religious practices" such as visiting saints and keep only the norms of Islamic "morality" and "rationality."[163] Thus, the modern "Tunisian woman" occupies an ambivalent position between authenticity and modernity.

POWER POLITICS AND THE RECEPTION OF AL HADDAD'S AND BOURGUIBA'S REFORMIST THOUGHT

According to Bhabha, there is a split "in the production of the nation" between the "accumulative temporality of the pedagogical, and the repetitious, recursive strategy of the performative."[164] This split in the process of writing the nation is best illustrated in Bourguiba's shift in his attitude toward the veil. If Bourguiba defended the veil in 1929, it was because unveiling entailed not only the loss of Tunisian identity but also the "Tunisian woman's" escape from her patriarchal role as mother and wife. "In following the fashion of the moment," Bourguiba wrote retroactively in 1960, "the woman [risks] being distracted from her milieu, cutting her ties with the past, and losing herself in an alien community." This "adventure into *Francisation*" means "scoff[ing] at her own mother and family." Letting France "lead our social evolution" means falling from the "Charybdis" of decadence to the "Scylla" of assimilation, as we concede "our fusion with the heart of French collectivity."[165] As a nationalist narrative, Bourguiba's speech seems split at the level of performance: While defending the Islamic veil as a symbol of Tunisian identity, Bourguiba relies on a Homeric/Western metaphor to convey the uniqueness of the "national identity" he is defending.

This split at the site of enunciation is often tied to a particular sociohistorical context. As he tries to negotiate a position from which to speak, Bourguiba often falls into contradictory positions. On the fortieth anniversary of al Haddad's death, Bourguiba delivered a speech where he justifies his 1929 position on the veil. In this speech, Bourguiba states that the Zaytuna Sheikhs used al Haddad as a scapegoat for their own participation in and silence over the Eucharist Congress that took place in Rue de la Montagne on 7–11 May 1930. The Catholic participants were "dressed in the costume of the crusaders" holding flags on which was written "The ninth Crusade." The "statue of the Cardinal Lavigerie was erected at the entry of the Medina holding the cross." "I felt provoked," Bourguiba writes; "[the Cardinal] intended to thrust the cross into this land, according to the doctrine they were professing in Algeria."[166] The Eucharist Congress was followed in 1931 by the commemoration of the fiftieth anniversary of the French colonization of Tunisia and the centennial of the French conquest of Algeria. Because of these events, Bourguiba remained silent over al Haddad's book even though he shared his views on the veil.

Even though after independence Bourguiba abolished the veil, polygamy, and the *habus* system, he did not implement al Haddad's call for gender equality in inheritance. Given the rivalry over the leadership of Tunisia between Bourguiba and Salah Ben Youssef,[167] Bourguiba had to cater to the Tunisian male clergy of the Zaytuna Mosque, most of whom were supporters of Bourguiba's political rival Ben Youssef.

Identifying with al Haddad, Bourguiba claims that he and al Haddad had common enemies: the colonial powers, the Old Destur, and the Zaytuna Sheikhs. According to Bourguiba, the controversy was created by *"les archéos"* (the archaic) and *"les enturbannés"*[168] (the turban-headed) of the Old Destur leadership—Ahmed Essafi, Salah Farhat, Mohieddine al Klibi—who wanted to get their revenge on al Haddad for denouncing their role in the failure of the union of Tunisian workers (CGTT) and the exile of Muhammad Alî al Hammi in 1925.

Even though he encountered resistance from the Zaytuna Mosque, Bourguiba's political power, class, and educational privileges allowed him to implement his feminist reforms. As al Haddad was a powerless and poor man of letters, his reformist ideas were conversely doomed to failure. In Tunisia, al Haddad's harshest critics were Muhammad Salah Ben Mrad[169] who wrote *Al Hidad 'ala Imraat al-Haddad* (*Mourning over al Haddad's Woman*), and Amor Ibn Ibrahim El Barri El Madani,[170] who wrote a long letter entitled "*Sayf al 'haq 'alâ man lâ yarâ al 'haq*" ("*The Sword of Justice on He Who Does Not See Justice*"). Both authors attacked al Haddad on his evolutionary conception of the Qur'an and for threatening their male privileges deriving from the Islamic laws of inheritance and the *habus* system. In the Islamic world, both the Egyptian newspaper *Al Ikhaa*[171] and the Algerian newspaper *Al Shihab*[172] accused al Haddad of apostasy and madness.

In addition to the colonial context, which turned the veil into a symbol of Tunisian identity, there was also a generational and class conflict between al Haddad and his opponents. The Old Zaytuna Mosque was led by the powerful and conservative old bourgeoisie of Tunis like Neifar, Ben Mrad, and Ben Achour who were working in tandem with the French colonial authorities.[173] The reformist movement of the 1920s and 1930s was led by people from a humble origin like al Haddad and Chebbi.[174] The latter, with the new rising bourgeoisie of the Sahel, often criticized the dogmatic teaching at the Zaytuna Mosque. Similarly, if Muhieddine al Kelibi, the leader of the Old Destur Party chose to attack al Haddad and repress the popular unionist movement of Muhammad Alî al Hammi, it was because the Old Destur was a conservative party that collaborated with the French authorities.[175]

I make the claim in this book that the fatwa against al Haddad was caused less by his call for unveiling and educating the "Tunisian woman" as in the Tunisian master narrative than by his call for gender equality in inheritance, which in his dialogic reading of the Qu'ran is not inimical to the "true" and egalitarian spirit of Islam. Many Tunisian reformers before al Haddad called for the education and unveiling of the "Muslim woman"—al Th'aalbi and Hassan Hosni Abdelwahab—yet not a single one of them was persecuted like al Haddad, which suggests that the latent cause for the fatwa against him was his call for gender equality in inheritance. In high school textbooks, only al Haddad's call to give the "Tunisian woman" a domestic education that would adequately prepare her to fulfill her future role as mother and wife is mentioned; his two subversive calls for equality in gender inheritance and condemnation of the marriage of the Muslim man to the non-Muslim woman have been totally suppressed by the patriarchal forces within the Tunisian academia. Among the dozens of articles and books written on al Haddad, only the CREDIF[176] publications mention his call for gender equality in inheritance. Because feminism is still a marginalized discourse in Tunisian academia, the 1990s new phase of Tunisian feminism led by female scholars is working from within the dominant discourse of the state to bring about social changes for Tunisian women.

In "No Longer in a Future Heaven," McClintock argues that in "bidding women to hold their tongues until after the revolution," male nationalists are in fact using "a strategic tactic to defer women's demands." "The lessons of international history," she says, show that "women who are not empowered to organize during the struggle will not be empowered to organize after the struggle."[177] The case of Tunisia provides a counterexample to McClintock's argument. Bourguiba's defense of the veil in 1929 did not prevent him from enacting after independence the PSC, which, despite its limits, granted Tunisian women rights unequaled in the rest of the Muslim world. Even though of a qualified patriarchal nature, the reformist thought of al Haddad and Bourguiba suggests that despite the essentialism, the changes encoded were still liberating for Tunisian women. In the 1990s, Tunisian feminists participated in many of the international conferences on women's rights in Africa, Asia, and the Middle East such as the Beijing Conference in September 1995. The law of 5 April 1996 allowed the spouses to have a premarital agreement where they decide to have a joint ownership of the properties acquired after marriage. Unlike the PSC of 1956, which recognized the "Tunisian woman's" rights only as mother and wife, Article 74 in the reforms of 1998 allowed the single mother to use a paternity test to sue the biological father for child alimony. However, the natural children are given the right to claim only the father's name. The single mother cannot use her own name to get welfare from the state.[178] Even today international laws regarding gender equality in inheritance and sexual orientation are not recognized in Tunisia because they are deemed incompatible with the "country's religious and cultural heritage."[179]

The history of Tunisian nationalism shows not only the political deployment of the "Muslim woman" in the nationalist effort to resist the French politics of assimilation but also her exclusion from the debate over women's role in the anticolonial struggle. As the nationalist newspapers of the time attest, most of the discourses on the "Muslim woman" in Tunisia were produced by men and for men.[180] Like the Islamic feminism of Mernissi, the female Orientalism of Eberhardt, and the psychoanalytic and feminist French theories of Fanon and Cixous, the discourse of Tunisian nationalism on the veil and the "Muslim woman" is quite ambivalent. A symbol of Islamic identity in Bourguiba's speeches during French colonial Tunisia, the veil became the symbol of backwardness in postcolonial Tunisia. This shows that rather than being static, the veil is a historically situated signifier. Similarly, in contrast with her function as a metaphor for the dislocation of home and language in French colonial Tunisia, the "Tunisian woman" came to embody the split between modernity and tradition in postcolonial Tunisia. While unveiling, work, and education were synonymous with an inevitable social progress, the Shari'a laws came to stand for an unchanging Tunisian essence that has to be jealously protected from the erosion of Western culture.

NOTES

1. *L'Action* is the Tunisian government's official newspaper after independence. Quoted in "Quoi de neuf pour les femmes?" *L'Action*, 7 Janvier 1957, 13(N).
2. All the translations from the Arabic and French in this chapter are mine except the quotations from Norma Salem's *Habib Bourguiba, Islam, and the Creation of Tunisia* (London: Croom Helm, 1984).
3. Homi Bhabha, ed., *Nation and Narration* (London: Routledge, 1994).
4. In "Critical Fanonism," Henry Louis Gates Jr. argues that in providing a psychoanalytic explanation for the split within the nationalist subject, Bhabha leaves out the role of history in the production of culture. Gates's criticism, however, seems based on the premise that the symbolic is a universal sign situated outside history. As a matter of fact, Bhabha does not deny the impact of history on the construction of the nationalist subject, as Gates claims. Bhabha clearly states that he does not "wish to deny" the "specific historicities" of "the cultural construction of nationness," in "DissemiNation: Time, Narrative, and the Margins of the Modern Nation," *Nation and Narration*, 292. Gates's criticism of Bhabha betrays a view that holds history to be divorced from human agency. Even though it takes into account the weight of history, this chapter argues that there is no history without agents of history, and no agents of history without discourse. See Gates, "Critical Fanonism," *Critical Inquiry* 17, no. 3 (Spring 1991): 475–70.
5. Bhabha, *Nation and Narration*, 2.
6. McClintock, "'No Longer in a Future Heaven': Gender, Race and Nationalism," *Dangerous Liaisons*, 92.
7. The concept of class in Tunisian society is somewhat problematic. In Tunisia, class is defined not just by money as in the United States, but also by ethnic and family history. My understanding and use of this term are therefore quite limited given the scarce research on this subject.
8. In 1911, the Zaytuna Mosque provided primary, high school, and higher education. Al Haddad did not study beyond the *Tatwi'* diploma, which he received at the end of his high-school education. For information about the educational system in the Zaytuna Mosque, see Ahmed Khaled, *Adhwâ Mina al Bi'a al Tunusiya 'alaa al Tahar Haddad wa nidhalu jil* (Tunis: Al dar al tunusiya li al nashr, 1985), 26–41.
9. This biographic information on al Haddad has been collected from Hédi Balegh's book *Les Pensées de Tahar Haddad* (Tunis: La Presse, 1993), 1–13.
10. Balegh, *Les Pensées de Tahar Haddad*, 7.
11. Norma Salem, *Habib Bourguiba, Islam and the Creation of Tunisia*, 31.
12. Following the arrest of the Tunisian nationalist leader Alî Balhouane, there was a large demonstration in the capital. The French army opened fire on the unarmed

Tunisian demonstrators. Dozens were killed, hundreds were wounded, and three thousands were arrested. The French colonial government dissolved the Neo Destur Party, executed many nationalist leaders and sent many others to jail in Fort Saint Nicolas in Marseilles.

13. Zeineb Ben Said Cherni, *Les Dérapages de l'histoire chez Tahar Haddad: Les Travailleurs Dieu et La Femme* (Tunis: Ben Abdallah, 1993), 40.

14. Abdelrazek Hammami and Zakiya Jouirou, *Al Mar'a fi al haraka al islahiya min al Tahar al Haddad ila Zine al Abidine Ben Ali* (Tunis: *Sharikat founoun li al rasm wa li al nashr wa assahafa*, 1999), 17. The publication of this book was sponsored by the Centre de Recherche, d'Etudes, de Documentation et d'Information sur la Femme, which was established by President Ben Ali as well as national and international organizations to endorse the rights and development of Tunisian women.

15. Quoted in Hammami, *Al Mar'a*, 17.

16. Quoted in Hammami, *Al Mar'a*, 18.

17. Quoted in Hammami, *Al Mar'a*, 19.

18. Quoted in Hammami, *Al Mar'a*, 20.

19. See Hafidha Chekir, *Le Statut des femmes entre les textes et les résistances: Le cas de la Tunisie* (Tunis: Chama, 2000), 11.

20. Quoted by Cherni, *Les Dérapages de l'histoire*, 140.

21. Quoted in Hammami, *Al Mar'a*, 28.

22. Quoted in Hammami, *Al Mar'a*, 27.

23. Quoted by Chekir, *Le Statut des femmes*, 12.

24. Bourguiba's attack on al Th'aalbi as an *"archéo"* and a *"larron"* after independence is caused by the political rivalry between the members of the Old and the Neo Destur as well as by Bourguiba's appropriation of the sole title of *"Le Libérateur de la femme Tunisienne."* As early as the 1910s, al Th'aalbi, a Zaytunian Sheikh like al Haddad, was calling for women's unveiling and education. The history of Tunisian feminism and nationalism till the late 1980s was centered on the personal cult of Bourguiba, "Le Combatant Supreme." See Bourguiba, *Tahar El Haddad, Vengé de ses détracteurs* (Tunis: Publications du Secrétariat d'Etat à l'Information, Janvier, 1976), 15.

25. Al Haddad, *Our Woman in the Shari'a Law and Society* (Tunis: Manshurat dar al ma'ârif li al tiba'a wa al nashr, 1997), 34.

26. Al Haddad, *Our Woman*, 24.

27. Al Haddad, *Our Woman*, 184–85.

28. Al Haddad, *Our Woman*, 184.

29. Al Haddad, *Our Woman*, 182.

30. Al Haddad, *Our Woman*, 190.

31. Al Haddad, *Our Woman*, 188–89.

32. Al Haddad, *Our Woman*, 190.

33. Quoted in Hammami, *Al Mar'a*, 26–27.

34. Al Haddad, *Our Woman*, 48.

35. Al Haddad, *Our Woman*, 214.

36. I am borrowing Eric Grekowicz's words in "Hybridity and Discursive Unrest in Late Colonial Anglophone Prose of South Asia (1880–1950)," Ph.D. diss., Michigan State University, 2001.

37. I shall return to this point later when I discuss the shift in Bourguiba's attitude toward the veil in terms of the power politics in colonial and postcolonial Tunisia.

38. Quoted by Muhammad Noomane, "*A L'Essor*," *Tunis Socialiste*, 11 Janvier 1929, 1 (N).

39. A cultural club frequented by the Socialist Party.

40. A Tunisian socialist lawyer who wrote against the veil in *Tunis Socialiste*.

41. Joachim Durel was the leader of the Socialist Party and the General Secretary for the French workers' union in Tunis.

42. Durel, "Réponses à quelques jeunes," *Tunis Socialiste*, 19 Janvier 1929, 1(N).

43. Bourguiba, "Le Voile," *L'Etendard Tunisien*, 1 Février 1929, 2(N).

44. Quoted in "La Polémique Bourguiba-Noomane," *L'Action Tunisienne*, 29 Octobre 1956, 17(N).

45. Bourguiba, "Le Voile," 1.

46. Quoted in "La Polémique Bourguiba-Noomane," 13.

47. Bourguiba, "Le Voile," 2.

48. Bourguiba, "Le Voile," 1.

49. Bourguiba, "Le Durrellisme ou le Socialisme boiteux," *L'Etendard Tunisien*, 1 Février, 1929, 1(N).

50. Fanon, "Algeria Unveiled," 35.

51. McClintock, "No Longer in a Future Heaven," 97.

52. Al Haddad, *Our Woman*, 94.

53. In the Maliki school of Islam, the husband can divorce his wife simply by saying three times that she is divorced.

54. Al Haddad, *Our Woman*, 113.

55. Al Haddad, *Our Woman*, 67.

56. Al Haddad, *Our Woman*, 28.

57. Al Haddad, *Our Woman*, 65.

58. Al Haddad, *Our Woman*, 46.

59. Al Haddad, *Our Woman*, 20.

60. Al Haddad, *Our Woman*, 9.

61. Al Haddad, *Our Woman*, 151.

62. Al Haddad, *Our Woman*, 57.

63. Cherni, *Les Dérapages de l'histoire*, 108.

64. Al Haddad, *Our Woman*, 23.

65. Al Haddad, *Our Woman*, 12.

66. Al Haddad, *Our Woman*, 33.

67. Bourguiba, "Coordination des services, respect des individus et libération de la femme," *Discours* 4 (5 Décembre 1957): 21.

68. Bahija M., "Le Coran impose-t-il le voile?" *L'Action*, 3 Février 1958, 18(N).

69. Bourguiba, "2ème Congrès National de L'UNFT," *Discours* 8 (13 Août 1960): 53.

70. Al Haddad, *Our Woman*, 55.

71. Bourguiba, "Deux fondements du statut personnel: dignité et cohésion nationale," *Discours* 2 (10 Août 1956): 129.

72. Al Haddad, *Our Woman*, 146–47.

73. Bourguiba, "Les Missions des femmes," *Discours* 10 (26 Décembre 1962): 205.

74. A land that is *habus* is a land that cannot be bought or sold. This system prevents not only the splitting up of property, but also the daughter's inheritance as the land is kept under the management of her brothers or uncles.

75. Al Haddad, *Our Woman*, 28–29.

76. Al Haddad, *Our Woman*, 32.

77. Al Haddad, *Our Woman*, 28.

78. Al Haddad, *Our Woman*, 160.

79. Al Haddad, *Our Woman*, 5.

80. Al Haddad, *Our Woman*, 121.

81. Al Haddad, *Our Woman*, 132.

82. Al Haddad, *Our Woman*, 158.

83. Al Haddad, *Our Woman*, 123.

84. Al Haddad, *Our Woman*, 124.

85. Al Haddad, *Our Woman*, 196.

86. Al Haddad, *Our Woman*, 209–10.

87. Bourguiba, "Libération de la femme et réforme des mœurs: tâche primordiale," *Discours* 4 (7 Avril 1958): 184.

88. Bourguiba, "Les Missions des femmes," *Discours* 10 (26 Décembre 1962): 193–94.

89. Article 23 of the PSC, which stipulates that the wife be obedient to her husband, was revoked only in 1993.

90. Quoted in "Bourguiba fait confiance aux femmes," *L'Action*, 7 Janvier 1957, 13(N).

91. Bourguiba, "Nous sommes tous fils d'une même mère," *Discours* 2 (12 November 1956): 242.

92. Mosse, *Nationalism and Sexuality: Respectability and Abnormal Sexuality in Modern Europe* (New York: H. Fertig, 1985), 17.

93. Mosse, *Nationalism and Sexuality*, 90.

94. Al Haddad, *Our Woman*, 189.

95. Quoted in "Bourguiba fait confiance aux femmes," *L'Action*, 7 Janvier 1957, 13(N).

96. Mosse, *Nationalism and Sexuality*, 37.

97. Mosse, *Nationalism and Sexuality*, 28.

98. Al Haddad, *Our Woman*, 185.

99. Bourguiba, "Les Missions des femmes," *Discours* 10 (26 Décembre 1962): 201–2.

100. I am using the Arabic-Arabic dictionary of Hassan Said al Karmi, *Al hadi ila lughati al 'Arab: Qamus 'arabi-'arabi*, s.v. "*umma*."

101. Al Haddad, *Our Woman*, 5.

102. Al Haddad, *Our Woman*, 179.

103. In his 1975 speech later published as *Tahar El Haddad*, Bourguiba makes the claim that al Haddad remained silent over the issue of naturalization in the early 1930s. Bourguiba's claim is inaccurate, for al Haddad did talk about the issue of

naturalization in "Naturalization is a Breach of the Protectorate Treaty," an article
he published in the *Al Umma* newspaper on 13 November 1923. If the issue of naturalization came to the fore in the 1930s, it was not because there were no naturalization laws prior to that date, but because of the impact of the 1929 economic
crisis and the introduction of the *tiers colonial*, which gave French citizens a mon-
etary incentive to immigrate to the colonies. See al Haddad, *Tahar al Haddad: Al
a'maal al kaamila* 1 (Tunis: Dar al arabiya li al Kitab, 1999), 229–38.

    104. Al Haddad, *Our Woman*, 53.

    105. Bourguiba, "Les Missions des femmes," *Discours* 10 (26 Décembre 1962):
203.

    106. Al Haddad, *Our Woman*, 59.

    107. Al Haddad, *Our Woman*, 60.

    108. Al Haddad, "The Birth and Being of the General Renaissance," in *Tahar al
Haddad: Al a'maal al kaamila* 1, 199.

    109. Al Haddad, "The Birth and Being of the General Renaissance," 201–2.

    110. 'Amor al Ghrayri , "Al Tabib li Assaydali: Hadher laha hadha al dawa wa hya
tabra bi idhni Allah," *Al Shabab* no. 4, 19 November 1936, 1(N). Source: Mahmud
Beyram al Tunsi, ed, *Al Shabab* (Tunis: Dar al Kutub al Wataniya, 2004). All the car-
icatures *from Al Shabab* were drawn by 'Amor al Ghrayri.

    111. Al Ghrayri, "The Joys of the Medina Sheikh," *Al Shabab* no. 10, 1 January
1937, 3(N).

    112. Al Ghrayri, "Maestro Boussa'dia," *Al Shabab* no. 13, 22 Janvier 1937, 6(N).

    113. Al Ghrayri, "Signore Mussolini to Tunisia—I Introduce You to Your Sister
Egypt through Tripoli," *Al Shabab* no. 10, 1 January 1937, 1(N).

    114. Hatim al Mekki, "Dernières Nouvelles Sportives: L'AFN A L'Entrainement,"
L'Action, 5 May 1958, 4 (N). "Mahmoud" is the official signature of the Tunisian car-
icaturist al Mekki.

    115. The Tangiers Conference was held by the Moroccan Istiqlal Party, the Alger-
ian National Liberation Front and the Tunisian Neo Destur Party to lay down the
founding stones of the Maghrebian union.

    116. Al Ghrayri, "This Rat Hole Must Be Destroyed like the Free Citizens De-
stroyed the Bastille,"*Al Shabab* no. 5, 26 November 1936, 1(N).

    117. Bourguiba, "Deux fondements du statut personnel: dignité et cohésion na-
tionale," *Discours* 2 (10 Août 1956): 135.

    118. Bourguiba, "2ème Congrès National de l'UNFT," *Discours* 8 (13 Août 1960):
59.

    119. Bourguiba, "Les Missions des femmes," *Discours* 10 (26 Décembre 1962):
200–201.

    120. Al Haddad, *Our Woman*, 218.

    121. Quoted in "Bourguiba fait confiance aux femmes," *L'Action*, 7 Janvier 1957,
13(N).

    122. Salem, *Habib Bourguiba*, 135.

    123. Salem, *Habib Bourguiba*, 136.

    124. According to Abdelwahab Bouhdiba, the Tunisian nation "came into being as
a result of Bourguiba's action" (Salem 183). In contrast, Hichem Djait made a dis-

tinction between a "national political personality" and a "cultural and ideological Tunisian personality" (185). It is the second personality, based on an imaginary civilizational, religious, and linguistic affiliation with the Muslim Middle East that was used by Bourguiba to legitimize his power and "the national political personality" (188). Neither the Tunisian men of letters Bouhdiba and Djait, nor Norma Salem, however, tried to examine how Bourguiba's concept of "personality" is implicated in the gender politics in colonial and postcolonial Tunisia. See Abdelwahab Bouhdiba, *A la recherche des normes perdues* (Tunis: Maison Tunisienne de l'Edition, 1973), 18–19. Also see Hichem Djait, *La Personnalité et le devenir Arabo-Islamique* (Paris: Seuil, 1974), 52–53.

125. Quoted in Khaled, *Adhwâ*, 398.

126. "Pin up d'hier et d'aujourd'hui," *L'Action*, 11 August 1958, 20(N).

127. Bourguiba, "Fraternité Arabe et collaboration avec l'Occident," *Discours* 3 (24 Octobre 1957): 288. Even though there was an infusion of non-Arabic people who came to Tunisia after the first Islamic conquests, the mythical Tunisian identity that Bourguiba constructs does not include the Turks, the Andalusian Jewish and Muslim immigrants, the Europeans, and the black Africans who came to Tunisia after the seventh century A.D., through conquest, exile, and slavery.

128. Quoted by Salem, *Habib Bourguiba*, 156.

129. Quoted by Salem, *Habib Bourguiba*, 150.

130. Bhabha, *Nation and Narration*, 300.

131. Hammami, *Al Mar'a*, 78.

132. According to Jean François Martin, the history of Tunisia and North Africa was revised in 1904 in French school manuals to emphasize the progress of French civilization and backwardness of the Arab-Islamic civilization. A French textbook published in 1916 stated: "At the moment of the French intervention, anarchy and chaos ruined Tunisia. Its land so fertile in the past became largely barren. The rural lands were ravaged by wars, and the poor inhabitants were under the pressure of the functionaries. France succeeded in establishing the reign of peace and order; it brought the country back into prosperity; and dedicated itself to give the indigenous population the tools to improve their own conditions." In Martin, *Histoire de la Tunisie Contemporaine: De Ferry à Bourguiba 1881–1956* (Paris: L'Harmattan, 1993), 99.

133. Al Haddad, *Our Woman*, 206.

134. Ahmed, *Women and Gender in Islam*, 196.

135. Article 207 of the PSC whereby the husband was liable only to a five-year imprisonment for the murder of his wife or accomplice caught in the act of adultery was repealed only in 1993 when new reforms were introduced to curb domestic violence.

136. Chekir, *Le Statut des femmes*, 129.

137. "Le Code va-t-il à l'encontre de la religion?" *L'Action*, 3 September 1956: 1(N.)

138. Bourguiba, "2ème Congrès National de l'UNFT," 61.

139. Quoted by Salem, *Habib Bourguiba*, 126.

140. Hammami, *Al Mar'a*, 80.

141. Hammami, *Al Mar'a*, 84.

142. Hammami, *Al Mar'a*, 88.

143. Quoted by Chekir, *Le Statut des femmes*, 127.

144. Tunisian women obtained the right to vote on 14 March 1957.

145. Bourguiba, "Les Missions des femmes," 199.

146. In 1993, the Tunisian woman obtained the right to give Tunisian citizenship to her children from a foreign father, though born abroad. However, this right is null and void without the father's consent.

147. Chekir, *Le Statut des femmes*, 92–93.

148. Chekir, *Le Statut des femmes*, 64.

149. Bourguiba, "Les Missions des femmes," 207.

150. See the myth *bété* in Denise Paulme, *La mère dévorante: Essai sur la morphologie des contes Africains* (France: Gallimard, 1976), 278.

151. Bourguiba, "Libération de la femme et réforme des mœurs: tâche primordiale," *Discours* 4 (7Avril 1954): 186–87.

152. Hammami, *Al Mar'a*, 29.

153. Al Haddad, *Our Woman*, 120–21.

154. Bourguiba, "Coordination des services, respect des individus et libération de la femme," *Discours* 4, (5 Décembre 1957): 21.

155. Bourguiba, "2ème Congrès National de l'UNFT," 60.

156. Bourguiba, "Libération de la femme et réforme des mœurs: tâche primordiale," 187.

157. In French colonial Tunisia, there were many other feminist organizations: L'Union Musulmane des Femmes de Tunisie created in 1936 by Bchira Ben Mrad, the daughter of Muhammad Salah Ben Mrad who fiercely attacked al Haddad's book; La Section Féminine de L'Association des Jeunes Musulmans (1944) directed by Mrs. Souad Khattech, wife of the president of this association Sheikh Muhammad Salah Ennaïfer (Marzouki 36); l'Union des Femmes de Tunisie (UFT) created in 1944 by the Tunisian Communist Party; l'Union des Jeunes filles de Tunisie at the end of World War II, which tried to cut across distinctions of race, religion, and political opinion" (97); and Le Club de la Jeune Fille Tunisienne in 1954 presided by Tawhida Farhat (36). After independence, these organizations slowly lost their political activism, as the state monopolized and thus controlled the Tunisian feminist movement by creating and sponsoring the UNFT in 1956 (157). From Ilhem Marzouki, *Le Mouvement des femmes en Tunisie au XXème siècle: Féminisme et politique* (Tunis: Cérès, 1993).

158. Bourguiba, "2ème Congrès National de l'UNFT," 59.

159. Bourguiba, "Les Missions des femmes," 195.

160. Marzouki, *Le Mouvement des femmes,* 189.

161. Quoted by Marzouki, *Le Mouvement des femmes*, 161.

162. Quoted by Marzouki, *Le Mouvement des femmes*, 173.

163. Quoted by Marzouki, *Le Mouvement des femmes*, 177.

164. Bhabha, *Nation and Narration*, 297.

165. Bourguiba, "2ème Congrès National de l'UNFT," 50.

166. Bourguiba, *Tahar El Haddad*, 22–23.

167. He challenged Bourguiba's leadership in two major ways: first, by claiming an Arab-Islamic identity rather than a specific Tunisian personality as Bourguiba did, and second, by rejecting the internal autonomy accords sanctified by the Neo Destur and supporting instead an independent and united Maghreb.

168. Bourguiba, *Tahar El Haddad*, 3–5.

169. Mentioned by Khaled, *Adhwâ*, 337.

170. Mentioned by Khaled, *Adhwâ*, 332.

171. Khaled, *Adhwâ*, 318.

172. *Al Nahdha*, 30 November 1930, 2(N).

173. Cherni, *Les Dérapages de l'histoire*, 67.

174. Marzouki, *Le Mouvement des femmes*, 32.

175. Cherni, *Les Dérapages de l'histoire*, 85–86.

176. To my present knowledge, the only Tunisian author who mentions al Haddad's call for gender equality in inheritance is Abdelrazek Hammami in his book *Al Mar'a*, whose publication was sponsored by the Centre de Recherche, d'Etudes, de Documentation et d'Information sur la Femme. The CREDIF center established by President Ben Ali on 7 August 1990 is funded by the state as well as national and international organizations for the purpose of endorsing women's rights and development in Tunisia.

177. McClintock, *Dangerous Liaisons*, 109.

178. Hammami, *Al Mar'a*, 128–29.

179. Hammami, *Al Mar'a*, 141.

180. There are few exceptions such as Habiba Menchari, the first Tunisian woman to speak unveiled in public, and Eve Nohelle, who wrote for the communist newspaper *Tunis Socialiste*.

Chapter Five

The House of the Prophet as a Technology of Power: Reinventing Domesticity and the Sacred in the Texts of Al Ma'arri, Al Naluti, Djebar, and Rushdie

Whereas the previous chapters studied the ideological production of the "Muslim woman" in the discourses of Orientalism, feminist theory, and Tunisian nationalism, this last chapter excavates the domestic politics underlying the House of the Prophet in *The Epistle of Forgiveness* (1032) by the Abbasid poet Abul Alâ al Ma'arri (973–1057), *Al Tawba* (*The Redemption*) (1992) by the Tunisian novelist Arusiyya al Naluti (1952–), *Loin de Médine: Filles d'Ismaël* (1991) by the Algerian writer Assia Djebar (1936–), and *The Satanic Verses* (1988) by Salman Rushdie (1947–). If this chapter focuses on the symbolic, it is because in many parts of the Islamic world the model of domesticity provided by the House of the Prophet is deployed as the final authority in promulgating laws affecting the lives of Muslim women. This explains why this powerful symbolic is being claimed today not only by the Islamists to justify women's seclusion but also by those who are on the margin of the dominant discourse of Islamic patriarchy; namely, those Muslim feminists who want to advance women's rights in Islamic societies. The major argument of this chapter is that the House of the Prophet is a technology of power[1] that is constantly changing its significance as it is being deployed and appropriated by different groups for various political reasons. Deployed as an instrument of political legitimation during the Abbasid dynasty, this powerful Muslim symbolic became a metaphor for corruption and political absolutism in al Ma'arri's divine comedy, a critique of social disparities in postcolonial Tunisia in al Naluti's *Al Tawba*, the symbol of Islam's sexual oppression of women in Rushdie's *The Satanic Verses*, and a means of self-empowerment in Djebar's feminist novel *Loin de Médine*.

This chapter is divided into three main sections. The first examines the House of the Prophet as a technology of power in Islamic memory. The second section focuses on al Ma'arri's divine comedy. Even though it is told from a male viewpoint, *The Epistle of Forgiveness* displays resistance toward

Abbasid gender ideology. In contrast with the Abbasid rulers' manipulation of this Muslim symbolic, al Ma'arri rejects the House of the Prophet as a technology of power and reconstructs it as a metaphor for social corruption and political absolutism. This second section also examines the reinvention of Muhammad's household in *Al Tawba* (*The Redemption*), a 1992 readaptation of al Ma'arri's divine comedy by the Tunisian novelist al Naluti.

The third section of this chapter focuses on Assia Djebar's feminist reconstruction of *Ahl al Beit* ("Muhammad's household") in *Loin de Médine*. This section starts by examining Djebar's subversive reading of the earlier discourses on the House of the Prophet. The central reading here holds that Djebar is reinventing Muhammad's household through the lens of both *écriture féminine* and Islamic feminism. Djebar's feminist construction of this sacred symbolic constitutes an act of self-empowerment allowing her—as the other within—to respond to the mental and physical violence perpetrated against Algerian women in the late 1980s and early 1990s by the Islamist groups such as the Islamic Salvation Front (FIS) and the Armed Islamic Group (GIA). The last part of this chapter will briefly compare Djebar's feminist project in *Loin de Médine* to Salman Rushdie's postmodern invention of the House of the Prophet in *The Satanic Verses*. This section will also examine Djebar's construction of a "liberal" or "spiritual" Islam versus an eternally repressive Arab culture.

EXCAVATING ISLAMIC MEMORY: THE HOUSE OF THE PROPHET AS A TECHNOLOGY OF POWER

In *Archaeology of Knowledge*, Foucault states that archaeology, rather than being a search for inventions, is to question and "uncover the regularity of a discursive practice"[2] without postulating an "original discourse."[3] It is from this Foucauldian perspective that this chapter examines the discourses on the House of the Prophet. Rather than postulating an authentic or a retrievable true model of Muhammad's life, this chapter examines the House of the Prophet as a semiotic object. As a sign, the House of the Prophet is tied to three levels of discourse: theological, etymological, and vernacular. In Islamic tradition, the expression *Ahl al Beit* ("People of the House") designates Muhammad's family. Even though it refers to the domestic/private self of Muhammad on the literal level, this expression is not separate from Muhammad's public self, for the second source of legislation in Islam after the Qur'an is the hadith, which is composed of Muhammad's statements and actions as reported by his wives or the *Sahaba* ("his disciples"). On the etymological level, the words *haram* ("sanctuary"), *harâm* ("sin"), *harîm* ("harem"), come from the same root "*h*r*m*," meaning sacred, and inviolable. In the North African vernacular, the word *dar* or *beit* ("house") is a synecdoche for family. "How is your house?" means "how is your wife/family?" In this sense, the House of the Prophet becomes a liminal or sacred space where the public and the domestic are conflated. This is why this chapter examines the House of the Prophet at the axes of gender, space, and temporal and spiritual power.

An overview of early Islamic history reveals that the House of the Prophet has always been used as an instrument of political legitimacy. According to the Muslim chronicler Tabari (839–923), al Hussein, the grandson of Muhammad, delivered at the Battle of Kerbala (Iraq)—just before being killed by the Umayyad troops—a speech where he claims his right to divine and political authority through his blood ties to the Prophet's household. He is not only the son of Fâtima and Alî (Muhammad's daughter and son in law), but also the nephew of the martyr Dja'far with the two wings, grand-nephew of Hamza (Muhammad's uncle), and his brother Hassan, who, according to the Prophet, will one day reign over paradise.[4]

Perhaps even more than the Umayyad, the Abbasid Caliphs justified their political and divine authority as members of the Prophet's family through Muhammad's paternal uncle al 'Abbas. Because the descendants of Alî[5] and their Shi'i supporters also presented themselves as heirs to Muhammad's spiritual and temporal heritage, the Sunni Abbasid rulers massacred almost all of the male descendants of Fâtima and Alî.[6] In his study of the term *ahl al beit*, Moshe Sharon examines how the Shi'i Muslims deployed *hadith al kisâ* to establish the idea of the Holy Five. According to this hadith, Muhammad took his *kisâ* (robe), "wrapped it around his son-in-law, his daughter and his two grandchildren and said 'O, Allah, these are my family (*Ahl Baytî*) whom I have chosen; take the pollution from them and purify them thoroughly.'"[7] Even though initially both Abbasids and 'Alîds claimed a common kinship to the House of Beni Hashim to legitimate their rule against Beni Umayya, when they finally came to power, the Abbasids modified and transformed the expression *ahl al beit* to include only Muhammad's uncle al 'Abbas. In the Abbasid version of *hadith al kisâ*, one reads:

> The Prophet came to 'Abbâs and his sons and said: "Come nearer to me." They all pushed against each other. He then wrapped them in his robe and said: "O, Allah, this is my uncle and the brother of my father, these are my family (*ahl baytî*); shelter them from the Fire in the same manner that I shelter them with my robe."[8]

In the Maghreb, both Mulay Idriss I, the founder of the Idrissid dynasty[9] in Morocco (788 A.D.), and 'Ubayd Allah al Mehdi, the founder of the Fatimid dynasty[10] (910 A.D.), which ruled over Egypt, Tunisia, and Eastern Algeria, came to power by claiming to be descendants of the Prophet by way of his daughter Fâtima and her husband Alî. Relying on the same claims, Mulay Rashid founded in 1666 the Alawit Cherifian dynasty,[11] from whom the present royal family of Morocco descends.

In his historical account of the Great *Fitna*, Hichem Djait traces the expression *Ahl al Beit* to the tribal structures of kinship in the pre-Islamic period of *Jahiliya*. If the Medina has been elevated to an "inviolable" or "sacred" space in Islamic memory, it is because the Islamic state has inherited
from the *Jahiliya* the "leading and religious"[12] functions that Quraish
(Muhammad's tribe) exclusively exercised during the Hajj ritual to the Qaaba
Sanctuary in Mecca.[13] However, both Sharon and Djait fail to include Muslim women in the House of the Prophet: the first by reading this Muslim symbolic as a metaphor for "family in the tribe"[14] and the second by erasing
Muhammad's daughters and wives from Muhammad's family tree.[15]

Today, in the face of unemployment, inflation, and poverty, the House of
the Prophet is being deployed not only by the Islamic right to justify women's
economic and social oppression but also by feminists such as Mernissi (*The
Veil and the Male Elite*), Ahmed (*Women and Gender in Islam*), and Djebar
(*Loin de Médine*). Whether they rely on the science of the hadith, *écriture
féminine*, or a Marxist approach, in excavating the archaeology of the House
of the Prophet, these Muslim feminists claim that they are resurrecting a spiritual Islam/a feminist revolution, which has been strangled in its cradle by Orthodox Islam.

REINVENTING THE HOUSE OF THE PROPHET: A STUDY
OF DOMESTIC AND POWER POLITICS IN
AL MA'ARRI'S SHI'I PARADISE

Abul Alâ al Ma'arri and His Garden: An Introduction

Born in 973 in Ma'arrat al Nu'mân, a small village between Aleppo and Dam-
ascus during the Abbasid dynasty (750–1258), Al Ma'arri lost his sight at the
age of four after contracting smallpox. Even though poor, his family held education in high esteem. His grandmother was recognized as a hadith transmitter. He was trained in Arabic lexicography, hadith transmission, Qur'anic
recitation, and Arabic literature.[16] His literary career was quite prolific: he
wrote many collections of poems such as *Saqt al Zand*, the *Luzumiyat*, *Al
Fusul wa al Ghayat* as well as a book entitled *Zajr al Nabih*, where he explains some misinterpreted verses in the *Luzumiyat*. He also wrote personal
letters and epistles, like *Risalat al Hana* (*The Epistle of Happiness*), *Risalat
al Mala'ika* (*The Epistle of Angels*), and *Risalat al Ghufran* (*The Epistle of
Forgiveness*). He lived during the reign of Caliph al Hakim bi Amr Illah, an
eccentric Fatimid ruler who encouraged the spread of mystical ideas such as
the doctrine of immanence (*al Hulul*).[17] Al Ma'arri resided in Baghdad for a
short period of time (1009–1010), where he visited its famous library *dar al*

'Ilm ("The House of Knowledge"). He soon retired to his home in Ma'arrat al Nu'mân after being publicly humiliated in the *majlis* (literary salon) of Abu al Qasim Alî al Sharif al Murtadhâ. Al Ma'arri was dragged by his leg from the house of al Murtadhâ for defending the Abbasid poet al Mutannabi, whom al Murtadhâ hated and despised.[18] After this incident al Ma'arri turned to asceticism and secluded himself for almost fifty years.

In his divine comedy,[19] al Ma'arri brings together poets from the *Jahiliya* period and Islam, not just to offer lessons in literary criticism but also to denounce the predicament of the man of letters reduced to composing panegyric poetry for the Abbasid Emirs and Viziers. Al Ma'arri's work comes in fact as a response to a letter from the panegyrist poet Ibn ul Qârih Alî Ibn Mansùr,[20] in which he apologizes for losing a letter he was charged to deliver to al Ma'arri. In his letter, Ibn ul Qârih explains how all of his belongings—including al Ma'arri's letter—were stolen and complains about the loss of morals. *The Epistle of Forgiveness* is an ironic response to the contrived literary style and the self-righteousness Ibn ul Qârih exhibits in his letter to al Ma'arri. In his letter, al Ma'arri tells Ibn ul Qârih that he cannot have access to heaven through panegyric poetry as he used to do on earth. Using Ibn ul Qârih's hypocrisy and corruption as example, al Ma'arri's divine comedy provides a social critique of Abbasid society and displays cynicism toward Islam's orthodox beliefs in hell, heaven, and redemption, through a literal presentation of the imagery of hell and paradise found in the Qur'an and Arabic poetry.

Al Ma'arri's attitude toward religion in *The Epistle of Forgiveness* cannot be understood without examining the political and religious strife that tore the Islamic world open in the tenth and eleventh centuries. In al Ma'arri's lifetime, many Caliphates appeared in Egypt, Baghdad, and Aleppo. They all used religion as a tool to justify their rise to power. Like the Abbasid dynasty, whose rulers claimed divine sovereignty through Muhammad's uncle, the Fâtimid rejected the Abbasid Caliphate in Baghdad, and ruled over Egypt and Aleppo by claiming direct descendency from Fâtima Azzahra, the daughter of Muhammad. In Baghdad, political power shifted hands from the Sunni Abbasid Caliphs to the Shi'i Buwayhid family, who were their Persian military commanders. Even though both the Buwayhid and the Fâtimid were Shi'ah, they were enemies. As Twelver Shi'is ("Twelve Imams"), the Buwayhid were happy to serve the Sunni Caliphate in opposing the conservatism of the Fâtimids, who were from the Isma'ili branch of the Shi'ah. In his *Luzumiat*, al Ma'arri reports the dispossession of Muhammad's descendants by the Abbasid dynasty, the weakness of the Abbasid ruler al Mansùr, and the rise to power of the Persians: "In the Wilderness were exiled Banu Hashim/And onto the hands of the *Daylam* [Persians] passed power."[21]

The House of the Prophet between Continuity and Resistance:
A Shi'i Heaven and a Monogamous Muhammad

An overview of al Ma'arri's Edenic garden reveals both conformity and resistance toward Abbasid gender ideology and the earlier discourses on the House of the Prophet. Whereas Alî (Muhammad's cousin and son-in-law), Ibrahîm (Muhammad's son), and Hamza (Muhammad's uncle) ride their horses and walk around freely on the Day of Reckoning, Fâtima is secluded[22] in her heavenly "abode" and comes out only once every "twenty-four hours of earthly time to greet her father Muhammad."[23] Fâtima is not to be seen: whenever she exits God's courtroom, a clerk "call[s] out to the people there to lower their eyes" until she passes. Even though she has the power of redemption, she runs her errands in Paradise only when chaperoned by her little brother Ibrahîm. During her intercession to Muhammad on behalf of Ibn ul Qârih, Fâtima does not fly alone with the latter: she first introduces him to her brother, and then they all fly together to see Muhammad. Reflecting the Abbasid segregation of the sexes, Ibn ul Qârih flies hanging from Ibrahîm's horse, not Fâtima's:

> Fâtima then said to her brother Ibrahîm (blessings on him) "Here is the man" [Ibn ul Qârih]. "Hang on to my horse" said he, and the horses of the company proceeded to pass through the throng, all nations and kindreds making way for them; and when the press became too close, they flew into the air, with me hanging on to the horse.[24]

As in the eighth- and ninth-century chronicles of Tabari, Ibn Saad, and Ibn Hisham, in al Ma'arri's afterlife, Fâtima and Khadija are trapped within the patriarchal roles of motherhood and wifehood: Fâtima as wife of Alî and mother of the two martyrs Hassan and Hussein, and Khadija as the Mother of the Believers and the mother of Muhammad's sons who died in infancy. Describing the House of the Prophet in the afterlife, Ibn ul Qârih observes:

> There was among them Alî the son of Husein and his two sons Muhammad and Zaid with others of the righteous and devout. With Fâtima (peace be upon her) was another woman equal to her in honor and dignity. They were told in answer to their enquiry that it was Khadijah the daughter of Khuwailid Ibn Asad Ibn Abdel Uzza. With her were youths riding on horses of light, and they were told they were Abdallah, Qâsim, Tayyib, and Tâhir, and Ibrahîm—sons of the Blessed Prophet.[25]

On the Day of Reckoning, Ibn ul Qârih is saved from hell only because Fâtima has interceded with Muhammad on his behalf. The idea that Fâtima could save someone from the flames of hell through intercession with her father is a common belief among the Shi'ah, who also believe that her two sons Hassan and Hussein, who were murdered by the Umayyad, are the only legitimate heirs to Muhammad's temporal and spiritual heritage. There is, indeed, a long tradition of Islamic literature where the Prophet's wives and daughters appear as the "matrons of paradise."[26] The idea that Fâtima would not save those who murdered her children and grandchildren was not unheard of in Abbasid society. About two centuries before al Ma'arri, the first chronicler of Islamic history Tabari reports a story Mousa Ibn 'Habib told him after the murder of Zaid:[27]

> A woman [told him] the following story: "On the night of the third day following Zaid's death, I saw in a dream a group of persons dressed in bright clothes and descending from the heavens who were gathered around Zaid, beating their faces, weeping and screaming, like our women do when they gather to cry over a dead person. One of them wearing a splendid garment shouted: 'O Zaid, they have killed you! O Zaid, they sent you to the gallows and exposed your nakedness! Definitely, they won't have the intercession of your grandfather on the Day of Resurrection!' I asked then one of her companions who that woman was. She told me: 'It is Fâtima, the daughter of the Prophet, the wife of 'Alî.'"[28]

In al Ma'arri's divine comedy, the preeminence of the House of the Prophet in the afterlife stands, on a symbolic level, for the restoration of their divine rights. This is why on the Day of Resurrection, only Muhammad's first wife; his daughter Fâtima; his five sons who died in infancy (Qâssim, Tâhar, Tayyib, Abdallah, and Ibrahîm); his grandson Hussein;[29] his great-great-grandsons Muhammad and Zaid; his son-in-law Alî; his paternal uncle Hamza, who died a martyr at the Battle of Uhud; and the Elect (other chosen members of his family), go back and forth between Heaven and God's courtyard, where the resurrected are fearfully waiting God's judgment.

In this afterlife family reunion, Muhammad's other wives are all absent, including his favorite wife Aïsha. Also striking is the absence of his other daughters from Khadija: Zeineb, Ruqayya and Um Kulthum. If these three daughters are absent, it is because from a Shi'i standpoint only the sons of Fâtima and Alî are Muhammad's legitimate heirs. Besides, Ruqayya and Um Kulthum were both married (one after the other) to 'Uthman Ibn 'Affan (644–56),[30] the third Muslim Caliph who gave power to his kinsman Mu'âwiya Ibn Abi Sufyan, the founder of the Umayyad dynasty, who fought against Alî in the Battle of Siffin, and persecuted the Prophet's grandsons Hassan and Hussein.

It is also the Elect who introduce Ibn ul Qârih to Fâtima, Alî, and Hamza. Describing the "Elect," Ibn ul Qârih states that they are "many members of the family of Abu Talib of both sexes, who had never touched wine or known doing wrong."[31] It is significant here that Muhammad's family is referred to as the "family of Abu Talib," who is Muhammad's uncle and father of Alî, and not as "the family of Abdul Muttalib," after his paternal grandfather, or "Beni Hashim," after the name of his clan. This is significant because the Abbasid rulers also presented themselves as the legitimate blood heirs to Muhammad's legacy. As a matter of fact, the Abbasid—who are the descendants of Muhammad's paternal uncle al 'Abbas son of Abdul Muttlalib son of Hashim—denied the political legitimacy of Alî Ibn Abi Talib through his marriage to Fâtima. Even though he was the father of Muhammad's only two grandsons (Hassan and Hussein), Alî and his descendants were denied legitimacy because inheritance, the Beni Abbas claimed, follows the father's line not the mother's. In his *Chronicle*, Tabari reports a correspondence between the Abbasid ruler Abu Ja'far al Mansur and Muhammad Ibn Abdallah (one of the descendants of Alî) where both lay claim to Muhammad's spiritual and temporal heritage. In the letter where he responds to the Abbasid ruler's promise to grant him his royal pardon "were he to give up his weapons and surrender,"[32] Muhammad Ibn Abdallah refuses to surrender and presents himself as the legitimate heir of Fâtima, the "principal heiress of Muhammad.[33] To this claim, Al Mansùr responds that the descendants of al 'Abbas are the real heirs because tribal honor has always been patrilineal, not matrilineal. "The nobility of origins," he says, "does not get transmitted by women, but through men." Because uncles are more important than cousins, the Caliphate should go to the descendants of Muhammad's uncle al Abbas, not those of his cousin Alî.[34] Thus, the absence on the Day of Reckoning of Beni al 'Abbas and the political power granted to Alî, his son Hussein, his grandson Alî, and his two great-grandsons Muhammad and Zaid[35] reflect the Shi'i belief that only Alî and his two sons Hussein and Hassan are Muhammad's legitimate heirs.

Even though Muhammad's favorite wife Aïsha is excluded from al Ma'arri's Shi'i afterlife, there is a hint concerning her alleged affair with Safwan Ibn al Mu'attal.[36] In Paradise, Ibn ul Qârih meets the Prophet's poet Hassan Ibn Thabit, who tells him that he entered heaven because he married Sirîn, the sister of Maryam the Copt, Muhammad's concubine and mother of his son Ibrahîm. Even though Ibn Thabit was flogged with the slave Mistah for spreading lies about Aïsha's reputation, Muhammad saved him because of the blood ties between the poet's son Abdul Rahman and the Prophet's own son Ibrahîm.[37] The story of Ibn Thabit's salvation shows that redemption is bestowed rather than earned. By making hypocrites like Ibn Thabit or profligate poets like al A'asha enter Paradise because of their kinship with the House of the Prophet or Muhammad's generosity, al Ma'arri is critiquing the Shi'i belief in the absolute power of the House of the Prophet on the Day of Reckoning.

In this Shi'i paradise, Aïsha is excluded not only because of her alleged affair with Safwan Ibn al Mu'attal, but also because she sided with Mu'âwiya (founder of the Umayyad dynasty) and fought against Alî—the Prophet's cousin and son-in-law—in the Battle of the Camel. Aïsha's participation in the first war where Muslim blood was shed caused many to blame her for creating *al fitna* ("chaos")[38] between Muslims. Besides this, the Shi'ah never forgot how she refused to let the corpse of Hassan be buried near the tomb of the Prophet. Aïsha claimed that the land where Muhammad's body was buried belonged to her. Because of this the body of Hassan "was buried in the cemetery of Baqî,"[39] not near his grandfather.

Al Ma'arri's divine comedy shows a departure from the earlier discourses on the House of the Prophet. For instance, the absence of the nine wives[40] Muhammad took after Khadija's death does not merely reflect the Shi'i belief that only the Prophet's descendants from Fâtima (daughter of Khadija) are his true legitimate heirs, but more important, al Ma'arri's own opposition and rejection of the institution of polygamy. In his invention of the House of the Prophet as a monogamous household, al Ma'arri makes Ibrahîm appear, not with his real mother, Muhammad's concubine Maryam the Copt, but with Muhammad's first wife Khadija and her sons Abdallah, Qâsim, Tayyib, and Tâhir.[41] Many Arab critics present al Ma'arri as a woman hater[42] for his portrayal of women in his *Luzumiat* as snakes,[43] irrational,[44] and dangerous, seductive creatures.[45] It is true that al Ma'arri has often expressed his hatred for women and procreation,[46] but he is also the Abbasid poet who has criticized polygamy and attacked Islam's holy wars for causing the enslavement and dishonoring of Arab women. In the *Luzumiat*, al Ma'arri makes sarcastic remarks about polygamous men: "Be content with the fourth of me he told his first wife after taking three others/ He rewards her if little satisfies her and stones her if she takes a lover/ He who marries two women can never reach the fifth or fourth of justice's pathway."[47] Al Ma'arri's criticism of polygamy is not unheard of in Abbasid times. As Ahmed demonstrates in *Women and Gender in Islam*, the Qarmatians, for instance, challenged the views of establishment Islam by rejecting polygamy, concubinage, and the wearing of the veil.[48] In the *Luzumiat*, al Ma'arri attacks all religions for turning people into "the bitterest of enemies" and wonders whether it "was not the Prophets' teachings, which permitted the enslavement and dishonoring of women among Arabs."[49] This is quite subversive given the fact that Muhammad's concubine, Maryam the Copt, was given to him as a gift. Muhammad's slave Selma was also a war captive. She was enslaved when her father Malik, head of the Beni Ghatafan, rebelled against Islam. Muhammad gave her as a gift to Aïsha, who later emancipated her.

Even though *The Epistle of Forgiveness* reproduces Muslim beliefs in the afterlife and in particular Shi'i beliefs in the divine authority and legitimacy of the House of the Prophet, al Ma'arri's description of resurrection and the House of the Prophet's absolute power of redemption borders on sarcasm and cynicism. An overview of *The Epistle of Forgiveness* shows that the House of the Prophet is a metaphor for social corruption and a satire of the absolute power of the Abbasid ruler. A corrupt and degenerate poet in his lifetime, Ibn ul Qârih gains access to heaven not through his good deeds, but thanks to his *pistons* ("personal acquaintances") and his talent as a panegyric poet. On the

Day of Reckoning, Ibn ul Qârih loses his Repentance Pass and tries to enter Paradise by bribing the angels guarding its gates with praise poetry. Plagiarizing the poetry of Imru' ul Qais, he composes verses "in praise of Radwan in the meter of the well-known verse: 'Rise ye two and let us weep for the memory of Habib and 'Irfan,'"[50] and he substitutes Radwan, the name of the doorkeeper of paradise, for 'Irfan. When Radwan refuses, he tries to bribe another guardian of heaven, Zufar, with "some verses rhyming in his name in the meter of Labid's verse,"[51] but in vain. He then composes a eulogy to Muhammad's uncle Hamza. Even though he does not save him, Hamza sends him to his nephew Alî[52] who summons the Judge of Aleppo to testify that Ibn ul Qârih has repented at the end of his life. Alî turns down his request of salvation and asks him to wait for his turn[53] to see Muhammad like everyone else. But Ibn ul Qârih does not give up:

> I then approached the noble family of the elect and said: "When I was in the mortal world I wrote a book at the conclusion of which I added these words: 'The blessing of Allah be upon our Lord Muhammad the seal of the prophets, and upon his family of elect and excellent persons.' These words must give me sanctuary (*hurma*) and the right of way (*wassila*)."[54]

As the above passage shows, Ibn ul Qârih wants to enter heaven not through his good deeds, but through the panegyric poetry he composed on earth in honor of Muhammad and his family. In Arabic, *wassila* means "instrument" or "means." The juxtaposition of the two words *wassila* and *hurma* ("sanctuary" and "sacred") reveals how through Ibn ul Qârih, al Ma'arri is denouncing the subjection of the sacred to ideological and political manipulation during the Abbasid dynasty. Just as the Abassid Caliphs used religion as a tool of political legitimacy, Ibn ul Qârih is using religious formula to have access to heaven.

At the request of Ibn ul Qârih, the Elect—to spare him the hardships of the long waiting line on Judgment Day—ask Fâtima to intercede with the Prophet on his behalf. Even though Muhammad finally grants him redemption,[55] Ibn ul Qârih's entry into heaven is ludicrous. As he is unable to keep his balance while crossing the purgatory, Fâtima "[orders] one of her handmaidens to help [him] across"[56] by carrying him piggyback. At the gate of heaven, Radwan the porter refuses to let Ibn ul Qârih in because he does not have his Repentance Pass with him. So Ibrahîm, the son of Muhammad, comes back to his rescue and kicks him "into Paradise."[57] In heaven, Ibn ul Qârih finally enjoys the blessings of heaven: fish sporting in pools of honey;[58] the rivers of wine, honey, and milk;[59] the jeweled pages;[60] heavenly houris[61] springing from apples and pomegranates, and so forth.

Throughout his divine comedy, Al Ma'arri's irony subverts the political machinery underlying the House of the Prophet and turns this Muslim symbolic into a metaphor for injustice and political absolutism. According to Aws Ibn Hajar, one of the poets Ibn ul Qârih visits in hell, there is no difference between the absolute power of the Abbasid king on earth and the House of the Prophet's absolute power of redemption in the afterlife: "People wickeder than I have entered Paradise, but the distribution of forgiveness is nothing but a lottery like the distribution of wealth in the world."[62] An ascetic and a cynic, al Ma'arri engages in the hegemonic discourses of the Abbasids and the Fâtimids only to mock them. Rather than deploying the House of the Prophet for some personal or political ends, al Ma'arri deploys this Muslim symbolic only to reveal its corruptive power as a tool of ideological manipulation. In his lifetime, al Ma'arri opposed not only the corruption of the Abbasid rulers in Baghdad—as his public humiliation at the salon of al Murtadha attests to— but also the Fâtimid regime in Egypt and Aleppo. Because al Ma'arri was a threat to the Fâtimid presence in Aleppo, the Isma'ili preacher Da'i al Du'ah started a correspondence with al Ma'arri asking him metaphysical questions and soliciting answers that could be used to give al Ma'arri the reputation of a "heretic" or "unbeliever."[63] A poor yet proud man of letters, al Ma'arri refused Da'i al Du'ah's offer of financial assistance, in the same way he turned down the other "Fâtimid attempts"[64] to bribe/control[65] him. In his *Luzumiat*, al Ma'arri attacks the Shi'i belief in the "*imamah*" (clergy), by stating, "there is no imam, but the mind."[66]

In his nihilistic worldview, al Ma'arri sees mankind as incurably corrupt: only sterility, castration, or floods can cleanse the world of their evil. Even though he opposes polygamy and women's enslavement in Islam's holy wars, al Ma'arri's reproduction of the traditional Islamic image of Fâtima and Khadija as mothers of the Believers reflects Abbasid patriarchal ideology. Finally, if al Ma'arri was able to reject the power politics underlying the House of the Prophet and live in seclusion, it was because of his double privilege of gender and education. During the fifty years he lived in seclusion, al Ma'arri was able to turn his home into a center for learning. It was his students and his maternal uncle who were providing him with food and other necessities of life.[67] An insider, on account of his gender and education, and an outsider, on account of his class, al Ma'arri's double position in Abbasid society recalls Foucault's statement that power is also extended to those who are "dominated": "It invests them, is transmitted by them and through them; it exerts pressure upon them, just as they themselves, in their struggle against it, resist the grip it has on them."[68]

After his humiliation at the Salon of al Murtadhâ, al Ma'arri became, in his own words, the inmate of three prisons: his "blindness," his "home," and his "body."[69] Al Ma'arri's imprisonment (except his blindness) recalls Foucault's claim that punishment is a "complex social function,"[70] "a political tactic," and a technology of the "soul"[71] that conceals its "materiality as an instrument and vector of power" over the body. Hardly a consequence of free will, the fifty years that al Ma'arri imposed on himself illustrate the "social" and political structure underlying the Abbasid technology of power, which affected not only al Ma'arri's "body," but also his soul, his "heart," "thoughts," "will," and "inclinations."[72]

Revisiting al Ma'arri's Male Paradise: Gender and Politics in Arusiyya al Naluti's *Al Tawba*

Born on the Island of Djerba in 1950, Arussiyya al Naluti belongs to the first generation of women novelists who started writing in Arabic in postcolonial Tunisia. A one-time teacher of Arabic literature, she is now working in the Tunisian Ministry of Education. In 1975, she published her first collection of short stories *Al Bou'd al Khamis* (*The Fifth Dimension*). Then, she wrote her first novel *Maratij* (*Locks*) in 1985, and finally *Tamas* (*Borderline*) in 1995. Besides this, she has written several scripts for Tunisian film and theater. In 1992, she wrote a readaption of al Ma'arri's garden in a play entitled *Al Tawba* (*The Redemption*).[73] The play, which consists of ten scenes or tableaux, was originally written for school-theater. It was meant to present al Ma'arri in a new light to the students of the baccalaureate. In an interview, al Naluti confesses that the play is part of her "unorthodox teaching" of al Ma'arri. Through this play, she wanted to present "a new vision or a new reading"[74] of this Abbasid poet.

In her theatrical readaptation of al Ma'arri's divine comedy, only Alî and Fâtima appear: they are introduced not through their names, but through their social status as the Emir[75] and the Lady.[76] In her reconstruction of al Ma'arri's divine comedy, al Naluti erases the religious conflict between Shi'i and Sunni Islam and places the issue of gender outside the paradigm of Islamic religion. By referring to Fâtima in terms of her class, al Naluti is recreating her as a social being, subverting thus not only her patriarchal construction in Islamic tradition as the mother of Hassan and Hussein but also Western feminists' tendency to overlook class differences between Muslim women.[77] At the same time, by downplaying the theme of religion and focusing instead on the social differences between the dwellers of Paradise, al Naluti subverts the unitary discourse of Tunisian nationalism and its occlusion of the social disparities tearing postcolonial Tunisia.

Commenting on the political context in which her play was produced, al Naluti states that her rewriting of *The Epistle of Forgiveness* was a means of escapism:

> The reading or rereading of a text in a particular moment is always a response to some particular circumstances even if we question an older text. In al Ma'arri's afterlife, the gehannam the damned are talking about is the gehannam of life and the

prison of the wretched. This arbitrariness that we find in the anti-hero Ibn ul Qârih—the biggest hypocrite and opportunist—encapsulates all of the maladies in al Ma'arri's age. The strangest thing is that when you pursue Ibn ul Qârih, you find him living among us today. How many Ibn ul Qârihs do we meet everyday? So Ibn ul Qârih, and al Ma'arri's manipulation of his character could happen at any time: yesterday, today, or tomorrow. Even if the author is unconscious when she/he questions an old text, this rereading stems from a particular ideological framework. This rereading reveals a specific reality and searches to express something.[78]

Hence, like, Mernissi, Ahmed, and Djebar, al Naluti is visiting the past to engage in the present. In al Ma'arri's text, al Naluti finds a vehicle through which she can carry her Marxist feminist critique of postcolonial Tunisia.

CLAIMING MUHAMMAD'S LEGACY: ASSIA DJEBAR'S FEMINIST REINVENTION OF THE HOUSE OF THE PROPHET IN *LOIN DE MÉDINE*

Born in French colonial Algeria in the town of Cherchell in 1936, Djebar is the most famous and prolific Francophone female novelist and filmmaker in the Maghreb. A historian by training and a novelist by vocation, Djebar is now exiled in the United States, where she teaches at New York University. At nineteen, she wrote her first novel *La Soif*, followed by *Les Alouettes naïves* (1967), *Poèmes de l'Algérie heureuse* (1969), *Rouge l'aube* (1970),[79] *Femmes d'Alger dans leur appartement* (1980), *L'Amour, La Fantasia* (1985), *Ombre Sultane* and *A Sister to Scheherazade* (1987). Her first film was *La Nouba des femmes du Mont Chenoua* (1977) followed by *La Zerda ou les chants de l'oubli* (1982). Her works—*Loin de Médine* (1991), *Vaste est la prison* (1995), and *Le Blanc de L'Algérie* (1996)—deal with the rise of the Islamist movement in Algeria and the seven-year Civil War[80] (1992–1997), which cost the lives of more than 100,000 people. Djebar's most recent works include *Les Nuits de Strasbourg* (1997), *Oran, Langue morte* (1997), and *Ces Voix qui m'assiègent* (1999). Like so many Algerians, Djebar lost members of her family and friends in the bloodbath that tore her country apart in the 1990s. In *Le Blanc de L'Algérie* and *Vaste est la prison*, two literary tributes for the victims of the Civil War, Djebar attacks the FLN socialist regime for paving the way for the theocratic discourse of the Islamists, through their own political absolutism and anti-intellectualism.

In contrast with Djebar's first novel *La Soif*, which tells the story of a young woman discovering her sexuality without a hint to the ongoing Algerian Revolution, *Loin de Médine* stands out as a piece of politically committed literature. In a 1993 interview with Clarisse Zimra, Djebar states that *Loin de*

Médine is "a response"[81] to the political situation in her homeland, especially to the bloody riots of October 1988, when young people took to the streets to contest the price of bread.[82] Declaring her engagement in the political debate and strife shattering Algeria, Djebar confesses that "*Médine* was conceived as a response to specific circumstances."[83] Rather than sitting on the margin of the dominant discourse of Islamic patriarchy, Djebar decides to answer back by reconstructing the House of the Prophet from a woman's standpoint. Just as the Islamists manipulate the sacred to justify women's seclusion and oppression, Djebar claims this powerful Muslim symbolic for the purpose of empowering Algerian women. Djebar's reinvention of the House of the Prophet through the lens of *écriture féminine*/French feminist aesthetics—that is, as body, voice, and movement—is triggered by the condition of Algerian women at the end of the 1980s and early 1990s. Claiming an Islamic state, Alî Ben Hadj, the head of the FIS, called for women's veiling and return home. In an article published in *Le Nouvel Observateur* on 22 July 1994, he stated:

> Women's natural place for expression . . . is the home. . . . In a true Islamic society, women are not meant to work and the head of state must allot them a wage. Thus, they will not leave their home but can devote themselves to the great mission of educating men. Woman produces [is a productrix of] men; she does not produce material goods but rather this essential thing that is a Muslim [male].[84]

"She Never Invents: She Re-creates": Djebar's *Loin de Médine* as a Strategic Rereading of Islamic Chronicles[85]

In *The Archaeology of Knowledge*, Foucault states that "the tools that enable the historians to carry out [their] work of analysis are partly inherited and partly of their own making."[86] A historian by training, Djebar's tools in excavating the House of the Prophet are also "partly inherited and partly [her] own."[87] In the Avant-Propos to her novel, Djebar acknowledges her indebtedness to the first Muslim historians—Ibn Hisham, Ibn Saad, and Tabari—who wrote their chronicles two centuries after Muhammad's death. However, she subverts the sets of rules through which the discourses on the House of the Prophet are formed. Rather than looking for coherence, Djebar's archaeology tries to describe "the contradictions"[88] and "the different spaces of dissension"[89] in the accounts of these earlier historians. As she confesses in her interview with Zimra about *Loin de Médine*, Djebar is filling those "blanks"[90] and the "dangerous/subversive"[91] "anecdotes"/fissures in the accounts of these Muslim chroniclers.

In opposition to the principles of continuity and closure in Tabari's originary narrative, Djebar does not provide straightforward answers. In his *Chronicle*, Tabari asserts that fear pushed the Queen of Yemen to marry Aswad, the murderer of her husband. In contrast, Djebar dismisses such easy answers and leaves the question suspended: "Was the Yemenite Queen a submissive victim or a false consenting prey?"[92] Was Firouz, the man who killed Aswad, the Queen's "lover" or simply her "cousin?"[93] To such questions, Djebar provides no answers. As she puts it: "Ambiguity envelops . . . the character of the Yemenite with a lamp. She disappears into oblivion: without honors, without other commentaries . . . her candle is gone out: silence falls on her."[94]

Djebar relies on the traditional methodology of the hadith only to subvert it. For instance, in Ibn Saad's *Tabaqat*, the hadiths[95] about the House of the Prophet are formed by two parts: first the *isnad* ("the chain of hadith transmitters") and the text of the hadith itself. The only Muslim women he mentions as the direct transmitters of the hadith are the mothers of the Believers, Aïsha and Um Salama, who besides their prestigious status as the wives of the Prophet, also came from the Quraish aristocracy. In *Loin de Médine*, Djebar subversively interferes with the "enunciative reordering"[96] of the hadith, by giving the power of transmission/enunciation not only to Muslim women of the upper classes, but also to non-Muslim women like Kerama the Christian or the slaves in Muhammad's household like Aïsha's slave Barira or Muhammad's sister-in law, Sirîn, who also was a slave before becoming the mother of Abdul Rahman, the son of the poet Hassan Ibn Thabit.[97]

In her rereading of Ibn Saad and Ibn Hisham, Djebar appropriates the orality of the hadith—which is the second source of legislation in Islam after the Qur'an/the written word of God—to resurrect the voices of these Muslim women who were silenced by the male Muslim chroniclers. In opposition to Foucault, whose archaeology is not preoccupied with the hidden meaning of discourse,[98] Djebar's archaeology digs up those feminine voices, which have been repressed by Tabari, Ibn Saad, and Ibn Hisham, so as to extract meaning. Among the Muslim women she gives voice to are Um Harem,[99] the maternal aunt of Anas Ibn Malik, the famous hadith transmitter and founder[100] of the Maliki rite, and her sister, Malik's mother, who spent most of her life silent. In reconstructing Malik's aunt as a *râwiya* ("hadith transmitter"/"story-teller"), Djebar is giving this gendered subaltern an equal status to that of the Muslim hadith scholars Bukhari, Muslim, and Malik. At the same time, in excavating this palimpsest of female voices, Djebar as historian/*râwiya*, is including herself—as the gendered subaltern—in the very construction of the sacred, turning therefore the orality of the hadith into an instrument of self-empowerment.

In *Loin de Médine*, Djebar states that her reading of the old Islamic chronicles triggered in her "the will to engage in *Ijtihad*."[101] Djebar's engagement in the dominant discourse of Islamic orthodoxy and deployment of the sacred is best expressed in the quotation she takes from al Ferdousi's *The Book of Kings*:

I may not have enough strength to reach the top of the fruit-loaded tree. However, he who sits in the shade of a powerful palm tree will be safe out of harm's way. Maybe I can find a place on a lower branch of this cypress tree, which far away extends its shade.[102]

Even though in the end, Djebar, as the gendered subaltern, can only aspire to occupy the lower branches of power, by sitting under the shade of the sacred as *râwiya* (transmitter) or *mujtahida* ("religious scholar"), she can keep herself/other women safe from the scorching sun of Islamic orthodoxy. It is from this marginal position that Djebar is returning to the House of the Prophet to advance the rights of Muslim women.

In contrast with the sacred persona of Muhammad in the Islamist narrative, Djebar's Muhammad seems a decentered and split subject. Even though he took many wives himself, Muhammad the father forbade his cousin and son-in-law Alî to take a second wife as long as he was married to his daughter Fâtima. These internal conflicts and contradictions not only reveal the "human presence"[103] of Muhammad, but also his love for his favorite daughter. Muhammad's "No" to Alî was uttered during prayer time, from his *minbar*, in the sacred space of the Mosque. Explaining why he is forbidding this marriage, Muhammad argues that Fâtima will be troubled in her faith and the daughter of the Prophet cannot live with Juwayriyah, the daughter of Abu Jahl, the enemy of God.[104] This public refusal is made by Muhammad the caring father, not the polygamous Prophet. Muhammad's notorious love for his daughter is being deployed here as a criticism of polygamy and as a model of the father-daughter relationship.

In her feminist reinvention of The House of the Prophet, Djebar focuses on the monogamous years in the lives of Muhammad and Alî. Fâtima "was the only wife in the life of her cousin Alî," just like her mother Khadija, who for twenty-five years remained Muhammad's only wife.[105] Whereas the Islamists and the Algerian Family Code of 1984 present polygamy as the symbol of an Islamic authentic identity, Djebar constructs Alî and Fâtima as a "couple."[106]

Djebar strategically uses Muhammad's public outcry that his daughter is "part of [him]" and that "whatsoever upsets her upsets [him]"[107] to rewrite a new script for the father-daughter relationships in present-day Muslim societies. In Arabic, a man who is "without a male descendant"[108] is called *abtar*, that is, "mutilated." Djebar's re-creation of Muhammad's relationship with his daughter constitutes a strategic act of grafting the daughter (the cut off branch/limb) to the father, and thus the feminine (Fâtima) into the sacred (Muhammad).

As a response to the increasing violence against women in Algeria, Djebar creates a Muhammad who is both tolerant and loving toward his daughters. Djebar reminds right wing Islamic groups that Muhammad did not kill his daughter Zeineb when she refused to convert out of love for her husband: "His daughter Zeineb did not join Islam for a long time out of love for her husband [Abu el 'Aç], whom she preferred to her father, who respected this love."[109] When her husband was made captive at the Battle of Badr, Zeineb sent as a ransom the pearl necklace she inherited from her mother, Khadija. Recognizing his wife's necklace, Muhammad, according to Tabari, "freed

Abu el 'Aç, gave him the money and the necklace and asked him to send Zeineb back to him because she is a Muslim."[110] Zeineb went back to her father. Later Abu el 'Aç converted to Islam and got remarried to Zeineb.

In opposition to the status of Aïsha and Fâtima as Mothers of the Believers in Islamic tradition, Djebar emphasizes their status as wives and beloved daughters. Djebar wonders why Fâtima appears in the early Muslim chronicles "only once, she is the mother of Hassan and Hussein."[111] Announcing her break with the cult of maternity so dear to the Muslim male chroniclers, Djebar declares:

> Islam, in its beginning, contented itself with adopting the maternal values found in Mary, the mother of Jesus (who remained chaste till his death). The theme of maternity has been so glorified and celebrated to the fullest in the preceding seven centuries of Christianity that it seems normal, then, to see it retreat. The Women-wives, the inheriting daughters rise, in this dawn of Islam, in a new modernity.[112]

In contrast with the construction of Aïsha in the popular memory of the Maghreb as Muhammad's favorite[113] wife, Djebar focuses on her pain "as a child-bride"[114] when Muhammad married Hafsa, the daughter of 'Umar. Also disruptive is Djebar's reading of Tabari's account of Muhammad's repudiation of his wife Sawda. When her father and two uncles are killed by the Muslim troops, Sawda cries out in pain, berating the Meccan captives and asking them why they were not killed like her father and uncles. Muhammad repudiates her when he hears that. But to keep her prestige as the Prophet's wife, she asks him to take her back, stating that in exchange, she will give all her nights to Aïsha.[115] Djebar's rereading of Tabari's account of this incident is quite subversive of the institution of polygamy: "More than the status of 'the favorite spouse,' that tradition will later make prevail, it is this status of 'double spouse' that matters at present."[116] After Sawda's repudiation, Aïsha enjoyed for a year the double[117] of the affective and sexual privileges she used to have when she had a co-wife. In contrast with the first Muslim historians who are bent on reporting every detail about Muhammad's young spoiled wife, Djebar focuses on Aïsha's pain every time her husband takes a new wife and on her happiness when for a year she had Muhammad exclusively for herself.[118] By focusing on the monogamous moments in Muhammad's lifetime, Djebar unearths and rewrites monogamy into the heart of the Sacred, undermining thus the Islamist narrative where Muhammad's life serves as a model to justify polygamy.

Looking through the Lens of Écriture Feminine: Djebar's Reinvention of the House of the Prophet as Voice, Body, and Movement

In *Loin de Médine*, Djebar reconstructs Fâtima as the "voice of contestation" and Aïsha as the "voice of transmission" and the "parole feminine."[119] On the death of Abu Bakr, 'Umar rudely orders the women to stop weeping because Muhammad forbade crying over the dead. Aïsha disputes his statement: "Umar Ibn el Khattab is wrong! He did not understand" what Muhammad said. "I testify that Muhammad allows us to weep over those who leave us." He forbade only screams, fits, and self-mutilations because they "could disturb the dead."[120] Aïsha's testimony is important not just because she is opposing the second Caliph of Islam, but also because she is standing up to defend her right to *ijtihad*, that is, her right to interpret the hadith. 'Umar's attempt to stop women from crying is presented by Djebar as one of the first attempts to stifle women's voices. This is why Djebar insists that Muhammad did not "scorn singing, and singers."[121] According to one of the *râwiyates*, "the Prophet charged his young wife Aïsha to send Zeineb el 'Ançariya"[122] — a famous singer from Médina—as a wedding gift to one of his friends among the 'Ançar. Djebar's claim that Muhammad loves singing and singers undermines the Islamist claim that a woman's voice is a *awra* ("nakedness") that has to be concealed through veiling and seclusion.

In the chapters "Voice" and "She Who Said No to Médina," Fâtima is defined as "the well-cherished daughter who said 'No.'" "No," to the people of Médina. "No," all the time. "No," for six months, till she died.[123] After Muhammad's death, Fâtima was denied her father's inheritance, including her husband's right of succession. Whereas Alî was busy with the funeral, the Medinese appointed Abu Bakr as the first Caliph in Islam. When she protested, Abu Bakr told her that Muhammad once said: "We the Prophets, we do not leave inheritance."[124] Contesting his literal interpretation of the hadith, Fâtima argued that the hadith was about the gift of prophecy, not property. To Abu Bakr's literal interpretation, Fâtima opposes many others: "Seek the content of Fâtima because her content is mine";[125] "Fear what angers Fâtima because this will anger me!"[126] and "He who loves Fâtima my daughter loves me."[127] The rejection of Fâtima's interpretation stands not only for the disinheritance of the Muslim daughter but also for women's exclusion from the field of *ijtihad*. As Djebar puts it:

> Fâtima, the one dispossessed from her rights, the first one at the head of a long and interminable procession of daughters whose disinheritance by fact [as opposed to by law] was often practiced by brothers, uncles, even sons, was attempting to install herself as legitimate in order to hold back Islam's unbearable feminist revolution during the seventh century of the Christian era.[128]

The ensuing political strife between the descendants of Alî and the clan of Beni Umayya over Muhammad's legacy will lead in the end to the split between Sunni and Shi'i Islam. Whereas in Islamic tradition the cause of this split is the dispossession of Alî and his two sons Hassan and Hussein, Djebar represents the disinheritance of the daughter as the latent or repressed cause for the "Great *Fitna*," that is, the split between the Shi'ah and the Sunna. In her rereading of Tabari, Djebar is challenging not only the Abbasid Sunni narrative where inheritance is constructed as patrilineal, but also the Shi'i erasure of the daughters of Fâtima and Alî from Muhammad's legacy. At the same time, Djebar is departing from the Shi'i construction of Aïsha as Mu'awiya's coconspirator in the Great *Fitna*. Hence, Djebar's excavation of the House of the Prophet reveals that the first bloodshed between Muslims was not spilled by Aïsha as some of the Shi'is claim, but by the repression of the feminine.

In her feminist invention of the House of the Prophet, Djebar asserts that in the first years of Islam, there were no restrictions on the movement of Muhammad's wives and daughters. For instance, in the Battle of Uhud, Aïsha was a nurse. Some people could still vouch they saw "Aïsha, her ankle bracelets jingling, go back and forth to attend to the wounded and give them water."[129] Also, in the expedition to Taif, Muhammad "took with him two of his wives: [Um] Salama and Zeineb."[130] Women's freedom to circulate unveiled was lost after the story of the necklace, in which Aïsha stood accused of having an affair with Safwan Ibn al Mu'attal.[131] During the expedition against the Beni Mostaliq, Muhammad took with him Aïsha. In the morning as they were leaving, Aïsha remembered that she forgot her seashell necklace where she made her ablutions. She left to look for her necklace without lifting up the curtain of her palanquin. Thinking she was still inside, the caravan left without her. In the wilderness of the desert, she met Safwan Ibn al Mu'attal who helped her join the caravan.[132] Then, the rumors started about her alleged affair with Safwan. Whereas for Mernissi the Medinese Hypocrites[133] attacked the House of the Prophet because of Muhammad's opposition to slave-prostitution, Djebar constructs this incident as a patriarchal attempt to control and violate the female body through veiling and seclusion. Although God proved Aïsha's innocence and condemned the slanderers in the Sura of Lights (33:59), in the same Sura, Muhammad's wives were ordered to wear the hijab. Commenting on the dire consequences of this incident, Djebar observes: "The ordeal of this long month of doubt; after [this] each woman of the Community of Islam, for fourteen centuries, will have in turn to pay her share: a day, a year, or sometimes the whole of her married life!"[134] Because of this lingering doubt, the body of the "Muslim woman" has to be cloistered. In *Loin de Médine*, even though God spoke in favor of Aïsha, there is still doubt lingering over the reputation of the "Muslim woman." As Sonia Lee puts it, "Not even God's word can bend the law of Médina."[135] In her rereading of the affair of the necklace, Djebar not only reinscribes cloistering and veiling as signs of *isyan*, that is, defiance of God's will, but also presents them "as a political technology of the body."[136]

The imposition of seclusion[137] on Muhammad's wives illustrates not only how patriarchal power relations "invest," and "subjugate" the female body, but also how they turn it "into an object of knowledge."[138] This complicity between knowledge and patriarchal power is manifest in the production of the "Muslim woman's" body as *fitna* ("chaos") and her voice as *awra* ("nakedness"). The doubt that still exists in the "Muslim man's" heart over Aïsha's/the "Muslim woman's" purity reveals a more "profound" subjugation than the "Muslim woman's" corporeal confinement: it is the patriarchal subjugation of the Muslim man's "soul."[139] For Djebar, patriarchy is a relation of power that dominates not only women's bodies, but also men's souls. Reversing the Christian and Sufi metaphor where the soul is trapped in the physical body, Djebar shows à la Foucault that it is "the soul [that imprisons] the body."[140]

As a response to Islamic patriarchy's control of the female body, in *Loin de Médine* Djebar strategically rewrites the feminine within the sacred and resexualizes the body of the Mothers of the Believers. Revisiting Tabari's account of the last days of Muhammad's life, Djebar states that it is in the "embrace"[141] of Aïsha that the Prophet has chosen to die. And that it was in Aïsha's bedroom[142] that he was buried. Djebar insists that there were no walls between the Mosque and the headquarters of Muhammad's wives.[143] As a sexualized and female space, Aïsha's bedroom is reconstructed by Djebar as the locus of the sacred. Because he is too weak to clean his own teeth, Aïsha used to chew the *souak* with her own teeth before giving it to him. "'In that last moment,' said Aïsha proudly in one of her hadiths, 'we exchanged our salivas.'"[144] Against Islamic traditional construction of Aïsha as the asexual Mother of the Believers, Djebar focuses on the life of sterility and sexual repression she has been condemned to at the age of nineteen: "She was only nineteen when Muhammad died. . . . Her honorific title [Mother of the Believers] caused her to be devoted to a life of sterility."[145]

The torture of a satirist-poetess unnamed by Tabari at the hands of Muhadjir Ibn Umayya, the executioner, provides another example of how power relations invest the female body. In the Wars of the Ridda,[146] a poetess from the tribe of Beni Kinda wrote many satires against the Prophet. As a punishment, Muhadjir pulled out her teeth and cut off her hands:

> She does not breathe, she doesn't utter one scream. "Why my teeth?" She wonders, her head spinning, about to faint. . . . As she falls down, she understands: her voice will whistle, her voice will squeak, her voice won't sing any of the stanzas, which at that very moment, were pressing up in her heart, as warm as the blood she was spitting.[147]

In describing the brutal unvoicing and dismembering of the poetess's hands, Djebar seeks to illustrate Islamic patriarchy's control of the female body through the exercise of brutal force. The predicament of the poetess of Beni Kinda provides a perfect example of what Foucault calls the "political technology of the body,"[148] which aims at dominating and subjugating the body through the brute exercise of power. Djebar's grafting of this poetess's tongue turns out to be a prophetic reading of Algeria's present, where intellectual women and men are having their throats cut by the FIS and the GIA.

In response to the claim of the FIS leaders that a woman's place is the home, Djebar reconstructs the women of Islam on the road. In the "avant-propos," Djebar states that she wants to resurrect "women in movement," whether "geographically or symbolically."[149] Djebar's women are either by themselves in the desert, in exile, runaways, in the Mosque, fighting in battles, or wandering in the desert. For instance, Um Salama, the fifth spouse of Muhammad, used to go to the Safa Hill where she would cry over the departure of her first husband Abu Salama, who migrated with Muhammad to Medina.[150] Likewise, Muhammad's daughter Ruqayya and two of his wives, Um Habiba and Sawda, exiled themselves to Abyssinia to avoid the persecution of Quraish.[151] Running away from her family in Mecca, the fifteen-year-old Um Kulthum—the half-sister of 'Uthman Ibn 'Affan, the third Caliph in Islam—crossed the desert to join the Muslims in Medina.[152]

It was also in the public and sacred space of the Mosque that Fâtima claimed her father's legacy. Addressing the Medinese during prayer time, she defiantly reprimands them for witnessing her disinheritance in silence: "Tell me O Believers, what has delayed you from coming to my rescue? What takes possession of you to the extent that you watch calmly my dispossession?" "Have you forgotten the Prophet when he said that every person is perpetuated in his children?"[153]

Also, in her resurrection of Esma the daughter of Abu Bakr—who is known in Islamic tradition "as the woman with the two belts" because she used to smuggle food to a cave where Muhammad and her father were hiding from Quraish—Djebar mentions that Esma was pregnant and crossing the desert by herself when she was bringing food to the Prophet and Abu Bakr.[154] In "'Filles d'Agar,' Dit-Elle," Djebar brings Ishmael's mother back to life. Abandoned by Abraham, Hagar—whose Arabic name *Hajar*[155] means "exile"—is the first woman in Arabia to be denied the legitimate/sacred line. Looking for water, the wandering mother goes back and forth between Safa and Merwa. Almost "naked," Hagar is dancing and praying under the watchful "eye of the sun." Her body seems possessed by an "uncontrollable" and frenetic dance. To appease the "fever" of the "maternal body,"[156] Ishmael digs into the sand and the holy water of zem-zem springs forth. In this scene, Djebar is reinscribing the female body into one of the founding myths of Islam and Arab nationalism. After all, it is the movement of the female body that millions of Muslim pilgrims celebrate during al Hajj when they reenact Hagar's wanderings between Safa and Merwa. In this rereading of the story of Hagar, the holy water of zem-zem is rewritten as an amniotic miracle that comes about through Hagar's prayer through her body. This reinscription of the amniotic into the heart of the sacred is also evident in Djebar's presentation of the venerated persona of Aïsha[157] as *ma' al hayat* (the water of life).[158] By including the female body as part of the foundational myths of Islam, Djebar, like the mystical poet Ibn Arabi, is emphasizing the feminine dimension of the divine. Thus, in Djebar's novel, female agency is located not only on the level of the symbolic—through her engagement with the patriarchal discourse of Islamic orthodoxy—but also on the transgressive site of the semiotic. The novel ends with a symphony of women's voices and on a note that emphasizes the presymbolic relation between mother and child (Hagar and Ishmael) and the redemptive powers of the holy water of zem-zem, which Djebar reconstructs along the lines of what Kristeva calls the "chora."

The House of the Prophet and the Question of Female Agency in *Loin de Médine* and *The Satanic Verses*

In contrast with the death of the author in Foucault's archaeology, Djebar presents herself as a committed author. In her interview with Zimra, Djebar confesses that her novel is triggered not only by the street riots in Algeria but also by the controversy following the publication of Rushdie's book. Djebar's statement that her novel is a response to "the Rushdie affair"[159] invites us to compare Djebar's feminist invention of the House of the Prophet with Salman Rushdie's postmodern construction of this Muslim symbolic in *The Satanic Verses*.

One of the central issues that led to the fatwa[160] against Rushdie is his desacralization of the House of the Prophet. In his postmodern rejection of all monologic discourses, Rushdie undermines the religious authority of this Muslim symbolic by turning it into a brothel. In *The Satanic Verses*, the House of the Prophet is sullied morally and spatially. On the ethical level, the twelve whores working in The Curtain (name of the brothel) have assumed the identities of the twelve wives of the Prophet. Under the prostitutes' insistence, Baal, the pimp-poet, accepts the role of "husband of the wives of the former businessman, Mahound."[161] Spatially, it is as an antimosque or anti-Qaaba that Rushdie presents The Curtain:

So in the Prophet's absence, the men of *Jahiliya* flocked to The Curtain, which experienced a three hundred per cent increase in business. For obvious reasons it was not politic to form a queue in the street, and so many days a line of men curled around the innermost courtyard of the brothel, rotation about its centrally positioned Fountain of Love much as pilgrims rotated for other reasons around the ancient Black Stone.[162]

In *The Satanic Verses*, the equation between the House of the Prophet (sacred) and The Curtain (profane) has a double function: first to denounce women's seclusion and second to undermine the institution of polygamy. In Arabic the word *hijab* means not only "curtain," but also "veil." In the Qur'an, the Sura of the Veil (33:53) designates the House of the Prophet as a space that is visually and morally forbidden.[163] Before dying Muhammad has decreed that none of his wives should marry after him. As a result, the "Mothers of the Believers" became sexually forbidden (*muharramat*). Today, this Sura is often quoted to justify women's seclusion and oppression. According to Mernissi, the wearing of the veil in early Islam was the demarcating line between free women and slaves. It is the Hypocrites who pushed Muhammad to accept "a slave-holding solution"[164] whereby only free women had to wear the veil and thus be protected; the slaves remained unveiled and subjected to *ta'arrudh*, that is, "sexual abuse." From this perspective, Rushdie's equation between the brothel and the House of the Prophet implies that far from being a sign of respectability, the veil stands for the degradation of Muslim women; both the secluded woman and the prostitute are enslaved by patriarchy.

The parallel between the House of the Prophet and The Curtain reveals a parallel between the institution of polygamy in Islam and the practice of polyandry in *Jahiliya*. When he returns to *Jahiliya*, Mahound closes down the brothels and arrests the prostitutes[165] because they are committing what the Qur'an views as *zina* ("fornication"), a sin punishable by flogging if the "culprit" is single, and stoning to death if married. If Islamic tradition constructs *Jahiliya* as preculture and dismisses it as a period of moral decadence, it is because women's sexual self-determination was asserted in pre-Islamic Arabia. All those practices in which a woman could choose more than one sexual partner are condemned by orthodox Islam as *zina*. Therefore, in equating polygamy (The House of the Prophet) with polyandry (The Curtain), Rushdie is deconstructing the institution of polygamy by basing it on *zina*.

Whereas in *The Satanic Verses* Rushdie creates a dichotomy between a monologic and male-centered Islam and a polyphonic gender-transgressive *Jahiliya*, Djebar creates the feminine and the polyphonic at the heart of the sacred. In resurrecting the daughters of Islam, Djebar is creating a symphony of transgressive female voices inside the house of Islam. Rushdie's novel raises many questions in regard to Muslim women's agency: What are the political consequences of undermining Islamic patriarchy by announcing his feminist agenda from the transgressive site of the *Jahiliya*, which is dismissed by most Muslims today as a profane pre-Islamic period? How can the "Muslim woman" speak in a text that already erases her agency within Islamic history?

While not denying the subversive power of irony, my reading of the history of Islamic feminism makes me question the universalist claim under Bakhtin's[166] assertion that parody is the only effective site of critique. For Muslim activists, Rushdie's postmodern equation of the House of the Prophet with a brothel as well as his erasure of female agency within an Islamic symbolic order are quite disabling. In locating female agency within the *Jahiliya* period, Rushdie tends to endorse the Islamist narrative, where the issue of women's rights is quickly dismissed as either *kufr*/*jahl*[167] ("un-Islamic"/"ignorance") or an instance of cultural imperialism. For instance, in the year 2000, Saïd Saadi, the Moroccan secretary of state for social affairs, was accused of apostasy because he wanted to reform the *Mudawanna* (the Moroccan family/Shari'a laws).[168] Because he received some financial aid from the United Nations Development Program to carry out his reforms, the Islamists inside Le Parti de la Justice et du Développement (PJD) launched a campaign throughout the country denouncing his reformist project as a new form of "colonization financed by the Occident and the Zionists."[169]

It is also from a Western perspective that Rushdie embraces the social and sexual rights of Muslim women. In *The Satanic Verses*, Rushdie traces women's seclusion to the birth of Islam. However, recent research indicates that veiling was apparently not introduced into Arabia by Muhammad, but already existed among the Jewish and Christian populations. As Ahmed has demonstrated in *Women and Gender in Islam*, Islam had brought no radical changes to the existing lifestyles in Arabia. It is Rushdie's position as outsider that makes him see Islamic civilization as disbarred from that pre-Islamic Middle Eastern past. In contrast with Rushdie, who leaves no room for the agency of the Muslim women in his self-Orientalist construction of the House of the Prophet, Djebar reinvents this powerful symbolic from the exclusive standpoint of Muslim women.[170]

In his postmodern reading of the Prophet's House, Rushdie creates a scene where a fifteen-year-old prostitute tries to turn on the grocer Musa by assuming the identity of Muhammad's young wife Aïsha:

> The fifteen-year-old whispered something in the grocer's ear. At once a light began to shine in his eyes. "Tell me everything," he begged. "Your childhood, your favorite toys, Solomon's-horses and the rest, tell me how you played the tam-

bourine and the Prophet came to watch." She told him, and then he asked about her deflowering at the age of twelve, and she told him that, and afterwards he paid double the normal fee, because "it's been the best time of my life." "We'll have to be careful of heart conditions," the Madam said to Baal [the pimp].[171]

Blotting out the historical context where early marriages were a common practice among Muslims, Jews and Christians alike, Rushdie reconstructs Muhammad's love for his young wife Aïsha as a pedophiliac desire, leaving no chance for Muslim women to empower themselves by claiming Muhammad's legendary love for his wife. In contrast, in *Loin de Médine*, Djebar displays a subversive reading of Aïsha's childhood. The fairy tales that Aïsha used to tell her playmates are turned into a symbol of women's voices.[172] Aïsha was also on the swing playing with her friends when her Mother Um Rouman calls her in to dress her up for her betrothal to Muhammad.[173] The mother's call for her daughter to go inside—as Arab customs required the brides to do—marks the beginning of Aïsha's seclusion once she has become a wife, and later the Mother of the Believers. This leads us to examine the dichotomies Djebar creates between spiritual and political Islam on the one hand and Arab culture and Islam on the other hand.

Beyond the Ghetto of Cultural Essentialism

Like Mernissi and Ahmed, Djebar creates a strategic dichotomy between political/orthodox Islam and spiritual Islam. Whereas 'Umar, Khalid Ibn al Walid, and Muhadjir stand for a political and violent Islam, Muhammad and Abu Bakr represent a more tolerant and humane version of Islam. Upon hearing what happened to the poetess of Beni Kinda, Abu Bakr sends a letter of reprimand to Muhadjir in which he states: "Neither a Muslim nor an apostate, she could, by the poetic power which is her weapon, choose whomever she wanted to be a victim of her satires."[174] It is on the basis of this spiritual Islam that Muslim feminists like Mernissi, Djebar, and Ahmed build their feminist agendas in Morocco, Algerian, and Egypt.

In contrast with her other novels (notably, *Fantasia* and *A Sister to Scheherazade*), in *Loin de Médine* Djebar presents an essentialized and homogenous view of Arab culture. Commenting on the consequences of the story of Aïsha's necklace, she observes: "Each woman of the Community of Islam, for fourteen centuries, will have [to pay the price] a day, a year, or sometimes the whole of her married life!"[175] Djebar's "mummification"[176] of Arab culture might stem out of a position of political insurgency against the patriarchal oppression of women in pre–Civil War Algeria; however, by ignoring the heterogeneity of Islamic tradition, and its constant change through time, Djebar not only dehistoricizes Arabic/Islamic culture but also falls within the ahistorical time of the Islamist/Orientalist narrative. Djebar's ambivalence embodies the "doubled vision"[177] of the feminist subject, who, according to de Lauretis, inhabits a space that is inside/outside the dominant ideology.

Djebar's construction of the "Muslim woman" as voice and her presentation of the veil as a fixed negative signifier also recall the logocentric division between silence/speech in French *écriture féminine*. Even more problematic are Djebar's views on the Arabic language. In her interview with Zimra, Djebar states that she refuses to translate *Loin de Médine* into Arabic and that she will allow its translation only if she can "work right along with the translators."[178] Because of the religious conventions in Arabic, which put a lot of constraints on the author, she prefers to write in the secular and "neutral mode" of the French language.[179] Comparing Arabic to the status of Latin in medieval and early Renaissance Europe, she declares that "a staid conformism has bogged the language down for the past five or seven centuries. A comparable situation prevailed in Europe, say, when people had to write in Latin, Europe's religious language."[180] Djebar's statement that conformism has impeded the growth of Arabic displays a colonial or Eurocentric evolutionary understanding of time and culture. In equating the status of Arabic with the status of Latin in medieval Europe, Djebar places herself into the "panoptical time" of French culture and language and relegates Arabic language and culture into what McClintock calls "an anachronistic"[181] space.

Djebar's assertion that Arabic has not grown over the last "five or seven centuries"[182] implies that Arabic as a language and culture is dead. This also betrays an implicit view that associates backwardness and religious fanaticism with Arab culture and language. Explaining why she refuses to translate her book into Arabic, she states:

> Non-Arabic people must realize that, wherever or whoever one is, even if one is a communist writer writing a communist piece, as soon as one writes or pronounces the name of the Prophet, one must immediately follow it with the requisite formula, "may the blessing of God be with him." Were one to omit the formula, it would immediately signify hostility to Islam.[183]

Two questions surface here: If she refuses to translate her book into Arabic, then how can Djebar, the politically committed writer,[184] reach out for the millions of Algerian women who are either illiterate or speak only Arabic? Second, if Arabic is such an oppressive language, does this mean that the "Arab Muslim woman" can speak only in English and French? Djebar's statement that Arabic has not grown for seven centuries would seem to ignore the transgressive Arabic literature written by Maghrebian women such as al Naluti's *Tamas* (*Borderline*) and Ahlam Mostghanemi's *Memory in the Flesh* (Algeria).

In separating Islam from Arab culture, feminists like Ahmed, Mernissi, and Djebar, are not simply defending Islam against the Christian West, they are also sending back to the West its recently constructed dichotomy between an oppressive Arab culture and a tolerant and spiritual Islam. In the 1990s, the U.S. politics of cultural liberalism made it politically incorrect to slander Muslims and Islam; Arabic as language and culture, however, remained somewhat suspect. Since the events of 11 September 2001, this binarism, which was initially situated on the left, has been recuperated and deployed by the nationalistic war propaganda to justify the war against Afghanistan: "We are not attacking Islam. Islam is a peaceful religion! We are not after the Afghan people! We are after the members of al Qaeda, those foreign Arab terrorists who have destroyed Afghanistan."

What the excavation of the House of the Prophet reveals is that the script of Islamic domesticity has never been static or monolithic: it gets changed and reinvented for various ideological reasons. The four works examined in this chapter reveal four different or contradictory scripts of Islamic domesticity. The novels of Rushdie and Djebar in particular reveal two contradictory models of domesticity: Whereas in *The Satanic Verses* the "Muslim woman" is produced as powerless and degraded by Islam, in *Loin de Médine* she is educated, eloquent, powerful, and free.

Focusing on the enunciative sites from which these discourses on the House of the Prophet are made, this chapter reveals that it is the privilege of education and gender that made al Ma'arri reject the House of the Prophet as a technology of power and live isolated from the rest of the world. Similarly, al Naluti's emphasis on the class conflict in her reinvention of the House of the Prophet reflects her double marginalization as a left-wing gendered subaltern. In contrast with Rushdie, who erases Muslim women's agency through his reproduction of the universalism underlying Bakhtin's gender-blind theory of parody, Djebar engages in the dominant discourse of Islamic orthodoxy and claims the House of the Prophet for the purpose of advancing women's rights in Algerian society. Eventually, just as the "Muslim woman" has been reinvented for various political reasons, the model of domesticity underlying the House of the Prophet—as an enclosed space and a political economy with direct implications on the lives of Muslim women—has always been an unstable yet powerful signifier.

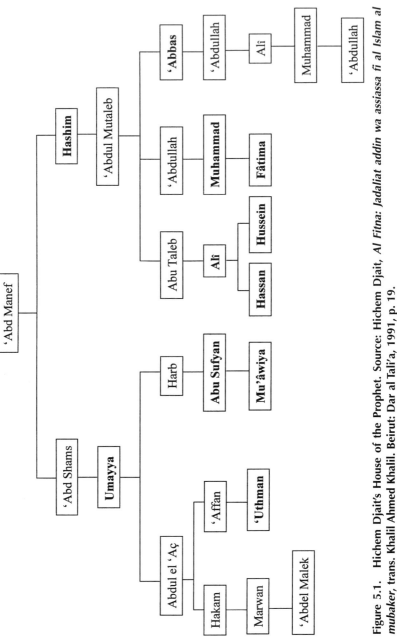

**Figure 5.1. Hichem Djait's House of the Prophet. Source: Hichem Djait, *Al Fitna: Jadaliat addin wa assiassa fi al Islam al mubaker*, trans. Khalil Ahmed Khalil. Beirut: Dar al Tali'a, 1991, p. 19.
*Names in bold are in the original Arabic text.**

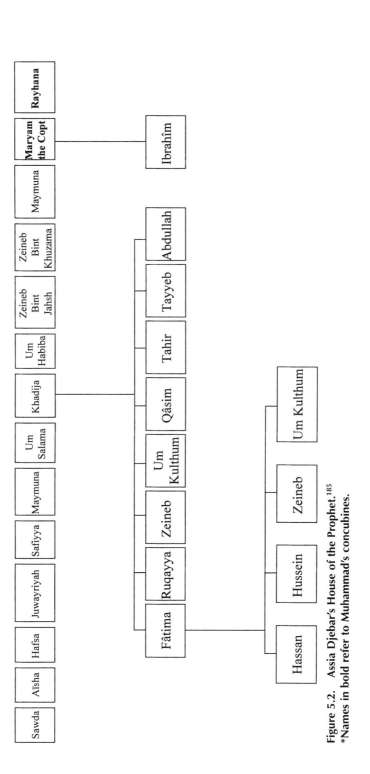

Figure 5.2. Assia Djebar's House of the Prophet.[185]
*Names in bold refer to Muhammad's concubines.

NOTES

1. Foucault, *Discipline and Punish: The Birth of the Prison*, trans. Alan Sheridan (New York: Pantheon Books, 1977), 24.

2. Foucault, *Archaeology of Knowledge*, 145.

3. Foucault, *Archaeology of Knowledge*, 148.

4. Mentioned by the Muslim historian Abou Ja'far Muhammad ibn Jarîr Ibn Yazid Tabari, *Chronique* 5/6, trans. Hermann Zontenberg (Paris: Sindbad, 1989), 42–43.
Unless indicated otherwise, all of the quotations from Tabari and Djebar from the French are mine. I am also using the conventional English spelling of the Arabic proper names.

5. Alî Ibn Abi Talib (656–61) is Muhammad's son-in-law and the fourth Caliph in Islam.

6. For more information see Tabari's *Chronique* 5/6.

7. Moshe Sharon, "*Ahl al Bayt*—People of the House," *Jerusalem Studies in Arabic and Islam* 18 (1986): 172.

8. Quoted by Sharon, "*Ahl al Bayt*," 177.

9. Charles André Julien, *Histoire de l'Afrique du Nord: Des origines à 1830*, vol. 2, 4th ed. (Tunis: Cérès, 2003), 54.

10. Julien, *Histoire de l'Afrique du Nord*, 71–78.

11. Julien, *Histoire de l'Afrique du Nord*, 330–33.

12. Djait, *Al Fitna: Jadaliat addin wa assiassa fi al Islam al mubaker*, trans. Khalil Ahmed Khalil (Beirut: Dar al Tali'a, 1991), 20.

13. The Qaaba is also called *beit Ibrahim* (the House of Abraham). In the Qur'an, Abraham and his son Ishmael are referred to as *ahl al beit* (2:125, 127; 3:97; 5:2, 97; 8:35; 22:26, 29, 33; 52:4, etc.). Mentioned by Sharon, "*Ahl al Bayt*," 171.

14. Sharon, "*Ahl al Bayt*," 181.

15. In tracing the genealogy of the Prophet, Djait erases all female progenitors and progeny of Muhammad. Djait's exclusive focus on the male descendants of Beni Hashim and Beni Umayya (the two branches of 'Abd Manaf) betrays a male bias that excludes Muslim women not only from the House of Islam but also from history and politics. See Djait's family tree in *Al Fitna*, 19.

16. Tahar K. al Garradi, *The Image of Al Ma'arri as an Infidel among Medieval and Modern Critics* (Ph.D. diss., University of Utah, 1987), 12.

17. Al Ma'arri, *Risalatu ul ghufran: A Divine Comedy*, ed. Kamil Kilany, trans. G. Blackenbury (Cairo: Al Maaref Printing and Publishing House, 1943), 7.
Unless otherwise indicated, all the quotations and references in English are from Blackenbury's translation of *The Epistle of Forgiveness*. The translations from al Ma'arri's *Luzumiat* are all mine.

18. Edouard Amin al Bustani, *Abu al Alâ al Ma'arri: Muta'amil fi al dhulumat* (Beirut: Beit al hikma, 1989), 19–21.

19. *Risalat al Ghufran* is believed to have been written in 1032, but there is no unanimous agreement over this matter among Arab critics. The dates for the other works are not known. I am deliberately translating al Ma'arri's *Risalat al Ghufran* as *The Epistle of Forgiveness* to emphasize its creative and epistolary aspects, which are lost in Black-

enbury's Eurocentric classification of the work in the Dantean divine comedy, a literary genre that appeared in Italy almost two centuries after Al Ma'arri's death.

20. The Arabic names are spelled exactly as they were in Brackenbury's 1943 translation.

21. Al Ma'arri, *Luzum maa laa yalzam: Luzumiat* II (Beirut: Dar Sadr, n.p.), 472.

22. According to Ahmed, the Abbasids imported the custom of secluding women from Byzantium and Iran. See *Women and Gender in Islam*, 55.

23. Al Ma'arri, *A Divine Comedy*, 83.

24. Al Ma'arri, *A Divine Comedy*, 84.

25. Al Ma'arri, A Divine Comedy, 84.

26. In Shi'i literature, both Maryam and Fâtima "are mentioned together as the matrons of paradise and Fâtima is even called *al-batûl* ('the virgin'), a most appropriate description for the female figure in the Islamic version of the Holy Family," in Sharon, "*Ahl al Bayt*," 173.

27. He is the son of Alî, son of Hussein, son of Alî, son of Abu Talib killed by the Abbasids. He appears in al Ma'arri's Paradise with his brother Muhammad along the side of their grandfather Hussein.

28. Tabari, *Chronique* 5/6, 264–65.

29. It is possible that the absence of Hassan is caused by his abdication in the year 41 of the Hijra. After his murder, his children and all the family of Alî went to live in Mecca with Hussein, who came to symbolize what is left of Muhammad's household. See Tabari, *Chronique* 5/6, 14 and 17.

30. According to Tabari, Ruqayya married 'Uthman after she was repudiated by her husband 'Utba, son of Abu Lahab (Muhammad's uncle), who fought against the new religion his nephew brought to Arabia. Muhammad's other daughter Zeineb was also repudiated by Abul el 'Aç because she was the daughter of Muhammad. However, because he loved her, her husband later converted to Islam, and took back his wife. See Tabari, *Chronique* 3, 172–73. 'Uthman was at first married to Ruqayya. After her death, and at Muhammad's request, he married her sister Um Kulthum.

31. Al Ma'arri, *A Divine Comedy*, 83.

32. Tabari, *Chronique* 5/6, 344.

33. Tabari, *Chronique* 5/6, 344–45.

34. Tabari, *Chronique* 5/6, 346–47.

35. Al Ma'arri, *A Divine Comedy*, 84.

36. I shall return to the story of the necklace more fully in the section on Djebar. For more information on this alleged affair, see Tabari, *Chronique* 3, 237–39.

37. Al Ma'arri, *A Divine Comedy*, 66.

38. The word *fitna* also means power of seduction.

39. Tabari, *Chronique* 5/6, 17.

40. There is no unanimous agreement among Muslim scholars over the exact number of Muhammad's wives. Most of them, however, mention the following: Sawda (daughter of Zama'a), Aïsha (daughter of Abu Bakr), Hafsa (daughter of 'Umar), Zeineb (daughter of Khuzama), Um Salama (daughter of Abu Umayya, son of Moghira, his cousin), Zeineb bint Jahsh (divorced by his adoptive son Zaid), Juwayriyah (daughter of 'Harith. From the tribe of Beni Mostaliq), Um Habiba (daughter of Abu Sufyan.), Maymuna (his cousin), Safiyya (a Jewish woman he married after his expedition to Khaybar).

He also took two concubines: Maryam the Copt (she was given to him as a gift by Mo-qauqas. She became the mother of Ibrahîm) and Rayhana (a captive from the Beni Quraizha).

41. Al Ma'arri, *A Divine Comedy*, 84.

42. See al Bustani, 117–18.

43. Al Ma'arri, *Luzumiat* II, 81.

44. Al Ma'arri, *Luzumiat* I, 196, 298.

45. Al Ma'arri, *Luzumiat* I, 63.

46. In his *Luzumiat*, al Ma'arri's misogyny is undeniable. "Castration," he says, "is better than marriage" (II: 47). To keep at bay women's evil, he advises men to teach them "home spinning, weaving, and let aside writing and reading" (I: 63). However, to present al Ma'arri as the epitome of Abbasid misogyny is a one sided reading of his oeuvre, for there are many passages in the *Luzumiat* and *The Epistle of Forgiveness* where he openly expresses his sympathy toward women. His ambivalent attitude to-ward women has to do with his pessimistic view toward life and mankind in general. It is "woman" as the symbol of life and procreation that he has issues with. Address-ing *al dunia* ("life")—which is gendered as female in Arabic—he writes: "Were you my wife I would divorce thee, but you are my mother, how can I escape thee?" (II: 148) This love/hate relationship is also clear in another verse where he describes him-self as a dog barking over the rotten corpse of life: "Dogs gathering or barking over a corpse, and perhaps am I the meanest of them all" (I: 114).

47. Al Ma'arri, *Luzumiat* II, 140.

48. Ahmed, *Women and Gender in Islam*, 66.

49. Al Ma'arri, *Luzumiat* I, 228.

50. Al Ma'arri, *A Divine Comedy*, 75.

51. Al Ma'arri, *A Divine Comedy*, 77.

52. Al Ma'arri, *A Divine Comedy*, 80.

53. Al Ma'arri, *A Divine Comedy*, 82.

54. Al Ma'arri, *A Divine Comedy*, 82–83.

55. Al Ma'arri, *A Divine Comedy*, 85.

56. Al Ma'arri, *A Divine Comedy*, 85.

57. Al Ma'arri, *A Divine Comedy*, 87.

58. Al Ma'arri, *A Divine Comedy*, 29.

59. Al Ma'arri, *A Divine Comedy*, 28.

60. Al Ma'arri, *A Divine Comedy*, 31.

61. Al Ma'arri, *A Divine Comedy*, 103.

62. Al Ma'arri, *A Divine Comedy*, 136.

63. Al Garradi, *The Image of Al Ma'arri*, 52.

64. It is reported that the Fâtimid Caliph al Mustansir Billah offered him financial assistance, but al Ma'arri refused. Mentioned in al Garradi, *The Image of Al Ma'arri*, 39. As the Egyptian scholar Taha Husayn put it: "Glory and benefit were never inac-cessible to him, but he resisted their temptation," *Tajdid dhikra Abi al Alâ* (Cairo: Dar al Ma'arif, 1963), 155.

65. Al Garradi, *The Image of Al Ma'arri*, 53.

66. Al Ma'arri, *Luzumiat*, I: 66.

67. Al Bustani, *Abu al Alâ al Ma'arri*, 24.

68. Foucault, *Discipline and Punish,* 27.

69. Quoted in Taha Husayn, *Ma'a Abî al Alâ fi Sijnih* (Cairo: Dar al ma'aarif bi misr, 1971), 19.

70. Foucault, *Discipline and Punish*, 23.

71. Foucault, *Discipline and Punish*, 30.

72. Foucault, *Discipline and Punish*, 16.

73. Even though the play was produced for Tunisian school-theater, it has never been published. I am using here a copy of the original script that Arusiyya al Naluti has written for the play.

74. Arusiyya al Naluti, interview by Lamia Ben Youssef, tape recording. Tunis, Tunisia, 17 July 2001.

75. Al Naluti, *Al Tawba* (Unpublished manuscript, 1992), 4: 19.

76. Al Naluti, Al Tawba, 6: 23.

77. Mohanty, "Under Western Eyes," 204.

78. Personal interview, 17 July 2001.

79. Djebar's only book in Arabic.

80. The Civil War broke out between the Algerian government and the Islamist groups because of the failure of the FLN socialist regime, high unemployment, and the severe economic crisis in the 1980s, all of which led in the end to the victory of the FIS (Islamic Salvation Front) in the municipal elections of June 1990. The government arrested the FIS leaders Abbas Madani and Ali Ben Hadj. Even though they were freed shortly thereafter, Madani and Ben Hadj were once more sentenced to twelve years in prison in July 1992 because the FIS was about to win the legislative elections. In December 1991, the government cancelled the elections claiming that the FIS was committing electoral fraud. Both the Kabileans and women of Algeria took to the streets because they were afraid that the establishment of an Islamic state would lead to the Arabization of the country and the loss of women's rights. Then the armed conflict between the government and the Islamists broke out. President Chadhli Ben Jedid resigned and was replaced by Muhammad Boudhiaf, a former FLN leader, who despite his political reforms, was assassinated on 29 June 1992. The bloodshed continued till Abdelaziz Bouteflika won the presidential elections in 1999 and negotiated a truce with the FIS. The government will grant total amnesty for the Islamists provided that they surrender and give up their weapons. The FIS leaders, notably its leader Abbas Madani, accepted his plan. But the GIA (Armed Islamic Group), an extremist faction that broke away from the FIS, is still continuing the war against the "apostate regime" of Bouteflika.

81. Assia Djebar Interview, "'When the Past Answers Our Present': Assia Djebar Talks About *Loin de Médine*," Clarisse Zimra, *Callaloo* 16, no. 1 (Winter 1993): 126.

82. Djebar, "When the Past Answers Our Present," 119.

83. Djebar, "When the Past Answers Our Present," 122–23.

84. Zimra's translation in "Not So Far from Medina: Assia Djebar Charts Islam's 'Insupportable Feminist Revolution,'" *World Literature Today* 70, no. 4 (Autumn 1996): 827.

85. "She never invents: she recreates." These words originally describe Aïsha's power of hadith transmission in *Loin de Médine* (300).

86. Foucault, *The Archaeology of Knowledge*, 3.

87. Djebar, *Loin de Médine*, 5.

88. Foucault, *Archaeology of Knowledge*, 151.

89. Foucault, *Archaeology of Knowledge*, 152.

90. Djebar, "When the Past Answers our Present," 122.

91. Quoted in Zimra, "Not So Far From Médina," 825.

92. Djebar, *Loin de Médine*, 20.

93. Djebar, *Loin de Médine*, 24.

94. Djebar, *Loin de Médine*, 28.

95. For more information on the feminist revisions and deployment of the hadith by Mernissi, Djebar, and Driss Charaïbi, see George Lang's essay: "Jihad, *Ijtihad*, and Other Dialogical Wars in *La Mère du Printemps*, *Le Harem Politique*, and *Loin de Médine*," in Kenneth Harrow's *The Marabout & the Muse* (Portsmouth: Heinemann, 1996).

96. Foucault, *Archaeology of Knowledge*, 56.

97. As *um walad* or "mother of child," a Muslim woman who is a slave can no longer be sold according to Islamic law.

98. For Foucault, "archaeology tries to define not the thoughts, representations, images, themes, preoccupations, that are concealed or revealed in discourses; but those discourses themselves, those discourses as practices obeying certain rules. . . . [Archaeology] does not seek another, better-hidden discourse. It refuses to be allegorical." *Archaeology of Knowledge*, 138–39.

99. Djebar, *Loin de Médine*, 187.

100. Djebar, *Loin de Médine*, 178.

101. "*Ijtihad*" means creative intellectual effort in matters of religion. It is usually perceived as a male prerogative by Islamic orthodoxy, in Djebar, *Loin de Médine*, 6.

102. Djebar, *Loin de Médine*, 7.

103. Djebar, *Loin de Médine*, 210.

104. Djebar, *Loin de Médine*, 71.

105. Djebar, *Loin de Médine*, 57.

106. Djebar, *Loin de Médine*, 69.

107. Djebar, *Loin de Médine*, 74.

108. Djebar, *Loin de Médine*, 58.

109. Djebar, *Loin de Médine*, 61.

110. Tabari, *Chronique* 3, 173.

111. Djebar, *Loin de Médine*, 62.

112. Djebar, *Loin de Médine*, 211.

113. Djebar, *Loin de Médine*, 128.

114. Djebar, *Loin de Médine*, 275

115. Djebar, *Loin de Médine*, 271.

116. Djebar, *Loin de Médine*, 272.

117. In his early days in Medina, Muhammad was married to Aïsha and Sawda only.

118. Djebar, *Loin de Médine*, 271.

119. Djebar, *Loin de Médine*, 292.

120. Djebar, *Loin de Médine*, 259.

121. Djebar, *Loin de Médine*, 126.

122. Djebar, *Loin de Médine*, 125–26.

123. Djebar, *Loin de Médine*, 67.

124. Djebar, *Loin de Médine*, 79.

125. Djebar, *Loin de Médine*, 83.

126. Djebar, *Loin de Médine*, 85.

127. Djebar, *Loin de Médine*, 84.

128. Djebar, *Loin de Médine*, 79.

129. Djebar, *Loin de Médine*, 279.

130. Djebar, *Loin de Médine*, 201.

131. Aïsha was accused of having an affair with Safwan Ibn al Mu'attal, and not Soffyan Ibn al Mu'attal as Djebar wrote in *Loin de Médine*.

132. Djebar, *Loin de Médine*, 278.

133. Mernissi, *The Veil and the Male Elite*, 131–80.

134. Djebar, *Loin de Médine*, 288.

135. Lee, "Daughters of Hagar: Daughters of Muhammad," *The Marabout and the Muse: New Approaches to Islam in African Literature*, ed. Kenneth Harrow, 60.

136. Foucault, *Discipline and Punish*, 30.

137. Mernissi claims that it is political Islam—that is, the strong male opposition to Muhammad's egalitarian project—which led to the imposition of the veil and thus to the failure of spiritual Islam. See *The Veil and the Male Elite*, 179.

138. Foucault, *Discipline and Punish*, 28.

139. Even though Foucault does not talk about gender and Islamic patriarchy in *Discipline and Punish*, I find his theory of power as a technology of the soul quite useful in analyzing and understanding the mechanism through which Islamic patriarchy maintains its grip on both men and women. See Foucault, *Discipline and Punish*, 30.

140. Foucault, *Discipline and Punish*, 30.

141. Djebar, *Loin de Médine*, 289.

142. Djebar, *Loin de Médine*, 13.

143. During Muhammad's lifetime, there was no separation between the apartments of his wives and the Mosque. It was the Umayyad who destroyed the apartments of Muhammad's wives and turned everything into a Mosque. Ibn Saad recounts this hadith: "'Ata al Khurasani heard 'Umar Ibn Abi Anas say: I saw the apartments of the wives of the Apostle of Allah, may Allah bless him, constructed of palm leaf stalks and on their doors were curtains of black hair (wool). I was present when the epistle of al Walid Ibn 'Abdl al Malik was read containing the order to take the apartments of the wives of the Prophet, may Allah bless him, within the Mosque of the Apostle of Allah, may Allah bless him. I never saw (people) [more weeping] than on that day." Ibn Saad's *Tabaqat* 1, trans. Moinul Haq and H. K. Ghanzanfar (Karachi: Pakistan Historical Society, 1967), 593.

144. Djebar, *Loin de Médine*, 11.

145. Djebar, *Loin de Médine*, 43.

146. In the Islamic master narrative, the Wars of the *Ridda* are those wars waged by the first Caliph Abu Bakr against the Arabian tribes who declared apostasy and rebelled against Islam after Muhammad's death.

147. Djebar, *Loin de Médine*, 121.

148. Foucault, *Discipline and Punish*, 26.

149. Djebar, *Loin de Médine*, 5.

150. Djebar, *Loin de Médine*, 53.

151. Djebar, *Loin de Médine*, 215.

152. Djebar, *Loin de Médine*, 159.

153. Djebar, *Loin de Médine*, 82.

154. Djebar, *Loin de Médine*, 51.

155. The word *hijra* ("immigration or exile") refers also to the Islamic calendar, which starts with the date of Muhammad's exile from Mecca to Medina.

156. Djebar, *Loin de Médine*, 302–3.

157. In Arabic, the verb *yarwi* (present tense) means both to "tell" and to "quench one's thirst." As storyteller or râwiya, Aïsha (whose name means "alive" in Arabic) embodies this duality between transmission/life or telling/birthing.

158. Djebar, *Loin de Médine*, 264.

159. Quoted in Djebar, "When the Past Answers Our Present," 123.

160. In February 1989, the Iranian leader Ayatollah Ruhollah Khomeini issued a fatwa or religious decree against the author and publishers of *The Satanic Verses* for blasphemy against Islam.

161. Rushdie, *The Satanic Verses* (Dover: The Consortium, 1988), 383.

162. Rushdie, *The Satanic Verses*, 381.

163. I am using here Mernissi's terminology in *The Veil and the Male Elite*, 93.

164. Mernissi, *The Veil and the Male Elite*, 178.

165. Mernissi, *The Veil and the Male Elite*, 390.

166. See "Carnival Ambivalence," *The Bakhtin Reader: Selected Writings of Bakhtin, Medvedev and Voloshinov*, ed. Pam Morris (London: Edward Arnold, 1994), 206–7.

167. In Arabic, both the words *jahl* and *jahiliya* signify ignorance. In the Islamic masternarrative, the pre-Islamic period called *Jahiliya* is constructed as a period of *jahl* ("ignorance") and preculture.

168. Saadi wanted to abolish polygamy and unilateral repudiation, impose divorce courts, and raise marriage age for women from fifteen to eighteen.

169. Benchemsi, "Maroc: minijupes contre tchadors," 36.

170. Djebar, "When the Past Answers Our Present," 124.

171. Rushdie, *The Satanic Verses*, 380.

172. Djebar, *Loin de Médine*, 300.

173. Djebar, *Loin de Médine*, 270.

174. Djebar, *Loin de Médine*, 122–23.

175. Djebar, *Loin de Médine*, 288.

176. Bhabha, *The Location of Culture*, 78.

177. De Lauretis, *Technologies of Gender*, 10.

178. Djebar, "When the Past Answers Our Present," 127.

179. Djebar, "When the Past Answers Our Present," 129.

180. Djebar, "When the Past Answers Our Present," 129.

181. McClintock, *Imperial Leather*, 36–37.

182. Djebar, "When the Past Answers Our Present," 129.

183. Djebar, "When the Past Answers Our Present," 129.

184. Djebar talks about her political commitment in her interview with Zimra, "When the Past Answers our Present," 122–23.

185. Only a few of Muhammad's women actually lived together as co-wives. For example, during his marriage to Khadija, Muhammad maintained a monogamous relationship.

Conclusion

As this book demonstrates, the "Muslim woman" as a fixed category has always been invented and produced to serve various political ends, whether in the discourse of Maghrebian feminism, Female Orientalism, French psychoanalytic feminism, or Tunisian nationalism. In the writings of the two Muslim activists, Mernissi and Djebar, the early "Muslim woman" is strategically reinvented as eloquent, free, and independent to show that gender equality rather than being a Western import is at the heart of Islam's egalitarian project. The invention of the "Muslim woman" from this theological framework is important because as Azza Karam puts it: "[Any] feminism that does not justify itself within Islam is bound to be rejected by the rest of society, and is therefore self-defeating."[1] The second chapter examined how the "Muslim woman" has been instrumental in defining Eberhardt's European identity as the Other Within. In this sense, the Maghreb, with its geography and women, becomes a technology of space where European identity is projected and negotiated. Chapter 3 argues that the construction of the veiled "Muslim woman" as silent and voiceless in French psychoanalytic feminism derives not only from the primacy of the specular in Western metaphysics but also from the same Orientalist impulse that Said discusses in *Orientalism*. In the writings of Bourguiba and al Haddad, the invention of the "Tunisian woman" as the mother of the nation and symbol of the *umma* is part of the Tunisian republican nationalist project, which, to resist the French politics of assimilation, has claimed an authentic precolonial Islamic identity. The last chapter argues that the House of the Prophet has always been deployed as a technology of power. Because it is constantly being claimed by the hegemonic and marginal groups, the script of domesticity underlying this powerful Muslim symbolic has always been plural and unstable. While in the right-wing Islamic narrative Muhammad's wives and daughter appear veiled and secluded, they are reinvented as free and independent in Djebar's feminist re-creation of this sacred Muslim symbolic.

In the nineteenth-century American play *Mohammed, the Arabian Prophet: A Tragedy, in Five Acts* (1850), the House of the Prophet is reinvented from a male-centered point of view, even though its author, George H. Miles,[2] was claiming to tell "the naked history"[3] about Muhammad. Whereas Khadija and Fâtima are constructed after the Victorian model of the angel in the house, Aïsha is presented as a castrating figure because of her excessive sexuality and transgression of women's traditional gender roles. In this American tragedy, the faithful and dutiful wife Khadija dies "victim of excessive love"[4] for her "Lord" and master Muhammad. In contrast with her eloquence and re-bellion in the narratives of Tabari and Djebar, the nineteenth-century American Fâtima is silent, except in those passages where she expresses her love and loyalty to her husband Alî. When Muhammad asks her to leave her husband, whom he wrongly suspects of having an affair with Aïsha, Fâtima refuses to listen to her father: she is a wife first, a daughter second.[5]

When Aïsha first appears on the stage, she is introduced through her excessive Oriental sexuality:

> Her blushing cheeks, made fragrant by her breath,
>   Excels the Persian rose,—her ruby lips
>   Mother unblemished pearls,—upon her brow
>   Aspiring scorn divided empire holds
>   With soft attraction, and with every motion
>   New graces flutter round her buoyant limbs.[6]

As soon as Muhammad sees her, he becomes her slave. 'Umar, who witnesses the scene, says: "She'll govern him!"[7] At the Battle of Badr, Fâtima stays at home after bidding farewell to her husband Alî. In contrast with this model of patriarchal womanhood, Aïsha, the "enchantress,"[8] is "reveling in blood"[9] and fighting alongside Alî in the male space of the battlefield. Whenever the Muslim fighters forsake "hope" and "[embrace] despair," she would encourage men to go back to battle. In the field of war as well as love, Aïsha's manliness constitutes a threat to Alî's masculinity:

> In the field of Beder, she follows Ali:
>   What a pretty sword!
>   How clean and bright!—bright as thy glancing
>   Eye.
>   Ali: Bright!—would it were—
>   Ayes. What?—out with it!
>   Ali. Red!

Red as thy coral lips!—Forgive me, lady,
But I have promised to achieve a name,
Ere night, or perish; and the day declines,
And hark!—the contest burns, —whilst I, chained here,
When every Moslem wields a dripping blade,
Flourish this gewgaw![10]

The conflation of the sexual and war imagery in this passage points to Alî's fear of emasculation. Whereas the other men's blades are burning and dripping in blood, Alî feels "chained" and effeminized by Aïsha's flirtatious behavior. As her eyes linger on his sword/phallic weapon, he stops fighting and starts stuttering. Reflecting the nineteenth-century patriarchal construction of war as the symbol of masculinity, Alî runs away from Aïsha to make a "name" for himself at the Battle of Badr.

In this American tragedy, Muhammad's tragic flaw seems to be his inability to control his home, especially his young wife's sexuality. He dies poisoned by Aïsha and Sufyan. When Alî and Fâtima come to his rescue it is too late, the poison has taken its effect. Muhammad asks forgiveness from Alî and gives him the Caliphate instead of 'Umar. As a punishment for Aïsha, Muhammad declares that none of his wives shall be permitted to marry again after his death: "Henceforth my soul must be thy only love."[11] Miles adds a footnote in the end of his play explaining that this "punishment so far as concerned Aïsha, was rather formal than real."[12]

In this American invention of the House of the Prophet, Muhammad's affection for Aïsha—which is being reclaimed today by Muslim feminists to advance women's rights—is dismissed and condemned as lust. When Muhammad asks Aïsha why she betrayed him after he had "showered" her with "the wealth of ransomed cities,"[13] she reiterates the medieval Christian construction of Muhammad as a lascivious false prophet:

When man discards
The pearl of chastity, he cannot ask
His wife to treasure it. Ay, make the earth
As full of houris as thy Paradise!
Free all thy slaves, and marry all their wives!
Indulge thy lust—

Published two years after the 1848 Seneca Falls Convention, this play reflects not only medieval Christianity's construction of Muhammad, but more important, it betrays patriarchal anxieties over women's roles in nineteenth-century America. In this American tragedy, rather than reflecting a more historically realistic understanding of Muhammad's household, the House of the Prophet—as a domestic space and a political economy—was instrumental in redefining and negotiating gender identity in nineteenth-century America. If this play won the prize for best American tragedy in 1849, it is because it hit some sensitive nerve at home, especially after first-wave feminists like Elizabeth Cady Stanton and Lucretia Mott started their campaign for women's suffrage and the reform of the marital and property laws, which bound American women to an inferior legal status.

In a like manner, the shift in Bourguiba's construction of the veil as the symbol of Islamic identity in French colonial Tunisia to his postcolonial construction of a mythical Punic past where women were unveiled shows that cultures, rather than being fixed, are always invented and negotiated in the present. Bourguiba's ability to claim a past and a future for the Tunisian woman suggests that rather than culture being a given, it is primarily a relation of power. Similarly, the three fatwas against Rushdie, al Haddad, and Bourguiba's PSC and the public humiliation of al Ma'arri at the literary salon of al Murtadha and his seclusion afterward for almost half a century show that patriarchy is a relation of power that subjugates and dominates both men and women.

As this book demonstrates, the discourses on the "Muslim woman" are never monolithic: they are different and contradictory at times, depending on the configurations of power involved in the process of enunciation. In contrast with Said's claim that in the imperial field "race takes precedence over both class and gender,"[14] I have shown in this work that class and gender are as important as race in the construction of the "Muslim woman" in the fields of female Orientalism, nationalism, and feminism. This work also shows that no discourse is situated outside power; power visits even the dominated like Al Ma'arri, Djebar, Eberhardt, and al Haddad.

This examination of the process of enunciation invites a further investigation of the reception of these discourses. Who is reading the books by Djebar, Mernissi, and Rushdie? Why is al Ma'arri almost unknown in the West? Why didn't *Loin de Médine*, despite its English translation, achieve in the West the notoriety of Rushdie's *The Satanic Verses* or even Djebar's other novels like *A Sister to Scheherazade* or *Women of Algiers*? Of all the rich medieval Arabic literature, why is *The Arabian Nights* almost the only Arabian medieval tale taught in American universities?

First, neither an exotic Oriental text like *The Arabian Nights*, an autobiography of an oppressed Muslim woman, nor a tale about Oriental despotism and tyranny, *The Epistle of Forgiveness*, continues to remain absent from all discussions of Arabic culture and literature in the Western academia, despite the latter's English translation in 1943.[15] Second, as Said puts it, one way of denying a people their humanity is to deny them literary creativity; hence the scarcity of critical material and courses containing Arabic literary master-pieces in American universities. Suzanne Pinkney Stetkevych's "Intoxication and Immortality: Wine and Associated Imagery in al Ma'arri's Garden" is one of the very few articles written in English about *The Epistle of Forgiveness.* Even though Stetkevych focuses exclusively on al Ma'arri's mingling of Qur'anic and pre-Islamic poetic imagery—with almost no reference to the theme of homosexuality in this Abbassid divine comedy—her article was published in a book called *Homoeroticism in Classical Arabic Literature.*[16]

The popularity of Rushdie's *The Satanic Verses* and Djebar's *A Sister to Scheherazade* or *Women of Algiers* cannot be dissociated from the commodi-fication of Islamic Otherness in the Western world. The publication of works written by postcolonial writers does not mean that the relations between the "First" and "Third World" have become less hegemonic. This unequal bal-ance of power manifests itself in the choice of books and authors published and studied in Western academia. While Rushdie's book brought millions of dollars to its publishers, there was no demand for Djebar's feminist construc-tion of the House of the Prophet as a model of gender equality in *Loin de Mé-dine.* The English translation, *Far from Madina* (1994), went out of print and Quartet Books declared bankruptcy.

It is also this same marketability of the "Muslim woman" that Laura Bush was trying to sell on her 17 November 2001 radio address. Justifying the war under the cloak of feminism, she stated, "the fight against terrorism is also a fight for the rights and dignity of women." Because of the deployment of the U.S. military in Afghanistan, Muslim "women are no longer imprisoned in their homes. They can listen to music and teach their daughters without fear of punishment." Laura Bush's claim that this war is fought on behalf of Mus-lim women and children raises many questions: Why did the suffering of the "Muslim woman" in Afghanistan become visible only after 11 September 2001?

Even though numerous feminist films were produced on the situation of Afghan women before September 11—*Shroud of Silence* (1996); *Women with Faces: Inside Free Afghanistan* (1998); *Kabul Kabul* (2000); and *Behind the Veil: Afghan Women under Fundamentalism* (2001) released just before the September 11 attacks—only Saira Shah's *Inside Afghanistan: Behind the Veil* was broadcast on CNN prior to the September tragedy (27 June 2001). After September 11, all of these films and documentary reports, to which the big networks had previously preferred the Lewinsky soap opera, came back from their shelves to answer the call of war propaganda. Like material goods, the suffering of Afghan women is produced according to the law of supply and demand. When no American lives are lost, these films, as well as the voices of RAWA (The Revolutionary Association of the Women of Afghanistan), the

Feminist Majority, and WAPHA (Women's Alliance for Peace and Human Rights in Afghanistan), remain frozen and shelved. In the aftermath of 11 September 2001, the big networks released these horrible images of Afghan women wearing the burqa and shot in the head in Kabul's public stadium to give an aura of legitimacy to the war against Afghanistan.

In this war, which is supposed to be fought on her behalf, the "Afghan woman" finds herself triply silenced: by the Taliban regime, American Christian patriarchy, and the complicity of some American women with the U.S. capitalist hegemony. The image of the veiled "Afghan woman" executed in Kabul stadium illustrates what Spivak calls "epistemic violence." Because of the visual and moral binarism underlying the meaning of the veil in Western epistemology, the veil can only be read as a negative signifier. In this scene, the "Afghan woman" is silenced not only by the Taliban regime but also by the big networks. What is emphasized in this scene is the "Afghan woman's" helplessness and suffering, not her agency; for to be punished, this anonymous woman veiled in black must have resisted and broken one of the misogynist rules of the Taliban regime that forbids women to work, to read and write, to leave home unescorted, to wear perfume, to watch from windows, and so forth. In contrast with the Western image of the Madonna with child, the suffering "Afghan woman" is shown in the process of being beaten, standing by herself in the middle of ruins, shot in the head, standing like a specter in her black burqa, but almost never with her children. The absence of children suggests that the only thing these women need to be free is to remove the veil, which is the symbol of their Islamic Otherness. All other similarities with Western women are erased. The question that begs an answer is: Who is consuming the suffering of the "Afghan woman"?

Besides justifying the war, and perhaps more important than securing the support of the Muslim world in the U.S. war against al Qaeda and the Taliban regime, this so-called noble and feminist war is for the purpose of reassuring American women about the threat of losing their rights in the rise of the Christian right-wing groups to power. The frequently broadcast scene of the monstrous "Muslim man" shooting the veiled and helpless "Muslim woman" in the head serves as an instrument of ideological manipulation aimed at relieving American women's anxieties over the loss of their sexual rights. Commenting on the production of the "Third World" in Western media, the feminist postcolonial critic Roy Chow observes:

> The King Kong syndrome . . . is the cross-cultural syndrome in which the "Third World," as the site of the "raw" material that is "monstrosity," is produced for the surplus-value of spectacle, entertainment, and spiritual enrichment for the "First World." The intensive productivity of the Western newspapers leads to the establishment of clear boundaries. Locked behind the bars of our television screens,

we become repelled by what is happening "over there," in a way that confirms the customary view, in the U.S. at least, that ideology exists only in the "other" (anti-U.S.) country.[17]

Therefore, the brutal stadium scene not only serves the U.S. war propaganda but also functions as an instrument of patriarchal intimidation at home: as long as we don't shoot you in the head, be happy that we are shooting off only your reproductive rights. This commodification of the Muslim Other is also ideologically instrumental in eliding the class struggle in America and in making everyone believe that they are free and enjoying the blessings of freedom and democracy.

In the same radio address, Laura Bush observes that "Muslims around the world have condemned the brutal degradation of women and children by the Taliban regime." Laura Bush's statement reflects a shift in America's construction of Islam from "the straightjacket of Islam" rhetoric of the 1970s and 1980s to the "hijackers of Islam" discourse of the late 1990s, which postulates a division between the Good and the Evil Muslim, and sometimes between peaceful Islam and an eternally violent and misogynist Arab culture. This does not mean, however, that the demonization of Islam is over; the two discourses coexist. Commenting on the 11 September 2001 attack, Chris Matthews, the news anchor for MSNBC, stated that the terrorists attacked America because they were jealous of the liberty and freedom American women had. "They hate us," he says, "because our culture teaches us to respect women," while theirs teaches them to veil and seclude their women. On Fox News, Pat Robertson has also stated that the hijackers committed suicide because their religion teaches them violence and promises them *houris* in heaven.

While deploying the language of feminism and secular humanism in its war abroad, the U.S. patriarchal establishment is ironically waging a war against the feminist and civil rights groups at home. In the October Concert for New York, Senator Hillary Rodham Clinton was booed by the male audience consisting primarily of the male establishment of firefighters and policemen of New York City. The demonization of Hillary Rodham Clinton in the American conservative mass media did not start with the September 11 tragedy, but with the feminist backlash that struck America in the 1990s. Because she did not accept a secondary position behind Bill Clinton's back, Hillary Rodham Clinton was accused of supporting the "Black Panthers," of destroying "capitalism" through her "welfare reform plans," and of conniving with Muslim terrorists. The demonization and construction of Hillary Rodham Clinton as a "power-starved consort" has two objectives: first to prevent her from participating in the presidential elections on her own right, and second, as Frances E. Dolan argues, to disable and "curtail"[18] other women's efforts to have access to power.

THE TOMAHAWKS OF WESTERN CIVILIZATION: RETHINKING RACE, GENDER, AND CULTURE IN THE AFGHAN WAR

In the first weeks following the September 11 attack, all over the right-wing channels, especially Fox News, there was this sense that the highjackers had emasculated or raped America. Most of the news headlines were in the passive form: "America under attack," "Freedom under attack," "Democracy under attack." After the deployment of the American troops in Afghanistan, the masculinist-militarist discourse underscores a sense of rephallicization. The shift into the active voice underscores a sense of remasculinization: now, "America Strikes Back." In short, the war in Afghanistan has become a war between Islamic and Christian fundamentalist patriarchy: they have raped our democracy and freedom, it is payback time, let's penetrate their country and unveil/rape their women.

The narrative of America's moral innocence has to be viewed also in gendered terms. All over newspapers, freedom is presented as a little girl or a woman wearing the three colors of the Star Spangled Banner. EBay.com was even advertising a red, white, and blue bridal dress called Freedom. The September 11 hijackers raped the innocent/virgin America. To revenge their honor and protect their land/women against future attack, phallic/masculine Uncle Sam must hunt down the rapist and punish him. In this post–Cold War era, phallic America seeks to protect the effeminate values of freedom and democracy not only in the motherland but also abroad. The only superpower left, Uncle Sam vows to protect freedom/the female body of the nation all over the globe. In this new hegemonic world order, the body of America extends across the borders of the modern nation-state, to include remote and diverse areas such as North Korea, the Philippines, Indonesia, the Middle East, and central Asia.

This rephallicization of Uncle Sam is also inscribed in the shape, action, and the intimidating Indian names of the U.S. military arsenal. On the phallic Tomahawk cruise missiles, there were inscriptions such as "From the Firefighters of New York City," "This is from the World Trade Center," or "This is from Uncle Sam." Whereas Uncle Sam regained his manhood, the Taliban are running and hiding in caves like women. "Now, they know what it means to feel like a veiled woman!" The "hunting imagery" used by the military establishment and television anchors also reflects the manly character of the nationalistic rhetoric. In the Afghan war, Uncle Sam promises to "hunt down" and "smoke out" the terrorists who are hiding in caves like "rabbits" and "rats." They are not "men enough to come out in daylight and face us." At times the war discourse takes a homoerotic turn as when the phallic bombs in an encounter of death and life "penetrate" the feminine symbol of the cave to meet the emasculated male Muslim Other.

Not least significant are the intimidating Indian names the U.S. Department of Defense has given to its assault helicopters: the "Apache," the "Iroquois," the "Cayuse," the "Black Hawk," "Kiowa," and "Comanche" assault helicopters, not to mention of course the "Tomahawk" cruise missile. These Indian names not only illustrate a latent racism toward Native Americans, but more important a split within the American rhetoric of civilization and freedom. In contrast with al Qaeda's violence, which is "illegitimate" because the bin Laden terrorist network does not belong to a nation-state, the U.S. war on Afghanistan, which is a state-sanctioned form of violence, is seen as lawful and even "civilized."[19] However, even though the war is presented as a legitimate kind of violence, by giving Indian names to its weapons of death and destruction, the U.S. military establishment is projecting onto other ethnic groups their own violence, as they are unable or perhaps unwilling to admit the fact that violence is the hidden face of civilization. The Indian names given to the U.S. weapons, ironically, relocate this neocolonial Manichaeism within the heart of America's project "Enduring Freedom" or "Infinite Justice," that is, within the axis of good. Once the pioneers have exterminated the threatening Indian savages, the eradicated race is now safe enough to be symbolic for a "good"[20] cause.

Before 11 September 2001, neither the Algerian Civil War, nor the oppression of women in Afghanistan, Sudan, and Rwanda aroused the interest of the American mass media. In *Time* magazine, for instance, there was only one article on Algeria. The article, "Drumbeat of Death,"[21] shows two horrible pictures of an Algerian morgue and a murdered young boy. When the Taliban came to power in 1996, and at a time when reports were already coming from RAWA (Revolutionary Association of Women of Afghanistan) about the oppressive rules the Taliban imposed on women, Anthony Spaeth writes in the 14 October 1996 issue of *Time*: "For its part the U.S. cares little who governs Afghanistan as long as it is governed and stable—and not led by radical Muslims."[22] The article raises many questions: Who is a radical Muslim? Or, rather, when does one become a radical Muslim? Why aren't these "tough Islamic laws" in Afghanistan alarming to Spaeth?

Spaeth's article on Afghanistan in *Time* presents the violence against women in Afghanistan as part of the "austere" Islamic culture. In the name of cultural relativism, we must remain silent and accept these atrocities committed against women. As Bronwyn Winter superbly argues, "the two superficially contradictory" discourses of "Orientalism" and "multiculturalism" are not as contradictory as they appear: "They are different faces of the same essentializing and dehistoricizing of Muslim culture."[23]

During the visit of the Taliban official Sayed Rahmatuallah Hashimi to Washington, D.C., on 20 March 2001, Afghan women and men as well as members of the American feminist majority picketed outside the buildings of the U.S. government with "signs reading, 'Save Afghan Women,' 'Give me Liberty,' 'Stop Gender Apartheid' and 'US Don't Recognize the Taliban.'"[24] According to Joanne Stato and Karla Mantilla, one of the possible reasons for the meeting is to stabilize the region "in order to clear the way for a proposed oil pipeline from Central Asia, through Afghanistan, to Pakistan. The pipeline project has been planned by American companies since the mid 1990s."[25] As usual, the American big networks did not bother to cover the Afghan women's protest in Washington. Thus, because the American giant oil companies[26] were making billions of dollars, and because those who were being slaughtered were not American citizens, and because the Taliban Sunni rulers were the sworn enemies of the Shi'i regime in Teheran, the Taliban could only be constructed by Spaeth as a moderate Islamic regime, its atrocities justified and hidden under the banner of Islamic culture.

Over the last two years, besides starvation and diseases, tons of bombs have been dropped on civilians, and the plight of Afghan women was slowly dropped by the mass media and the U.S. administration. The interim government of Afghanistan has included two women in its thirty cabinet positions, but this symbolic political inclusion was of no consequence. Women need food, clean water, medical supplies, and education for their children, not symbolic political representation. Upon hearing that the Northern Alliance stopped women from marching twice in Kabul after the fall of the Taliban regime, Ari Fleischer "dismissively" responded: "We're talking about different regions of the world where people have their own cultures and histories. . . . We cannot dictate every day's events to everybody all throughout Afghanistan."[27] In similar fashion to the Taliban and other ultra Orthodox Islamic groups, "culture" emerges in the discourse of Fleischer as an excuse to deny Muslim women their rights. In 2002, the U.S. administration blocked the $134 million humanitarian aid intended to Afghanistan in the Supplemental Appropriations Act. Only $2.5 million was approved for the new Ministry of Women's Affairs in Afghanistan. So far, the United States has given them only $120,000, justifying the cut by the economic crisis in the United States.[28] Fleischer's comments provide the sharpest criticism of the U.S. feminist adventure in Central Asia. Whereas initially a dichotomy was created between a spiritual and tolerant Islam and an oppressive patriarchal Eastern culture, in the final chapter of the war, Islam and Eastern patriarchal cultures are strategically reconciled to deny Afghan women humanitarian aid, and in the bitterest of ironies, the "Muslim woman" is reunited—with the full blessing of the U.S. administration—to her austere Islamic culture and history.[29]

An overview of Afghan women's history shows that they have not always been subjected to an immemorial Islamic/Eastern patriarchal culture. In 1964, Afghanistan's Constitution gave basic rights to women, including the right to vote, to equal pay, and to education. In the 1950s, women made up almost half of the students, 70 percent of the teachers, 40 percent of doctors, and 30 percent of Afghanistan's civil servants.[30] It was Jimmy Carter who in 1979 ousted the socialist Afghan government under which Afghan women continued to enjoy these freedoms. This shows that rather than being inherited from the past or confined within particular geographical areas, cultures and civilizations are invented and maintained to express relations of power. Dismissing the conventional anthropological notion of culture as a set of social practices common to a special locale, nation, or tribe and also the defensive discourses produced by many Muslim scholars after September 11 that there is a true Islamic culture/civilization as opposed to the fake one represented by the West or the 9/11 highjackers, *The Production of the Muslim Woman* asserts that there is no homogeneous or unifying Islamic culture/civilization. My argument here is that cultural identity, as Harrow puts it, emerges from "contestation," from setting oneself against another; hence, it cannot be "confined within established borders."[31] Rather than focusing on the cultural differences between East and West, this study seeks to investigate the production of culture, that is, the hegemonic position from which a discourse articulating cultural and gender difference is enunciated, and the processes through which cultures are imposed, invented, and transformed.

In separating Islam from Arab culture, feminists like Ahmed, Mernissi, and Djebar are not simply defending Islam against the Christian West, they are also sending back to the West its recently constructed dichotomy between an oppressive Arab culture and a tolerant and spiritual Islam. In the 1990s, the U.S. politics of cultural liberalism made it politically incorrect to slander Muslims and Islam; Arabic as language and culture, however, remained somewhat suspect. Since the events of 11 September 2001, this binarism, which was initially situated on the left, has been recuperated and deployed by the nationalistic war propaganda to justify the war against Afghanistan: "We are not attacking Islam. Islam is a peaceful religion! We are not after the Afghan people! We are after the members of al Qaeda, those foreign Arab terrorists who have destroyed Afghanistan."

The Afghan war also shows that patriarchy is a relation of power that governs both sexes, not just women. The Taliban regime imposed restrictive rules not only on women but also on men. They had to follow a certain dress code, keep a beard, not listen to music, and so forth. For Afghan women, the complicity of Western feminism with corporate America is as oppressive as the Taliban regime.

In her 26 March 1999 "Women's Rights Address" in Tunis, Hillary Rodham Clinton also addressed the issue of violence against women in Algeria and Afghanistan. However, these beautiful feminist sentiments were of no political consequences for the women of Algeria and Afghanistan. The First Lady's feminist concern for her oppressed "Muslim sister" has been silenced by Hillary Rodham Clinton, the politician, who is too enmeshed with corporate America to take any action to stop the atrocities against women in Algeria and Afghanistan. It is equally hard to believe Madeleine Albright's concern for the plight of the "Muslim woman" after declaring on 12 May 1996 on *60 Minutes* that the sanctions against Iraq would be sustained at any price, even the lives of over half a million Iraqi children. This shows that patriarchy is to be redefined in terms of power, not gender.

THE PRODUCTION OF THE IRAQI "MUSLIM WOMAN"

In contrast with its "feminist crusade" in Afghanistan, the U.S. war machine deployed the trope of Eastern despotism, not feminism, to justify its invasion of Iraq. Once the "butcher of Baghdad" is out of the game, and once the liberator's dream of being received with flowers has vanished, the American administration resorts to refashioning the old trope of colonial feminism to justify its illegitimate occupation of Iraq. Faced with a majority of Iraqi Shi'is, the United States has created a strategic binarism this time, not between Islam and Oriental culture as in the Afghan war propaganda, but between civility or secularism and religious tyranny. This binarism is apparent in Paul Bremer's promise to oppose any attempt to make the Shari'a law the backbone of the future Iraqi Constitution and in Daniel Serwer's[32] vision of a civil society in Iraq:

> After more than three decades of Saddam Hussein's brutal dictatorship, a motivated and educated Iraqi citizenry is enjoying political pluralism, and diverse groups and elements of Iraqi society have been quick to flourish in the post-war environment. Innumerable newspapers and political parties have surfaced. But extremists of several types are seeking to impose their agendas on a deeply traumatized society. Iraqi democracy cannot be successful without a vigorous and home-grown civil society composed of nongovernmental organizations (NGOs), schools, business and industry, and others.[33]

While resisting multiculturalism and secularism at home, the current U.S. administration is ironically prescribing them as the condition for the emergence of any free and democratic society in the Middle East. In his statement regarding the WTC and Pentagon attacks, Pat Robertson blames—in bin

Laden fashion—feminists, secularism, and the civil libertarians for the attack against America. In this dangerous phase of evangelical imperialism, the Christian radical right has appropriated the slogans of American "civil libertarians" to launch their Armageddon against the Empire of the Beast. While on the domestic level, the Christian Coalition is fighting the separation between state and religion in education and all levels of government, in Iraq, the U.S. administration has transformed the language of the American left into a weapon to prevent the Shi'i majority from having access to power.

In Iraq, women worked as lawyers and university teachers as early as the 1920s.[34] After the 1958 Revolution, Iraqi women enjoyed many rights, such as the abolition of polygamy and the right to inheritance, education, divorce, and child custody. In 1990, however, Saddam enacted a new code whereby Iraqi women lost most of their rights. Because many Iraqi men died in the war against Iran, Saddam reinstituted polygamy to protect the "sanctity and longetivity of the family."[35] Under Article 427 of the Iraqi Penal Code, a rapist can be released if he marries his victim. Under Article 409, sentences for honor killings do not exceed three years of prison.[36] Under Saddam's regime, hundreds of women were tortured, raped, videotaped, and even beheaded in front of their families because of their political/religious views or because their husbands or fathers fell out of Saddam's favor.[37]

In November 2003, a delegation of Iraqi women leaders came to Washington, D.C. to voice their concern about women's condition in war-torn Iraq. Dismissing Iraqi women's pressing concerns, the White House press release mentions that this delegation came to Washington to thank President Bush for liberating them from Saddam's tyranny:

> A delegation of 18 Iraqi women leaders came to Washington, DC November 9–19 to convey to U.S. policymakers and the American public their gratitude to the United States for liberating them from a brutal dictator. In a Nov. 17 meeting with President Bush, a member of the Iraqi Governing Council, Songul Chapouk, asked President Bush, " . . . [do] not leave us, please at this time . . . Iraqi people like your forces. Thank you very much [for liberating us]."[38]

The silencing and subordination of Iraqi women is most conspicuous in the brackets affixed to the already selected excerpts of Songul Chapouk's speech. Even though a civil engineer by training and a member of the Iraqi Governing Council, Chapouk appears here helpless and infantilized not just to prop up the White House's narrative of liberation, but more important to justify the ongoing U.S. occupation of Iraq. In opposition to their presentation as dependent minors in the White House press release, in an article from the 3 December 2003 *New York Times*, Chapouk and Raja Habib Khuzai[39] appear very critical of the sexist U.S. policies in Iraq. Even though women form 60 percent of the

Iraqi population, Chapouk and Khuzai are "the only women" the U.S. administration appointed "on the 25-member Governing Council." Advocating a quota system after the Swedish, Norwegian, Danish, and Rwandan models, Chapouk and Khuzai call for Iraqi women's participation in all branches of government, including the committee responsible for drafting the new Iraqi Constitution. Rather than begging for the fatherly protection of the American military establishment, Chapouk and Khuzai are demanding leadership roles in the reconstruction of Iraq: "The women of Iraq are ready, willing and able to lead," they assert. "Only by making certain that they participate can the United States and Iraqi Governing Council plant seeds of inclusion, security, democracy, and stability."[40]

On International Women's Day, Secretary of State Colin L. Powell[41] congratulated Secretary of Agriculture Ann M. Veneman and Deputy Secretary of Defense Paul Wolfowitz for putting an end to Saddam's "republic of fear" and announced "two important initiatives for Iraqi women: the Women's Democracy Initiative and the U.S.-Iraq Women's Network." Iraqi women's "self-help centers," he euphorically observed, are now "blossoming from Baghdad to Babylon, from Basra and beyond." Women are attending "workshops on constitutional laws, on the independent media, on human rights and on how to build non-governmental organizations, [and] a civil society." Powell's "bright" vision of Iraq remains hollow, not just because no Iraqi woman has been invited to the Washington Treaty Room where her future is being decided for her by Powell, Veneman, and Wolfowitz, but also because on the same day the latter are celebrating their feminist achievements in Iraq, Houzan Mahmoud, the U.K. representative of the Organization of Women's Freedom in Iraq,[42] writes that since the U.S. occupation, "rape, abduction, 'honor killings,' and domestic violence have become daily occurrences"[43] for Iraqi women. When the Iraqi Governing Council (IGC) "proposed replacing the secular law with Sharia," Iraqi women took to the streets, but their protest received no coverage by the Arab and American press. Denouncing the Iraqi puppet government, Mahmoud observes:

> The groups represented by the IGC are irrelevant to Iraqis' demands and desire for freedom. American support for Islamist groups through the IGC exposes U.S. hypocrisy. The parties in the IGC have no legitimacy, and have not been chosen by Iraqis.
> Iraq's lack of basic rights for women and the rise of political Islam are the result of three wars and the ongoing occupation. The only way out of this chaos is through the direct power of the real people of Iraq—the progressive, secular masses.[44]

The Organization of Women's Freedom in Iraq states that 400 Iraqi women were raped in Baghdad between April–August 2003.[45] The real numbers must be higher because many rape victims do not speak out because of shame and fear of honor killing. According to Lauren Sandler, there are now millions of Iraqi women under "house arrest"[46] because of Saddam's release of criminals before the American invasion, the "crumbling of Iraqi law enforcement," and the indifference of the Coalition Provisional Authority to the plight of Iraqi women. On 24 August 2003, the Organization of Women's Freedom in Iraq demonstrated in Baghdad "against the abduction and murder of women since the war."[47] And again, the protest was ignored by the Arab and Western media.

Refuting Bremer's colonial feminism and secular humanism, the Iraqi Women's League[48] maintains that Iraqi women suffered not only from the fascist rule of Saddam but also from the UN economic sanctions of the 1990s and the Anglo-American attack against the "cultural, economic, and national institutions" of Iraqi "civilization."[49] The so-called reconstruction of Iraq is nothing but a veil "for the daylight robbery of [Iraq's] natural resources." While 70 percent of Iraqis are unemployed,[50] "Bremer is handing out contracts worth billions of dollars" to "multinational"[51] firms like Bechtel and Halliburton.[52]

In her 17 November 2001 radio address, Laura Bush remarked that Americans have been holding their families closer since September 11, and invites all of them to "join [the Bush] family in working to insure that dignity and opportunity will be secured for all the women and children of Afghanistan."[53] In opposition to the ideal of the Christian family in America, the Iraqi "Muslim woman" is produced in the U.S. rhetoric of civil society as the dangerous *hommesse* American patriarchy fears at home, that is, as an individual with no family, no history, no husband, no father, no sons, no brothers, no daughters, no mothers, and no sisters. In contrast with Bremer's colonial secularism, the Iraqi women seek not solely freedom from the Shari'a law, but also freedom from want and violence against their families. Their pressing concerns are food, water, medical supply, personal security for themselves and their families, and especially economic opportunities that, for the time being, are being generously given away to multinational corporations.

At least 10,000 Iraqis[54] have died since the Anglo-American invasion of Iraq, most of whom were children who died either of malnutrition or the U.S. and U.K. bombing of civilian residential areas. Under Saddam's tyrannical rule, there were numerous accounts of "women and children tortured in front of their husbands and fathers."[55] Today, there are also frequent accounts of Iraqi mothers who have watched their "young children's heads severed from their bodies"[56] by the weapons of the Coalition. While American children go to school, receive welfare and medical care, play in Chuck E. Cheese, and take trips to Capitol Hill and the Smithsonian Museum to build an American civil society, Iraqi kids are robbed of their childhood, schools, history, future, and dismissed as "collateral damage."

The history of the Ba'ath Party and the wanton destruction of Iraq's museums, national archives, Islamic library, state buildings, and economic infrastructure[57] show that cultures get not only produced, but also transformed and terminated. Because Iraq is perceived as the cradle of human civilization, and because in his myth of Arab nationalism Saddam heavily invested in "archaeological research and restoration"[58] to create "a strong sense of Iraqiness," the U.S. army deliberately allowed the ransacking of Iraq's national heritage "as a kind of cultural 'shock and awe'"[59] to destroy the very foundation from which Arab nationalism derives its power and capacity for *ba'ath*, i.e., regeneration and renewal.[60]

In an article published originally in *Le Monde Diplomatique*, Jean Baudrillard observes that the 9/11 attacks stem not from the U.S. policy of "dispossession and exploitation," but from "the hatred felt by those to whom we have given everything, and who can give nothing in return."[61] The terrorist attacks on the World Trade Center and the Pentagon constitute a symbolic act of humiliation against "global power"[62] by those who have nothing to give back:

> The worst thing that can happen to global power is not for it to be attacked or destroyed but for it to be humiliated. Global power was humiliated on 11 September because the terrorists inflicted an injury that could not be inflicted on them in return. Reprisals are only physical retaliations, whereas global power had suffered a symbolic defeat. War can only respond to the terrorists' physical aggression, not to the challenge they represent. Their defiance can only be addressed by vengefully humiliating the "others" (but surely not by crushing them with bombs or by locking them up like dogs in detention cells in Guantanamo Bay).[63]

Reading the looting of Baghdad's museums through Baudrillard's concepts of "global interchange" and "vengeful humiliation," Stephen Smith writes that for the United States, "an Iraqi is interchangeable with someone from al-Qaeda, who is interchangeable with any Arab, Muslim, Asian etc."[64] In this respect, the destruction of Iraq's historical heritage stands as a "retaliatory" symbolic humiliation against this non-Western interchangeable Other. However, neither Baudrillard nor Smith studies the role of gender in that symbolic exchange of retaliatory violence. Because the 9/11 male Muslim highjackers have raped the female body of the American nation, the U.S. policy of "vengeful humiliation" is carried out not only against Iraq's historical heritage but also against Iraqi women's honor, which the American military patriarchy perceives as Iraqi men's property. Far from being carried out for the sole purpose of extracting information, the violence against Iraqi women through rape and sodomization[65] was intended as a sort of symbolic humiliation of the Islamic patriarchal order, which locates family honor in the control of women's sexuality. The sexual humiliation of the Iraqi prisoners by men and women in the American military establishment shows that patriarchy is a relation of power that is exercised not only by both sexes but also against both sexes. In this new world order, the body of the Iraqi "Muslim woman" turned into an object of global exchange between Iraqi and American patriarchy; the exploitation titles to her honor and dignity, like the Iraqi oil fields, have passed from Iraqi to American hands.

The September 2003 killing of Iraqi Councilmember 'Akila al Hashimi shows the precarious situation of Iraqi women activists, who came to be seen by the Iraqi resistance as collaborators with the American and British invaders. During the Arab Summit in Tunis, on 22 May 2004, the issue of women's rights in the Arab world was perceived as an American neoimperialist ploy to divert the Arab world's attention from the daily massacres of Palestinian and Iraqi men, women, and children.

To the question "can the Muslim woman speak?" I would like to say yes, despite the horrendous times we live in. However, I have reservations about essentializing and holding Muslim women's voices as the unique sign of their liberation. Perhaps more than their voice or their orgasm, what Muslim women want, for the time being, is access to water, food, education, and social and economic opportunities for themselves and their families. Today, what they want most is to keep their children and families alive and safe from the Anglo-American bombs. Rather than dismissing the discourse of human rights as an imperialist or neocolonial mode, I believe in the strategic use of humanism.[66] Even though universalism was and continues to be at the service of imperialism, this concept needs to be critiqued, reevaluated, and deployed as part of a "transnational"[67] or planetary humanism that is based on social, economic, and political justice.

The worldwide opposition to the current raging wars in Afghanistan, Iraq, and Sudan shows a return to global ethics. The political mobilization of left-wing Western academics since the tragic events of 9/11 invites us to revise Spivak's premise that "there is no space from which the sexed subaltern can speak"[68] and her dismissal of white feminism as "white men saving brown women from brown men." What is happening today shows us that "white and brown Western women and men on the left are in a better position than any brown person to save brown women and men from the white/brown women and men on the far right," and that these groups of white and brown people like Judith Butler, Noam Chomsky, Alice Walker, Kenneth Harrow, Robert Fisk, Michael Moore, David Corn, John Krieger, and many others can speak on behalf of brown people when these brown men and women, alike, have no "space" from which to speak in either world. These are, indeed, sad and bleak times for Arab intellectuals and activists who feel powerless and full of self-contempt. Many of them feel paralyzed and unable to take it to the streets; their souls dominated by the hegemonic power of the Arab state.

After the September tragedy, many American secular humanists and feminists stood up to condemn the violence against the Arab and Muslim communities in America. All over the country, there were conferences where men and women from all faiths were invited to explain the social, economic, and political reasons behind the September 11 attack. This interest in hearing and understanding the other side reflects a new awareness that whatever happens outside the U.S. national borders will sooner or later come back to haunt America at home. Both the increasingly sophisticated communication technologies and the global hegemony of Western-based multinational corporations have turned the world into a beehive where everything is connected and interdependent.

Since the launching of the U.S. military operations in Afghanistan and Iraq, a new phase of feminism appeared in America, Britain, and some parts of the Arab world, which I would describe as wom(b)anism. Akin to Walker's concept of womanism, wom(b)anism is a motherly humanism that appeals to all parents to stop the insane violence against our children. Organizations like MADRE and the Iraqi Women's League, which includes Muslim, Christian, and Jewish members, are all trying to mobilize international feminist organizations, military families, and academia against war. All over the United States and Europe, interfaith organizations of mothers are sprouting to put an end to this unjustified and illegitimate war in the Middle East. John Krieger's poem "The Children of Iraq Have Names" shows that wom(b)anism is not restricted to women and that we should not *lose amal* or hope for the sake of our children:

> What do you call the children of Iraq?
> Call them Omar, Mohamed, Fahad.
> Call them Marwa and Tiba.
> Call them by their names.
> But never call them statistics of war.
> Never call them collateral damage.[69]

NOTES

1. Karam, *Women, Islamists and the State: Contemporary Feminisms in Egypt* (London: MacMillan Press, 1998), 11.

2. The introductory "Advertisement" section of the play mentions that *Mohammed* won $1,000 for being the best "tragedy, in five acts" in 1849. In the preface to the play, Miles states that he was inspired by Goëthe' s and Voltaire's accounts of Muhammad (vi). Miles, *Mohammed, the Arabian Prophet: A Tragedy, in Five Acts* (Boston: Phillips, Sampson & Company, 1850), microfilm, Michigan State University Library, 1583 Reel 369.7.

3. Miles, *Mohammed*, v.

4. Miles, *Mohammed*, 43.

5. Miles, *Mohammed*, 142.

6. Miles, *Mohammed*, 89.

7. Miles, *Mohammed*, 90.

8. Miles, *Mohammed*, 122.

9. Miles, *Mohammed*, 110.

10. Miles, *Mohammed*, 103.

11. Miles, *Mohammed*, 150–52.

12. Miles, *Mohammed*, 166.

13. Miles, *Mohammed*, 126.

14. Quoted from "Media, Margins and Modernity: Raymond Williams and Edward Said," in the appendix to Raymond Williams, *The Politics of Modernism: Against the New Conformists* (London: Verso, 1989), 196–97.

15. According to al Garradi, the first English translation of al Ma'arri's garden was by Reynold Alleyne Nicholson, "The Risalatu'l Ghufran by Abu'l 'Alâ al Ma'arri," *Journal of the Royal Asiatic Society* (1900), 637–721. I was, however, unable to have access to this first translation. Only Blackenbury's 1943 translation was accessible to me.

16. J. W. Wright Jr. and Everett K. Rowson, eds., *Homoeroticism in Classical Arabic Literature* (New York: Columbia University Press, 1997). Stetkevytch's article mentions but does not study thoroughly the issue of homosexuality in al Ma'arri's garden.

17. Chow, "Violence in the Other Country," *Third World Women and the Politics of Feminism*, ed. Chandra Mohanty (Bloomington: Indiana University Press, 1991), 84.

18. Frances E. Dolan, "The Dawn of the Hillary Clinton Backlash: An Introduction," *Genders* 33 (2001): 5.

19. Judith Butler, "Guantanamo Limbo," *The Nation*, 1 April 2002, 24(N).

20. This argument was collected from my informal discussions with my friend and colleague Vicky Ben Rejeb, who works in the Department of English at l'Institut Supérieur des Langues de Tunis.

21. "Drumbeat of Death," *Time* 6 October 1997, 50–51.

22. Spaeth, "A Peace that Terrifies: Tough Islamic Laws Rule in Afghanistan and the U.S., Russian and Pakistan Warily Eye the Fundamentalists," *Time* 14 October 1996, 62.

23. Winter, "Fundamental Misunderstandings: Issues in Feminist Approaches to Islamism," *Journal of Women's History* 13, no. 1 (Spring 2001): 2.

24. Joanne Stato and Karla Mantilla, "Afghan Women Protest Taliban in Washington," *Off Our Backs* 31, no. 4 (1 April 2001): 1.

25. Stato and Mantilla, "Afghan Women," 2.

26. According to a 1998 issue of *Genders*, the giant oil company UNOCAL wanted to make a pipeline from Turkmenistan to Pakistan that goes through Afghanistan and needed the cooperation of the Taliban to stabilize the region against drug dealers, "Muslim terrorists," and Shi'i Iran. In their 21 December 1998 update on the situation in Afghanistan, the editorial staff of *Genders* wrote that "UNOCAL [had] pulled out of the pipeline deal for [the moment], but recently American mineral/mining exploration executives visited Taliban in Kabul looking for deals," Robert Schultheis, "Afghanistan's Forgotten Women," *Genders* 28 (1998): 3, available at www.genders.org/g27/g27_afw.html.

27. Smith, "Using Women's Rights to Sell Washington's War, 4.

28. Alison Raphael, "Women Call on White House to Restore Aid," 20 August 2002, available at www.converge.org.nz/pma/cra0799.htm (15 May 2004).

29. In contrast with the visibility of the "Afghan woman's" burqa, the masculine control of global economy remains hidden. The dichotomy between "Eastern" vs. "Western" culture makes invisible the "patriarchal roots/routs of global capitalism" (10). The Bin Laden empire is indeed "tied to multiple investments such as General Electric, Goldman-Sachs, Merrill Lynch, Microsoft, and Boeing," Zillah Eisenstein, "Feminisms in the Aftermath of September 11," *Social Text* 20, no. 3 (Fall 2002), available at www.ithaca.edu/faculty/eisenste/docs/htmldocs/socialtext2.htm (8 May 2003).

As a matter of fact, it is the CIA who created the Taliban and bin Laden during the Cold War. As journalist Ken Silverstein remarks: "Though Reagan called the rebels 'freedom fighters,' few within the government had any illusions about the forces that the United States was backing. The Mujahedin fighters espoused a radical brand of Islam—some commanders were known to have thrown acid in the faces of women who refused to wear the veil—and committed horrific human violations in their war against the Red Army," in "Blasts from the Past," *Salon*, 22 September 2001, available at http://dir.salon.com/news/feature/2001/09/22/blowback/index.html (7 May 2003).

30. These figures are from Smith's "Using Women's Rights to Sell Washington's War," 3.

31. Harrow, "Shibboleths in the Production of Culture," n.p.

32. He is the Director of Peace Operations in the U.S. Institute of Peace.

33. Daniel Serwer, "Building Civil Society: An Overlooked Aspect of Iraq's Reconstruction?" 31 July 2003, available at www.usip.org/newsmedia/releases/2003/0731_NBiraq.htm (25 May 2004).

34. Mentioned in Lauren Sandler, "Veiled Interests: Iraqi Women Debate Religion, Democracy, and Head Scarves. But is Anyone Listening?" *Boston Globe* 31 August 2003, available at http://psychoanalystsopposewar.org/resources_files/Veiled_Interests__Iraqi_Women_Debate.htm (25 May 2004).

35. Sandler, "Women Under Siege," 29 December 2003, available at www.thenation.com/doc.mhtml%3Fi=20031229&s=sandler (14 May 2004).

36. Sandler, "Veiled Interests," 2.

37. See Robert Fisk's "Revealed: The Women Who Suffered Saddam's Tyranny," *The Independent* 23 January 2004, available at www.k1m.com/antiwarblog/archives/

000098.html (14 May 2004).

38. "Iraqi Women Leaders Come to Washington November 13–20," *The White House Press*, available at www.state.gov/g/wi/cal/26563.htm (15 May 2004).

39. An Iraqi doctor who was among the Iraqi women's delegation to Washington, D.C., on 9–19 November 2003.

40. Raja Habib Khuzai and Songul Chapouk, "Iraq's Hidden Treasure," *Women's World* 2 December 2003, available at www.wworld.org/crisis/crisis.asp?ID=429 (25 May 2004).

41. Secretary Colin L. Powell, "International Women's Day," 8 March 2004, available at www.state.gov/secretary/rm/30219.htm (14 May 2004).

42. The Organization of Women's Freedom in Iraq was founded on 22 June 2003.

43. Mahmoud, "An Empty Sort of Freedom: Saddam Was No Defender of Women, but They Have Faced New Miseries and More Violence Since He Fell," *The Guardian* 8 March 2004, available at www.guardian.co.uk/comment/story/0,3604,1164268,00.html (25 May 2004).

44. Mahmoud, "An Empty Sort of Freedom," 2.

45. Mahmoud, "An Empty Sort of Freedom," 1.

46. Sandler, "Women Under Siege," 1.

47. Sandler, "Veiled Interests," 2.

48. The Iraqi Women's League was founded in 1952 during the anti-British agitation in Iraq.

49. Iraqi Women's League, "Open Appeal to All Women's Organisations in the UK," available at www.globalwomenstrike.net/English/iraqiwomenleagueopenletter.htm (25 May 2004).

50. Figure mentioned in Yifat Susskind, "One Year Later: Women's Human Rights in 'Liberated Iraq,'" *MADRE: An International Women's Human Rights Organization* Spring 2004, available at www.madre.org/art_nl_1_2004.html (25 May 2004).

51. The Iraqi Women's League, "Open Appeal to All Women's Organizations in the UK," 2–3.

52. Henry A. Waxman, "Evidence of Waste of US Taxpayers' Dollars in Iraq Contracts," 6 October 2003, available at www.mees.com/postedarticles/oped/a46n40d02.htm (25 May 2004).

53. Laura Bush, "Radio Address by Mrs. Bush" 17 November 2001, available at http://www.whitehouse.gov/news/releases/2001/11/20011117.html (25 May 2004).

54. Susskind, "One Year Later," 5.

55. Fisk, "Revealed," 2.

56. Mentioned by David Krieger, President of the Nuclear Age Peace Foundation in "The Meaning of Victory," 3 April 2003, available at www.wagingpeace.org/articles/2003/04/03_krieger_meaning-victory_print.htm (25 May 2005).

57. For the destruction of Iraq's national patrimony see Fisk's "Library Books, Letters and Priceless Documents Are Set Ablaze in Final Chapter of the Sacking of Baghdad," *The Independent*, 15 April 2003, available at www.commondreams.org/views03/0415-07.htm (4 June 2004).

58. Maureen Clare Murphy, "Art, Music & Culture: Who Will Profit from Iraqi Museum Looting," *Electronic Iraq*, 4 May 2003, available at http://electroniciraq.

net/cgi-bin/artman/exec/view.cgi/14/744 (4 June 2004).

59. Stephen Smith's "Art, Music & Culture: Furious Envy-Baudrillard and the Looting of Baghdad," *Electronic Iraq*, 4 September 2003:1, available at http://electroniciraq.net/news/1065.shtml (4 June 2004).

60. According to Fiachra Gibbons, "one of the first acts of the war was an attack on the museum in Saddam's home town of Tikrit." See "The End of Civilization," *The Guardian Unlimited*, 2 April 2003: 2, available at www.guardian.co.uk/arts/features/story/0,11710,927788,00.html (4 June 2004).

61. Jean Baudrillard, "The Despair of Having Everything," trans. Luke Sandford, November 2002: 4, available at www.egs.edu/faculty/baudrillard/baudrillard-the-despair-of-having-everything.html (6 June 2004).

62. Baudrillard, "The Despair of Having Everything," 3.

63. Baudrillard, "The Despair of Having Everything," 4–5.

64. Smith, "Furious Envy," 2.

65. Rouba Kabbara reports cases of rape by "US and Iraqi jailers." She also reports a case where an Iraqi woman committed suicide because she was raped in front of her husband. Other Iraqi women asked Iraqi men to "find a way to kill [them]" because they have been raped at the prison of Abu Ghraib. See Kabbara's "Human Rights Groups: Iraqi Women Raped at Abu Graib Jail," *Middle East Online*, 29 June 2004: 1–3, available at www.middle-east-online.com/english/?id=10096=10096&format=0 (6 June 2004).

66. I am indebted in my discussion of humanism to Robbins's "Race, Gender, Class, Postcolonialism: Toward a New Humanistic Paradigm?" and Anthony C. Allessandrini's "Humanism in Question: Fanon and Said," in *A Companion to Postcolonial Studies*, ed. Henry Schwarz & Sangeeta Ray (Malden: Blackwell, 2000).

67. I am referring to Anthony Kwame Appiah's notion of "transnational" or "ethical" humanism in "Is the Post- in Postmodernism the Post- in Postcolonial?" in *Contemporary Postcolonial Theory: A Reader*, ed. P. Mongia (London: Arnold, 1996) and Appiah's *In My Father's House* (New York: Methuen, 1992).

68. Spivak, "Can the Subaltern Speak?" *Colonial Discourse and Postcolonial Theory*, ed, Williams and Chrisman, 130.

69. Krieger, "The Children of Iraq Have Names," 1 November 2002, available at www.wagingpeace.org/articles/2002/11/01_krieger_children-iraq.htm (25 May 2004).

Bibliography

Abdel-Jaouad, Hedi. "Isabelle Eberhardt: Portrait of the Artist as a Young Nomad." *Yale French Studies* 83, no. 2 (1993): 93–117.

Abdelwahab, Hassan Hosni. *Shahirat Attunisiyat*. 3rd ed. Tunis: Manshurat baktabat al manar, 1965.

Abitbol, Michel. *The Jews of North Africa during the Second World War*, trans. Catherine Tihanyi Zentelis. Detroit: Wayne State University Press, 1989.

"About al Haddad's Book." *Al Nahdha*. 30 November 1930: 2.

Ageron, Charles-Robert. *France coloniale ou parti colonial?* Paris: Presse universitaire de France, 1978.

Ahmed, Leila. "Western Ethnocentrism and Perceptions of the Harem." *Feminist Studies* 8, no. 3 (1982): 521–34.

———. *Women and Gender in Islam: Historical Roots of a Modern Debate*. New Haven, Conn.: Yale University Press, 1992.

Aijaz, Ahmed. "The Politics of Literary Postcoloniality." *Race & Class* 36 (1995): 1–20.

Alloula, Malek. *The Colonial Harem*, trans. Myrna Godzich and Wlad Godzich. Minneapolis: University of Minnesota Press, 1986.

Amselle, Jean-Loup. *Mestizo Logics: Anthropology of Identity in Africa and Elsewhere*, trans. Claudia Royal. Stanford: Stanford University Press, 1998.

Anderson, Benedict. *Imagined Communities: Reflections on the Origin and Spread of Nationalism*. London: Verso Editions, 1983.

Appiah, Kwame Anthony. *In My Father's House*. New York: Methuen, 1992.

———. "Is the Post- in Postmodernism the Post- in Postcolonial?" Pp. 55–71 in *Contemporary Postcolonial Theory: A Reader*, ed. P. Mongia. London: Arnold, 1996.

Arat, Zehra F. *Deconstructing Images of "The Turkish Woman."* New York: St. Martin's Press, 1998.

Auclert, Hubertine. *Les Femmes Arabes en Algérie*. Paris: n.p., 1900.

Ayoun, Richard, and Bernard Cohen. *Les Juifs d'Algérie: 2000 ans d'histoire*. Paris: Lattès, 1982.

Bakhtin, Mikhail. "Carnival Ambivalence." *The Bakhtin Reader: Selected Writings of Bakhtin, Medvedev and Voloshinov*, ed. Pam Morris. London: Edward Arnold, 1994.

Bal, Mieke, Jonathan Crewe, and Leo Spitzer, eds. *Acts of Memory: Cultural Recall in the Present*. Hanover, N.H.: Dartmouth College, 1999.

Balegh, Hédi. *Les Pensées de Tahar Haddad*. Tunis: La Presse, 1993.

Baudrillard, Jean. "The Despair of Having Everything," trans. Luke Sandford. November 2002: 1–8. Available at www.egs.edu/faculty/baudrillard/baudrillard-the-despair-of-having-everything.html (6 June 2004).

Beauvoir, Simone de, and Gisèle Halimi. *Djamila Boupacha*, trans. Peter Green. New York: Macmillan Company, 1962.

———. *The Second Sex*, trans. H. M. Parshley. New York: Alfred A. Knopf, 1968.

Behdad, Ali. *Belated Travelers: Orientalism in the Age of Colonial Dissolution*. Durham, N.C.: Duke University Press, 1994.

Behija, M. "Le Coran impose-t-il le voile?" *L'Action*, 3 Février 1958.

Benchemsi, Ahmed R. "Maroc: minijupes contre tchadors." *Jeune Afrique*, 21–27 Mars 2000: 34–37.

Berger, Anne-Emmanuelle. "The Newly Veiled Woman/Irigaray, Specularity, and the Islamic Veil." *Diacritics* 28, no. 1 (1998): 93–119.

Bhabha, Homi K. *The Location of Culture*. London: Routledge, 1994.

———, ed. *Nation and Narration*. London: Routledge, 1990.

Biondi, Jean-Pierre. *Les Anticolonialistes (1881–1962)*. Paris: Robert Laffont, 1992.

Boone, Joseph A. "Vacation Cruises; or, the Homoerotics of Orientalism." *Modern Language Association of America* 110, no. 1 (January 1995): 89–112.

Boudhina, Muhammad. *Mashahîr al Tunisiyîn*. Tunis: Manshurat Muhammad Boudhina, 2001.

Bouhdiba, Abdelwahab. *Sexuality in Islam*, trans. Alan Sheridan. London: Routledge Kegan Paul, 1985.

———. *A la recherche des normes perdues*. Tunis: Maison Tunisienne de l'Edition, 1973.

"Bourguiba fait confiance aux femmes." *L'Action* 7 Janvier 1957: 13.

Bourguiba, Habib. *Discours*. 11 vols. Tunis: Publications du Secrétariat d'Etat à l'Information, 1975.

———. "Le Durrellisme ou le Socialisme boiteux." *L'Etendard Tunisien*, 1 Février 1929: 1.

———. "Le Voile." *L'Etendard Tunisien*, 11 Janvier 1929: 1–2.

———. *Tahar El Haddad, vengé de tous ses détracteurs*. Tunis: Publications du Secrétariat d'Etat à l'Information, Janvier 1976.

Bujéga, Marie. *Énigme Musulmane: lettres à une Bretonne*. Tangier and Fez: n.p., 1933.

———. *Nos soeurs Musulmanes*. Alger: n.p., 1932.

Bush, Laura. Radio Address by Laura Bush to the Nation. Crawford, Tex.: White House News Releases. 17 November 2001. Available at www.whitehouse.gov/news/releases/2001/11/20011117.html. (6 May 2003).

Bustani, Edouard Amin al. *Abu al Alâ al Ma'arri: muta'amil fi al dhulumat*. Beirut: Beit al hikma, 1989.

Butler, Judith. *Gender Trouble: Feminism and the Subversion of Identity*. New York: Routledge, 1990.

———. *Excitable Speech: A Politics of the Performative*. New York: Routledge, 1997.

———. *Feminists Theorize the Political*. New York: Routledge, 1992.

———. "Free Press Interview with Judith Butler." Kerry Chance. 8 May 2003. Available at www.bard.edu/hrp/events/spring2002/butler_interview.htm (26April 2002).

———. "The Guantanamo Limbo." *The Nation*, 1 April 2002: 20–24.

———. "How Bodies Come to Matter: An Interview with Judith Butler." Interview with Irene Costera Meijer and Baukje Prins. *Signs* 23, no. 2 (Winter 1998): 275–86.

———. "Interview: Judith Butler (on Religion, Violence, and Patriotism)." *Common-Sense Online: The Intercollegiate Journal of Humanism and Free Thought*. Available at www.cs-journal.org/lll1/lll1features3.html (16 May 2004).

"Ce n'est pas une Kemalisation." *L'Action*, 3 September 1956: 8.

Charles-Roux, Edmonde. *Nomade j'étais: Les Années Africaines d'Isabelle Eberhardt 1899–1904*. Paris: Bernard Grasset, 1995.

———. *Un Désir d'orient: jeunesse d'Isabelle Eberhardt, 1877–1899*. Paris: Bernard Grasset, 1988.

Chekir, Hafidha. *Le Statut des femmes entre les textes et les résistances: Le Cas de la Tunisie*. Tunis: Chama, 2000.

Cherni, Ben Said Zeineb. *Les Dérapages de l'histoire chez Tahar Haddad: Les Travailleurs, Dieu et la femme*. Tunis: Ben Abdallah, 1993.

Chow, Roy. "Violence in the Other Country," ed. Chandra Mohanty. *Third World Women and the Politics of Feminism*. Bloomington: Indiana University Press, 1991.

Cixous, Hélène. *Hélène Cixous: Photos de racines*. Paris: Des femmes, 1994.

———. "The Laugh of the Medusa." Pp. 245–64 in *New French Feminisms: An Anthology*, ed. Elaine Marks and Isabelle de Courtivron. Amherst: University of Massachusetts Press, 1980.

Cixous, Hélène, and Catherine Clément. *The Newly Born Woman*, trans. Betsy Wing. Minneapolis: University of Minnesota Press, 1986.

———. *Les Rêveries de la femme sauvage: Scènes primitives*. Paris: Galilée, 2000.

Clancy, Julia Smith, and Frances Gouda. *Domesticating the Empire: Race, Gender, and Family Life in French and Dutch Colonialism*. Charlottesville: University of Virginia Press, 1998.

Clinton, Hillary Rodham. "Women's Rights—Address by First Lady Hillary Rodham Clinton." Tunis: United States Information Agency. 26 March 1999. Available at http://usinfo.state.gov/usa/womenusa/tunis2.htm (15 May 2004).

———. "Women's Rights—Remarks by First Lady Hillary Rodham Clinton." New York: United States Information Agency. 4 March 1999. Available at http://clinton3.nara.gov/WH/EOP/First_Lady/html/generalspeeches/1999/19990304.htm l (15 May 2004).

"CNN Using 1991 Footage of Celebrating Palestinians to Manipulate You." *Independent Media Center*. 17 September 2001. Available at www.casi.org.uk/discuss/2001/msg00834.html (2 June 2004).

Davies, Carole Boyce. *Black Women, Writing, and Identity: Migrations of the Subject*. London: Routledge, 1994.

Derrida, Jacques. *Of Grammatology*, trans. Gayatri Chakravorty Spivak. Baltimore: Johns Hopkins University Press, 1976.

——. *Spurs: Nietzsche's Styles*. Chicago: University of Chicago Press, 1978.

Djait, Hichem. *Al Fitna: Jadaliat addin wa assiassa fi al Islam al mubaker*, trans. Khalil Ahmed Khalil. Beirut: Dar al Tali'a, 1991.

——. *La Personnalité et le devenir Arabo-Islamique*. Paris: Seuil, 1974.

Djebar, Assia. *A Sister to Scheherazade*, trans. Dorothy S. Blair. London: Quartet, 1987.

——. *Fantasia: An Algerian Cavalcade*, trans. Dorothy S. Blair. Portsmouth: Routledge, 1993.

——. *Far from Madina*. London: Quartet Books, 1994.

——. Interview. "'When the Past Answers our Present': Assia Djebar Talks About *Loin de Médine*." Clarisse Zimra. *Callaloo* 16, no. 1 (Winter 1993): 116–31.

——. *La Soif*. Paris: Julliard, 1957.

——. *Loin de Médine: Filles d'Ismaël*. Paris: Albin Michel, 1991.

——. *Women of Algiers in their Apartment*, trans. Marjolijn de Jager. Charlottesville: University Press of Virginia, 1992.

Doane, Mary Ann. "Veiling over Desire: Close-ups of the Woman." Pp. 105–41 in *Feminism and Psychoanalysis*, ed. Richard Feldstein and Judith Roof. Ithaca, N.Y.: Cornell University Press, 1989.

Dolan, Frances E. "The Dawn of the Hillary Clinton Backlash: An Introduction." *Genders* 33 (2001). Available at www.genders.org/g33/g33_dolan.html (2 June 2004).

"Drumbeat of Death." *Time*, 6 October 1997: 50–51.

Durel, Joachim. "Réponses à quelques jeunes." *Tunis Socialiste*, 19 Janvier 1929.

Eberhardt, Isabelle. *Departures: Selected Writings*, trans. and ed. Karim Hamdy and Laura Rice. San Francisco: City Lights Books, 1994.

——. *Écrits sur le sable*. Paris: Bernard Grasset, 1988.

——. *Écrits intimes: lettres aux trois hommes les plus aimés*, ed. Marie-Odile Delacour et Jean-René Huleu. Paris: Payot, 1991.

——. *In the Shadow of Islam*, trans. Sharon Bangert. London: Peter Owen, 1993.

——. *The Oblivion Seekers*, trans. Paul Bowles. San Francisco: City Lights, 1972.

——. *The Passionate Nomad: The Diary of Isabelle Eberhardt*, trans. Nina de Voogd, ed. Rana Kabbani. London: Virago, 1987.

——. *Rakhil*. Paris: La Boîte à Documents, 1990.

Eisenstein, Zillah. "Feminisms in the Aftermath of September 11." *Social Text* 20, no. 3 (Fall 2002). Available at www.ithaca.edu/faculty/eisenste/docs/htmldocs/socialtext2.htm (8 May 2003).

Esonwanne, Uzoma. "Feminist Theory and the Discourse of Colonialism." Pp. 233–55 in *ReImagining Women: Representations of Women in Culture*, ed. Shirley Neuman and Glennis Stephenson. Toronto: University of Toronto Press, 1993.

Ezra, Elizabeth. *The Colonial Unconscious: Race and Culture in Interwar France*. Ithaca, N.Y.: Cornell University Press, 2000.

Fanon, Frantz. "Algeria Unveiled." Pp. 35–67 in *Studies in a Dying Colonialism*. New York: Monthly Review Press, 1965.

————. *Black Skin, White Masks*, trans. Charles Lam Markmann. New York: Grove Press, 1967.

————. *The Wretched of the Earth*. New York: Grove Press, 1963.

Farah, Madelain. *Marriage and Sexuality in Islam: A Translation of al-Ghazali's Book on the Etiquette of Marriage from the Ihya'*. Salt Lake City: University of Utah Press, 1984.

Faulkner, Rita A. "Assia Djebar, Frantz Fanon, Women, Veils, and Land." *World Literature Today* 70, no. 4 (Fall 1996): 847–55.

Fernea, Warnock Elizabeth. *In Search of Islamic Feminism: One Woman's Global Journey*. New York: Doubleday, 1998.

Fisk, Robert. "Revealed: The Women Who Suffered Saddam's Tyranny." *The Independent* 23 January 2004. Available at www.k1m.com/antiwarblog/archives/000098.html (14 May 2004).

Flanders, Laura. "Algeria Unexamined: Tens of Thousands Dead and It's Barely News." *On the Issues* 7, no. 2 (Spring 1998): 24–28.

Flaubert, Gustave. *Flaubert in Egypt: A Sensibility on Tour*, trans. Francis Steegmuller. Boston: Little, Brown, and Company, 1972.

————. *Salammbô*. New York: Modern Library, 1929.

Foucault, Michel. *The Archaeology of Knowledge and the Discourse on Language*, trans. A. M. S. Smith. New York: Pantheon Books, 1972.

————. *Discipline and Punish: The Birth of the Prison*, trans. Alan Sheridan. New York: Pantheon Books, 1977.

————. *The Order of Things: The Archaeology of the Human Sciences*, trans. Alan Sheridan. New York: Vintage Books, 1973.

Fraiman, Susan. "Jane Austen and Edward Said: Gender, Culture, and Imperialism." *Critical Inquiry* 21 (Summer 1995): 805–21.

Fraser, John Foster. *The Land of Veiled Women: Some Wanderings in Algeria, Tunisia and Morocco*. London: Cassell and Company, LTD, 1913.

Freud, Sigmund. *Beyond the Pleasure Principle*, trans and ed. James Stratchey. New York: Liveright Publishing Corporation, 1961.

————. *Three Contributions to the Theory of Sexuality*, trans. A. A. Brill. New York: E. P. Dutton & Co., 1962.

Gafaiti, Hafid. "The Blood of Writing: Assia Djebar's Unveiling of Women and History. *World Literature Today* 70, no. 4 (Autumn 1996): 813–22.

Gallop, Jane. *Reading Lacan*. Ithaca, N.Y.: Cornell University Press, 1985.

Garradi, Tahar K. al. "The Image of al Ma'arri as an Infidel among Medieval and Modern Critics." Ph.D. diss., University of Utah, 1987.

Gates, Louis Jr. "Critical Fanonism." *Critical Inquiry* 17, no. 3 (Spring 1991): 457–70.

Gibbons, Fiachra. "The End of Civilization." *The Guardian Unlimited*, 2 April 2003: 1–5. Available at www.guardian.co.uk/arts/features/story/0,11710,927788,00.html (4 June 2004).

Gikandi, Simon. *Maps of Englishness: Writing, Identity in the Culture of Colonialism*. New York: Columbia University Press, 1996.

————. *Reading the African Novel*. London: James Currey, 1987.

Gilman, Sandra L. "The Jewish Nose: Are Jews White? Or, The History of the Nose Job." In *Encountering the Other(s): Studies in Literature, History, and Culture*, ed. Gisela Brinker-Gabler. Albany: State University of New York Press, 1995.

Gobineau, Arthur de. *Essai sur l'inegalité des races humaines*. Paris: Librairie de Jacob, 1933.

Grekowicz, Eric. "Hybridity and Discursive Unrest in Late Colonial Anglophone Prose of South Asia (1880–1950)." Ph.D. diss., Michigan State University, 2001.

Grosz, Elizabeth. *Sexual Subversions: Three French Feminists*. St. Leonards: Allen & Unwin, 1989.

Guillory, John. *Cultural Capital: The Problems of Literary Canon Formation*. Chicago: University of Chicago Press, 1993.

Gupta, Akhil, and James Ferguson, eds. *Culture, Power, Place: Explorations in Critical Anthropology*. Durham, N.C.: Duke University Press, 1997.

Haddad, Tahar al. *Imra'atuna fi al shari'a wa al mujtama'*. Tunis: Manshurat dar al ma'ârif li al tiba'a wa al nashr, 1997.

———. *Tahar al Haddad: Al a'maal al kaamila*. Tunis: Dar al arabiya li al kitab, 1999.

Hammami, Abdelrazek, and Zakiya Jouirou. *Al Mar'a fi al haraka al islâhiya min al Tahar al Haddad ila Zine al Abidine Ben Ali*. Tunis: Sharikat funûn li al rasm wa li al nashr wa assahâfa, 1999.

Hansen, Karen Tranberg. *African Encounters with Domesticity*. New Brunswick, N.J.: Rutgers University Press, 1992.

Harrow, Kenneth W. *The Marabout & the Muse: New Approaches to Islam in African Literature*. Portsmouth: Heinemann, 1996.

———. "Shibboleths in the Production of Culture." Paper presented at the 27th Annual Conference of the African Literature Conference, Virginia Commonwealth University, Richmond, Virginia, 4–8 April 2001.

Hecox, Doug. "The Military Indian (Name) Giving." Available at www.gridlockmag. com/dewey/indians.html (2 June 2004).

Hendricks, Margo. "Managing the Barbarian: The Tragedy of Dido, Queen of Carthage." *Renaissance Drama* 23 (1992): 165–88.

Hersh, Seymour M. "Torture at Abu Ghraib." *The New Yorker*. 10 May 2004: 1–7. Available at www.newyorker.com/printable/?fact/040510fa_fact (6 June 2004).

Hilgar, Marie-France. "L'Histoire de Didon et La Légende surfaite du pieux Enée." *Papers on French Seventeenth Century Literature* 21 (1984): 127–38.

Hill, Douglass E. "Albright's Blunder." *Irvine Review*. Available at www.irvinereview. org/guest1.htm (15 May 2003).

Hoodfar, Homa. "The Veil in Their Minds and on Our Heads: Veiling Practices and Muslim Women." Pp. 248–79 in *The Politics of Culture in the Shadow of Capital*, ed. Lisa Lowe and David Lloyd. Durham, N.C.: Duke University Press, 1997.

Hountondji, Paulin J. *African Philosophy: Myth and Reality*, trans. Henri Evans and Jonathan René. Bloomington: Indiana University Press, 1983.

Hourani, Albert. *A History of the Arab Peoples*. Cambridge, Mass.: Belknap Press of Harvard University Press, 1991.

Husayn, Taha. *Tajdid dhikra Abi al Alâ*. Cairo: Dar al ma'aarif, 1963.

——. *Ma'aa abi al Alaa fi sijnih*. Cairo: Dar al ma'aarif bi misr, 1971.

Hynes, William J. "Mapping the Characteristics of Mythic Tricksters: A Heuristic Approach." In *Mythical Trickster Figures*, ed. William J. Hynes and William G. Doty. Tuscaloosa: University of Alabama Press, 1993.

Ibn Hazm. *The Ring of the Dove: A Treatise on the Art and Practice of Arab Love*, trans. A. J. Arberry. London: Luzac, 1953.

Ibn Sa'd. *Kitab al tabaqat al kabir*, trans. S. Moinul Haq and H. K. Ghazanfar. Vol.1. Karachi: Pakistan Historical Society, 1967.

"Iraqi Women Leaders Come to Washington November 13–20." *The White House Press*. Available at www.state.gov/g/wi/cal/26563.htm (15 May 2004).

Iraqi Women's League. "Open Appeal to all Women's Organisations in the UK." Available at www.globalwomenstrike.net/English/iraqiwomenleagueopenletter. htm (25 May 2004).

Irigaray, Luce. *An Ethics of Sexual Difference*, trans. Carolyn Burke and Gillian C. Gill. Ithaca, N.Y.: Cornell University Press. 1993.

——. *Speculum of the Other Woman*, trans. Gillian C. Gill. Ithaca, N.Y.: Cornell University Press, 1985.

——. *This Sex Which is Not One*, trans. Catherine Porter. Ithaca, N.Y.: Cornell University Press, 1985.

——. "Veiled Lips." *Mississippi Review* 11, no. 3 (1983): 98–118.

Jakobson, Roman. *Selected Writings II: Word and Language*. The Hague and Paris: Mouton, 1971.

Jones, Ann Rosalind. "Inscribing Femininity: French Theories of the Feminine." Pp. 80–112 in *Making a Difference: Feminist Literary Criticism*, ed. Gayle Greene and Coppélia Kahn. London: Methuen, 1985.

Julien, Charles André. *Histoire de l'Afrique du Nord: Des origines à 1830*. Vol. 2. 4th ed. Tunis: Cérès, 2003.

Kabbara, Rouba. "Human Rights Groups: Iraqi Women Raped at Abu Graib Jail." *Middle East Online*, 29 June 2004: 1–3. Available at www.middle-east-online.com/english/?id=10096=10096&format=0 (6 June 2004).

Kahf, Mohja. *Western Representations of the Muslim Woman: From Termagant to Odalisque*. Austin: University of Texas Press, 1999.

Karam, Azza. *Women, Islamists and the State: Contemporary Feminisms in Egypt*. London: Macmillan Press, 1998.

Karmi, Hasan Said al. *Al haadi ila lughati al 'arab: Qamus 'arabi-'arabi*. Beirut: Dar lubnan li attiba'a wa al nashr, 1991.

Khaled, Ahmed. *Adhwâ mina al bi'a al tunusiya alâ al Tahar Haddad wa nidhalu jil*. Tunis: Al dar al tunusiya li al nashr, 1985.

Khalifa, Rashad, trans. *The Quran: The Final Testament*. Tucson: Islamic Productions, 1989.

Khuzai, Raja Habib and Songul Chapouk. "Iraq's Hidden Treasure." *Women's World* 2 December 2003. Available at www.wworld.org/crisis/crisis.asp?ID=429 (25 May 2004).

Kobak, Annette. *Isabelle: The Life of Isabelle Eberhardt*. London: Chatto & Windus, 1988.

Krieger, David. "The Children of Iraq Have Names." 1 November 2002. Available at www.wagingpeace.org/articles/2002/11/01_krieger_children-iraq.htm (25 May 2004).

———. "The Meaning of Victory." 3 April 2003. Available at www.wagingpeace. org/articles/2003/04/03_krieger_meaning-victory_print.htm (25 May 2005).

Kristeva Julia. *Powers of Horror: An Essay on Abjection*, trans. Leon S. Roudiez. New York: Columbia University Press, 1982.

———. *Revolution in Poetic Language*, trans. Margaret Waller. New York: Columbia University Press, 1984.

Lacan, Jacques. *Écrits*, trans. Alan Sheridan. New York: W. W. Norton & Company, 1977.

———. *Le Séminaire de Jacques Lacan*. Paris: Édition du Seuil, 1981.

———. *The Seminar of Jacques Lacan Book XX: On Feminine Sexuality, The Limits of Love and Knowledge, 1972-1973*, trans. Bruce Fink, ed. Jacques-Alain Miller. New York: W.W. Norton & Company, 1999.

"La Polémique Bourguiba-Noomane." *L'Action Tunisienne*, 29 Octobre 1956: 17.

Largueche, Dalenda, and Abdelhamid Largueche. *Marginales en terre d'Islam*. Tunis: Cérès, 1992.

Laskier, Michael M. *North African Jewry in the Twelfth Century: The Jews of Morocco, Tunisia, and Algeria*. New York: New York University Press, 1994.

Lauretis, Teresa de. *Technologies of Gender: Essays on Theory, Film, and Fiction*. Bloomington: Indiana University Press, 1987.

Lazreg, Marnia. *The Eloquence of Silence*. New York: Routledge, 1994.

———. "Feminism and Difference: The Perils of Writing as a Woman on Women in Algeria." Pp. 326–48 in *Conflicts in Feminism*, ed. Marianne Hirsche and Evelyn Fox Keller. New York: Routledge, 1990.

"Le Code va-t-il à l'encontre de la religion?" *L'Action*, 3 September 1956.

Lewis, Reina. *Gendering Orientalism: Race, Femininity and Representation*. London: Routledge, 1996.

Lowe, Lisa. "The Orient as Woman in Flaubert's *Salammbô* and *Voyage in Orient*." *Comparative Literature Studies* 23, no. 1 (Spring 1986): 44–58.

Lyons, Harriet D. "Presences and Absences in Edward Said's *Culture and Imperialism*." *Canadian Journal of African Studies* 28, no. 1 (1994): 101–5.

Ma'arri, Abul Alâ al. *Luzum maa laa yalzam: Luzumiat*. Beirut: Dar Sadr, n.p.

———. *Risalatu ul ghufran: A Divine Comedy*, trans. G. Blackenbury, ed. Kamil Kilany. Cairo: Al Maaref Printing and Publishing House, 1943.

———. *Risalatu ul ghufran*, ed. Ali Hassan Fa'ur. Beirut: Dar al Kutub al 'ilmiya, 1998.

MacMaster, Neil, and Toni Lewis. "Orientalism: From Unveiling to Hyperveiling." *Journal of European Studies* 28 (1998): 121–35.

Mackworth, Cecily. *The Destiny of Isabelle Eberhardt*. New York: The Ecco Press, 1975.

Mahmoud, Houzan. "An Empty Sort of Freedom: Saddam Was No Defender of Women, but They Have Faced New Miseries and More Violence Since He Fell." *The Guardian* 8 March 2004. Available at www.guardian.co.uk/comment/story/0,3604,1164268,00.html (25 May 2004).

Makaryk, Irena R. *Encyclopedia of Contemporary Literary Theory: Approaches, Scholars, Terms.* Toronto: University of Toronto Press, 1993.

Martin, Jean François. *Histoire de la Tunisie Contemporaine: De Ferry à Bourguiba 1881–1956.* Paris: L'Harmattan, 1993.

Marzouki, Ilhem. *Le Mouvement des femmes en Tunisie au XX ème siècle: Feminisme et politique.* Tunis: Cérès, 1993.

McClintock, Anne, Aamir Mufti, and Ella Shohat, eds. *Dangerous Liaisons: Gender, Nation, & Postcolonial Perspectives.* Minneapolis: University of Minnesota Press, 1997.

——. *Imperial Leather: Race, Gender and Sexuality in the Colonial Contest.* New York: Routledge, 1995.

McMillan, James F. *Housewife or Harlot: The Place of Women in French Society 1870–1940.* New York: St. Martin's Press, 1981.

Melman, Billie. *Women's Orients: English Women and the Middle East, 1718–1918: Sexuality, Religion and Work.* Ann Arbor: University of Michigan Press, 1992.

——. "Transparent Veils, Western Women Dis-Orient the East." Pp. 433–65 in *The Geography of Identity*, ed. Patricia Yaeger. Ann Arbor: University of Michigan Press, 1996.

Mernissi, Fatima. *Beyond the Veil: Male Female Dynamics in Muslim Society.* London: Al Saqi Books, 1985.

——. *Chahrazad n'est pas Marocaine: autrement, elle serait salariée!* Casablanca: Le Fennec, 1991.

——. *Islam and Democracy: Fear of the Modern World*, trans. Mary Jo Lakeland. Reading, Mass.: Addison-Wesley, 1991.

——. *Dreams of Trespass: Tales of a Harem Girlhood.* Reading, Mass.: Addison-Wesley, 1994.

——. *The Veil and the Male Elite: A Feminist Interpretation of Women's Rights in Islam*, trans. Mary Jo Lakeland. Reading, Mass.: Addison-Wesley, 1991.

Michaelson, Scott, and David E. Johnson, eds. *Border Theory: The Limits of Cultural Politics.* Minneapolis: University of Minnesota Press, 1997.

Miles, George H. *Mohammed, the Arabian Prophet: A Tragedy, in Five Acts.* Boston: Phillips, Sampson & Company, 1850. Microfilm. Michigan State University Library, 1583 Reel 369.7.

Moses, Claire Goldberg. *French Feminism in the 19th Century.* Albany: State University of New York Press, 1984.

Mosse, George L. *Nationalism and Sexuality: Respectability and Abnormal Sexuality in Modern Europe.* New York: H. Fertig, 1985.

Mostghanemi, Ahlam. *Memory in the Flesh*, trans. Baria Ahmar Sreih. Cairo: American University in Cairo Press, 2000.

Mudimbe, V. Y. *The Invention of Africa: Gnosis, Philosophy, and the Order of Knowledge.* Bloomington: Indiana University Press, 1988.

Murphy, Maureen Clare. "Art, Music & Culture: Who Will Profit from Iraqi Museum Looting." *Electronic Iraq.* 4 May 2003: 1–3. Available at http://electroniciraq.net/cgi-bin/artman/exec/view.cgi/14/744 (4 June 2004).

Murrmann, Mark. "Campus Watch Raises Specter of McCarthyism." *North Gate News Online*. University of California-Berkeley, 18 September 2002. Available at www.campus-watch.org/survey.php/id/14 (8 May 2003).

Naluti, Arusiyya al. *Al Tawba*. Unpublished play, 1992.

———. *Maratij*. Dar demeter li al nashr, 1985.

———. Personal interview by Lamia Ben Youssef. Tape recording. Tunis, Tunisia, 17 July 2001.

———. *Tamas*. Tunis: Dar al janub li al nashr, 1995.

Narayan, Uma. "Essence of Culture and a Sense of History: A Feminist Critique of Cultural Essentialism." *Hypatia—A Journal of Feminist Philosophy* 13, no. 2 (Summer 1998): 96–106.

Nashat, Guity, and Judith E. Tucker. *Women in the Middle East and North Africa: Restoring Women's History*. Bloomington: Indiana University Press, 1999.

Nietzsche, Friedrich. *The Gay Science*, trans. Walter Kaufmann. New York: Vintage Books, 1974.

Noomane, Muhammad. "A L'Essor." *Tunis Socialiste*, 11 Janvier 1929.

O'Loughlin, Katrina. "The Spectre of the Veiled Dance: The Transvestic and European Constructions of the 'East.'" *Ariel* 50 (1996): 230–46.

Ortigues, Marie Cécile, and Edmond. *Oedipe Africain*. Paris: Plon, 1966.

Oushakine, Serguei Alex. "On American Academics Critical of Israel." 20 September 2002. Available at http://lists.partners-intl.net/pipermail/women-east-west/2002-September/001882.html (15 May 2003).

Paulme Denise. *La mère dévorante: Essai sur la morphologie des contes Africains*. France: Gallimard, 1976.

"Pin-up d'hier et d'aujourd'hui." *L'Action*, 11 Août 1958: 20.

Plato. *The Republic*, trans. Tom Griffith, ed. G. R. F. Ferrari. Cambridge: Cambridge University Press, 2000.

Powell, Colin L. "International Women's Day." 8 March 2004. Available at www.state.gov/secretary/rm/30219.htm (14 May 2004).

Pratt, Mary Louise. *Imperial Eyes: Travel Writing and Transculturalism*. London: Routledge, 1992.

Prochaska, David. *Making Algeria French: Colonialism in Bône, 1870–1920*. Paris: Editions de la maison des sciences de l'homme, 1990.

"Quoi de neuf pour les femmes?" *L'Action*, 7 Janvier 1957: 13.

Raphael, Alison. "Women Call on White House to Restore Aid." 20 August 2002. Available at www.converge.org.nz/pma/cra0799.htm (15 May 2004).

Rose, Jacqueline. "Edward Said Talks to Jacqueline Rose." *Critical Quarterly* 40, no. 1 (Spring 1998): 72–89.

Roudinesco, Elisabeth. *Jacques Lacan*, trans. Barbara Bray. New York: Columbia University Press, 1997.

Rousseau, Jean-Jacques. *Politics and the Arts: Letter to M. D'Alembert on the Theatre*, trans. Allan Bloom. Ithaca, N.Y.: Cornell University Press, 1989.

Rubie, Jennie. "Is this a Feminist War?" *Off Our Backs* 31, no. 10 (November 2001): 12–14.

Rushdie, Salman. *The Satanic Verses*. Dover: The Consortium, 1988.

Said, Edward W. *Culture and Imperialism*. New York: Vintage Books, 1993.

———. "Identity, Authority, and Freedom: The Potentate and the Traveler." *Boundary 2* 21, no. 3 (Fall 1992): 1–18.

———. *Orientalism*. New York: Vintage Books, 1979.

Salem, Norma. *Habib Bourguiba, Islam and the Creation of Tunisia*. London: Croom Helm, 1984.

Sandler, Lauren. "Veiled Interests: Iraqi Women Debate Religion, Democracy, and Head Scarves. But is Anyone Listening?" *Boston Globe* 31 August 2003. Available at http://psychoanalystsopposewar.org/resources_files/Veiled_Interests__Iraqi_Women_Debate.htm (25 May 2004).

———. "Women Under Siege." 29 December 2003. Available at http://www.thenation.com/doc.mhtml%3Fi=20031229&s=sandler (14 May 2004).

Schehr, Lawrence R. "*Salammbô* as the Novel of Alterity." *Nineteenth Century French Studies* 17, nos. 3–4 (Spring–Summer 1989): 326–41.

Schultheis, Robert. "Afghanistan's Forgotten Women: News and Commentary." *Genders* 28 (1998): 1–5. Also available at www.genders.org/g27/g27_afw.html.

Schwarz, Henry, and Ray Sangeeta, eds. *A Companion to Postcolonial Studies*. Malden: Blackwell, 2000.

Serwer, Daniel. "Building Civil Society: An Overlooked Aspect of Iraq's Reconstruction?" 31 July 2003. Available at http://www.usip.org/newsmedia/releases/2003/0731_NBiraq.htm (25 May 2004).

Shapiro, Ann-Louise. *Breaking the Codes: Female Criminality in Fin de Siècle Paris*. Stanford: Stanford University Press, 1996.

Sharon, Moshe. "*Ahl al Bayt*—People of the House." *Jerusalem Studies in Arabic and Islam* 18 (1986): 169–84.

Shohat, Ella. "Notes on the 'Post-Colonial.'" Pp. 126–39 in *The Pre-Occupation of Postcolonial Studies*, ed. Fawzia Afzal Khan and Kalpana Seshadri Crooks. Durham, N.C.: Duke University Press, 2000.

Silverstein, Ken. "Blasts from the Past." *Salon*, 22 September 2001. Available at http://archive.salon.com/news/feature/2001/09/22/blowback/ (7 May 2003).

Smith, Sharon. "Using Women's Rights to Sell Washington's War." *International Socialist Review*. January–February 2002. Available at www.isreview.org/issues/21/afghan_women.shtml (5 April 2003).

Smith, Stephen. "Art, Music & Culture: Furious Baghdad and the Looting of Baghdad." *Electronic Iraq*. 4 September 2003: 1–8. Available at http://electroniciraq.net/news/1065.shtml (4 June 2004).

Spaeth, Anthony. "A Peace That Terrifies: Tough Islamic Laws Rule in Afghanistan as the U.S., Russia and Pakistan Warily Eye the Fundamentalists." *Time*, 14 October 1996: 62.

Spillers, Hortense. "All the Things You Could Be by Now: If Sigmund Freud's Wife Was Your Mother: Psychoanalysis and Race." *Boundary 2* 23, no. 3 (Autumn 1996): 75–141.

Spivak, Gayatri Chakravorty. *A Critique of Postcolonial Reason: Toward a History of the Vanishing Present*. Cambridge, Mass.: Harvard University Press, 1999.

———. *The Postcolonial Critic: Interviews, Strategies, Dialogues*. New York: Routledge, 1990.

Stato, Joanne, and Karla Mantilla. "Afghan Women Protest Taliban in Washington." *Off Our Backs* 31, no. 4 (1 April 2001): 1.

Stetkevych, Suzanne Pinkney. "Intoxication and Immortality: Wine and Associated Imagery in al Ma'arri's Garden." Pp. 210–32 in *Homoeroticism in Classical Arabic Literature*, ed. J. W. Wright Jr. and Everett K. Rowson. New York: Columbia University Press, 1997.

Susskind, Yifat. "One Year Later: Women's Human Rights in 'Liberated Iraq.'" *MADRE: An International Women's Human Rights Organization* (Spring 2004). Available at www.madre.org/art_nl_1_2004.html (25 May 2004).

Tabari, Abou Ja'far Muhammad ibn Jarîr Ibn Yazid Tabari. *Chronique*, trans. Hermann Zotenberg. 6 vols. Paris: Sindbad, 1989.

Tate, Claudia. "Freud and His 'Negro': Psychoanalysis as Ally and Enemy of African Americans." *Journal for the Psychoanalysis of Culture & Society* 1, no. 1 (Spring 1996): 53–62.

Thomas, Sue. "Difference, Intersubjectivity, and Agency in the Colonial and Decolonizing Spaces of Hélène Cixous's 'Sorties.'" *Hypatia* 9, no. 1 (Winter 1994): 53–69.

Tunsi, Mahmud Beyram al, ed. *Al Shabab, 29 October 1936–12 Mars 1937*. Tunis: Dar al Kutub al wataniya, 2004.

Virgil. *The Aeneid*, trans. C. H. Sisson. Manchester: Carcanet Pess, 1986.

Yaeger, Patricia, ed. *The Geography of Identity*. Ann Arbor: University of Michigan Press, 1996.

Young, Robert J. C. *Colonial Desire: Hybridity in Theory, Culture, and Race*. London: Routledge, 1995.

Waxman, Henry A. "Evidence of Waste of U.S. Taxpayers' Dollars in Iraq Contracts." 6 October 2003. Available at www.mees.com/postedarticles/oped/a46n40d02.htm (25 May 2004).

Williams, Brackette F., ed. *Women Out of Place: The Gender of Agency and the Race of Nationality*. New York: Routledge, 1996.

Williams, Raymond. *The Politics of Modernism: Against the New Conformists*. London: Verso, 1989.

Williams, Patrick, and Laura Chrisman, eds. *Colonial Discourse and Postcolonial Theory: A Reader*. New York: Columbia University Press, 1994.

Winter, Bronwyn. "Fundamental Misunderstandings: Issues in Feminist Approaches to Islamism." *Journal of Women's History* 13, no. 1 (Spring 2001): 9.

Woodhull, Winnifred. "Unveiling Algeria." *Genders* 10 (Spring 1991): 113–31.

———. "Feminism and Islamic Tradition," *Studies in Twentieth-Century Literature* 17, no. 1 (1993): 27–44.

Zimra, Clarisse. "Not so Far from Medina: Assia Djebar Charts Islam's 'Insupportable Feminist Revolution.'" *World Literature Today* 70, no. 4 (Autumn 1996): 823–34.

Zmerli, Sadok. *A'lâm Tunisiyûn*, ed. Hamadi Sahli. Beirut: Dar al gharb al islamî, 1986.

Index

About the Author

Lamia Ben Youssef Zayzafoon is a Tunisian scholar who holds a Maîtrise in English literature and language from l'École Normale Supérieure of Sousse and a Ph.D. degree in English from Michigan State University. She taught English literature at the Institut Supérieur des Langues de Tunis and the Faculty of Arts & Humanities of Sousse, Tunisia. Research areas include postcoloniality, African literature of the diaspora, feminist and Islamic studies, and creative writing.